MEMORIES

Etta Wilson Lawrence

MEMORIES

By

Etta W. Lawrence

1st books – rev. 6/7/00

ABOUT THE BOOK

"Memories" is an anthology, which includes biographical material about the author, her predecessors, her siblings and her children. Also included are many true stories collected over her lifetime, which have been told, retold and remembered.

Some of these stories are rendered in the colloquial dialects of the times and locations. She describes moments of elation and triumph over difficulties and other times of overwhelming tragedy and sorrow. She includes a time line of all of the many places she has lived over her life of eighty-two years. You will marvel at her tremendous capacity to recall and narrate the details of events spanning so many years.

CREDITS

Grateful acknowledgement is made to the following for permission to reprint material controlled by or provided by them:

To: The Unitarian/Universalist Fellowship for use of the poem "We Remember Them" Number 720 of their Hymnal.

To: My Grandmother Bette and Grandfather Erv for having told and retold many of these stories to my mother, who told them to me.

To: Mama "Evie" who repeated her parents and grand parents stories to me.

To: Aunts: Dallie, Maude, Sue, Ethel and Great Aunt Bessie. Uncles: Ernest, Little Doc, Sanford, Evard, and Collie for telling and retelling me some of the stories contained herein.

To: My brothers: Jim, George, Howard's Family and Leo and my sister Lela for giving me pertinent information that I could use.

To: My daughter, Vicki, who has encouraged me and prodded me to complete this book.

To: My husband, Harry, who made my efforts to put all these stories together and have them printed a reality. Without his help this would have been a futile effort on my part.

To: All my friends who have listened to me talk about this project and those who have encouraged me along the way.

Before you read "My Story" (Chapter 5) please understand that I felt compelled to explain how certain events affected me. Maybe that was because it was therapeutic for me to get it off my chest or maybe it was because I just didn't know when to quit. Whatever....it's done.

Hobo Signs

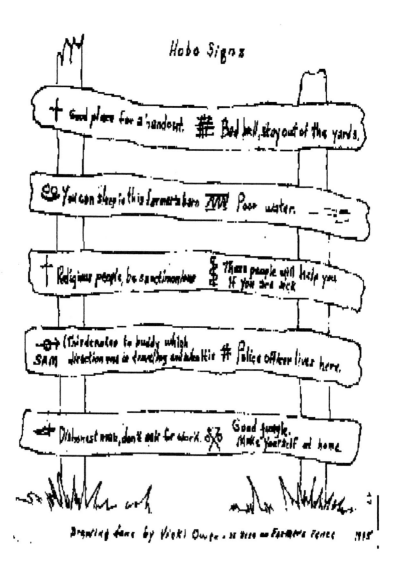

+ Good place for a handout.   ╫ Bad bull, stay out of the yards.

∞ You can sleep in this farmer's barn   ⊞ Poor water.   ⸗

† Religious people, be sanctimonious   § These people will help you if you are sick

SAM ⟶ (Circdenotes to buddy which direction you are traveling and who it is)   ╫ Police officer lives here.

⟵ Dishonest man, don't ask for work.   ✂ Good jungle. Make yourself at home.

work

Drawing done by Vicki Owens - as seen on Farmers Fence   1915

Dedicated to the memory of:

Lynn Eldy Thayer and Terry Owen Thayer

Table of Contents

Chapter 1 - MY PREDECESSORS 3
  Bettie and Erv 3
  The Panther 4
  Erv's Pigs 4
  Great Aunt Bessie 7
  Eva Modena 10
  Rolling Store 10
  Aunt Dallie 12
  Press and David 13
  Cousin Odie 14
  Family of Henry and Eva 14
  Hart County 18
Chapter 2 - MY SIBLINGS 23
  Jim 23
    Jim's Straw Hat 23
    The Barn 24
  Little Ralph 33
  George 34
    Colt in Waterhole 35
    The Bull Story 36
  Howard 39
    Howard's Electric Dance 42
  Leo 42
  Lela 44
Chapter 3 - MAMA 49
  Mama and Frank 49
  The Traveling Tombstone 55
  We Remember Mama 57
Chapter 4 - MANY MANY MOVES 77
  Prior to 1920 77
  Snake Story 79
  The Biggest Snake in Hart County 80

Chapter 5 - ABOUT ME 97
  My Story 98
  Oklahoma 102
  New Found Religion 104
  Trip to Georgia 110
  The Whorehouse 112
  The Cottage 119
  Christmas - 1942 121
  The Preacher 125
  Truck Driver 127
  Changes in My Life 132
  Bermuda Story 136
  Beta Sigma Phi 149
  The Cruise 156
  Down to Earth 158
  Retirement 162
  With John 162
  Hiawassee Haven 168
  The Motor Home 170
  Square Dancing 172
  With Ben 172
  Life with Harry 177
  Harry's Story 178
Chapter 6 - MY CHILDREN 189
  Vicki 189
    Sons-A-Bitches 193
  Lynn 210
    The Butterfly 216
    We Remember Them 239
  Terry 240
    To Visit Roy Rogers 244
    Society Avenue 251
    "Wings in the Wind" 261
Chapter 7 - AFTER 267
  The Estate Sale 267

Room Mates 268
Europe 269

INTRODUCTION

This book, 'MEMORIES', is a collection of stories for my three Children, seven Grand Children, eleven Great Grandchildren and one Great Great Grandson and... on to anyone interested enough to read it..

Everyone may not agree with my version. That is their privilege. If they don't like what I have written, they are free to write or tell their own version. We all know that three, or more, people can witness an event and each will have his or her interpretation. Sometimes very different.

I tried to never exaggerate but am guilty of having told the same story slightly different at times because of something I forgot or remembered in retelling. Be that as it may, this is the way I Think, Talk and Write.

I didn't realize it at the time, when I was seven, as I began by making notes about stories told to me; keeping a diary; saving newspaper clippings that interested me and writing hundreds of letters, and keeping copies, to friends and relatives that any of it would turn out to be invaluable as I tried to put all this in book form.

My notes show that I started to write "Scraps of Family History", my first book, in 1954. A divorce and raising three teenagers along with a full-time job delayed my writing until the 1980s, when I did quite a bit. A second marriage that lasted eighteen years; and coping with being a widow delayed me again. I remarried and became a widow the second time after eight years; laid it aside again until 1991. I dilly-dallied now and then and finally got serious about it in 1993. It was finally finished in 1999 with the help of my fourth husband.

It took many hours to sort this all out and make it interesting enough that anyone would read and absorb, at least some of it. If they do, that will be my reward.

Whether I'd have the courage and stamina to put my collection of notes, letters and copies together I'd never have known if I hadn't tried it.

I hope that I remembered all the details correctly but please forgive me if I haven't. Some memories have gone back almost eighty years and were remembered better than what happened yesterday. I have drawn on my memory bank to the fullest extent.

I've lived to the ripe old age of eighty-two years, as of January, 1999, to actually get serious enough to finish it.

SO HERE IT IS!!!..."MEMORIES"...FOR WHAT IT'S WORTH.

NOTE: All three of my children encouraged me to do these stories, many that they loved to hear when they were young children. They preferred my stories to those in Nursery Books because mine were very real to them.

There are some stories, written separately, added within the main story about a person i.e., 'The Butterfly' in Lynn. 'To Visit Roy Rogers' was inserted in Terry. Many others follow the main story about an individual but it was difficult to work it in as part of it.

I will be forever sorry that I did not have this compilation of stories finished when I lost both my sons, Lynn and Terry in October 1996. They died in a fiery plane crash at the airstrip behind Terry's house. There are stories about that too.

CHAPTER 1

MY PREDESSORS

MY PREDECESSORS

GREAT GRANDPARENTS

Thomas was born in August 1837 and died in July 1938 but his tombstone shows a different birth date. My mother always said that he lived to be almost 101. Sarah Ann Emily was born in 1839 and married Thomas in August 1867. He was 30 and she was 28. She was a round-faced woman of ample build. My mother, Eva, looked very much like her and had her hazel eyes.

Many stories were told about Great Grandpa, Tom. He was a small short man, just over five feet, with fine features and piercing blue eyes. The only time that I can remember seeing him was the year before he died. At that time he had very thin hair and a sparse goatee.

In his younger days he would lie down and have somebody measure him and then would jump that distance flat-footed. He would get behind his mule and take a running jump landing on the mule's back when he was well up in years. Everyone knew Tom. He carried the mail on horseback for many years.

BETTIE AND ERV

Granpaw, William Ervin, was called 'Erv'. He was tall, about six feet, had lots of dark brown hair which often fell across his brow. His eyes were very blue and he loved to joke and tell stories, especially about his Moonshiner days. He was one of fifteen children who each had large families. I counted one-hundred-one grandchildren on that branch of the family. He was about eighteen when he married his schoolteacher, Mary Elizabeth 'Bettie'.

I never knew Granmaw's real name until I saw it in her personal Bible that Aunt Maude, Margies's mother, had until she died early in 1994

Several of the men and a couple of the women, in Granpaw's family, developed some kind of an illness that affected their walk and speech. All of them, including my Uncles, my mother's brothers, were in their late seventies when they were afflicted. It

3

seems to be some kind of heredity thing and no Doctor, that I have asked, has ever been able to determine what it was. So far, it has not affected my brothers. All three are over seventy. We lost Howard before he was seventy. I just got word, October 1999, that George, at seventy-eight, has Parkinson's disease. That must have been what my Uncles had. My heart aches for him.

Because of this, my cousin Margie Nell, has donated her body to Medical Science in hopes that some key may be found to help our own children. Possibly, because of such different combinations of blood in our marriages, this will eventually be erased from the family.

Granmaw Bettie was a tiny woman, about five feet tall with dark hair that she wore in a bun on the top of her head. She was full of life and her brown eyes would sparkle when she told some of her stories, many that we had heard before but we persuaded her to tell them again. She was a fantastic storyteller and would make all the noises to demonstrate her point.

THE PANTHER

My favorite one was about the panther, which she always pronounced 'painter', that climbed up on the roof of their house and tried to get into the windows. Granmaw heard the noise, grabbed her shotgun and ran out on the el-shaped porch.

She could see it sitting up there screaming. Granmaw would stop at that point and scream like a woman being attacked. Her scream would make the hair stand up on the back of your neck.

Suddenly, the panther made a leap at her. She just got into the house and slammed the door as the panther took a piece out of her dress-tail; old fashioned name for long skirt. He clawed the porch floor and Granmaw showed us the claw marks that were forever there until the house was destroyed years later by fire

ERV'S PIGS

Granpaw loved his family and tried to support them by

farming some dirt-poor land. When that failed he turned to making Corn Liquor. 'White Lightn' as locals and revenue officers called it.

Mama told us of many times he would get drunk, he became an alcoholic, called 'drunkard' in those days, beat all of them and threaten to burn the house down with them in it. When he was drunk, he roared and the children knew to stay out of his way. When he was sober, he tried to make up for his poor behavior and would sleep it off in the barn.

One particular incident comes to mind that happened when my mother, Eva, was about twelve.

Grandpa was clever, even though he only went to third grade. Revenue Officers, "revenoors" to the locals, knew that he had made several stills and had broken them up but had never caught him at or near one. He knew every inch of the mountains and could hide out for days. He could out-run the 'revenoors' and be sitting calmly at home when they came.

Many of the houses, in the South, were built up off the ground several feet. By bending over a person could see anything stored underneath. He made the children crawl underneath and clean out everything in sight. The only thing visible was the chimney, which came down to below ground level.

He cleaned all the ashes out of the fireplace in the kitchen and started digging. As soon as he got the hole deep enough he had Mama and the other children carry buckets of dirt out and spread it around on the ground so it wouldn't look suspicious.

After endless buckets of dirt he had dug himself a space big enough to stand up in and to build his copper still. He perfected it and finished off with a drain, a wooden trough, under-ground that led directly to the hog pens. He knew the hogs would eat the mash. The smoke went directly up the chimney beside the trap door he had made for himself under half of the wide chimney floor. He was quite proud of his accomplishment. This was the best "likker" he had ever made and orders were rolling in. Revenoors heard that he was in business again and came to the house several times looking for the still. They looked under the house but could see nothing. They gave up for awhile.

A neighbor stopped to visit and look at some fat pigs Granpaw had for sale. As they stood by the fence, the man remarked on how good the pigs looked... then he looked again. The pigs all seemed to be hogging it, pardon the pun, at one trough and then running around like crazy.

The man said, "If'n I didn' know better, I'd say them pigs was drunk". He left with a healthy looking pig. The next 'revenoor' he saw he told about Erv's pigs. He got a reward after the 'revenoors' came back and threatened to burn the house down if Granpaw didn't tell them where the still was.

Granpaw had to give in and tell. He got six months in jail and that ended his career as the best "Likker man" in Habersham County.

His moonshine days were over. He and the family, still at home, moved to Towns County. They bought a small farm with an old house on Fodder Creek near Hiawassee, Georgia.

After one of Granmaw's stories, while we were still sitting on the porch, on my first trip back to Georgia, Granpaw asked me the reason I had left home. It seemed to be of great concern to him.

I felt free to tell Granpaw that I had left after a bitter argument with Mama about my wearing pants to go target practicing with my brother, Jim, my boy friend and several others, when I was almost nineteen. Granpaw was very sympathetic to me and said "you'll just have to let her have her say, but you know what's right and wrong so don't pay her no mind".

He thought I should live my own life especially since I had been living away from home and supporting myself for two years. He seemed relieved that I hadn't turned out 'bad' as Mama considered me to be because I just couldn't accept her ideas of religion.

Granmaw had already told me about Mama running away when she was sixteen to marry a neighbor who was considerably older than she was. She got mad and walked home when he, David the Sweetheart that Mama had told me about many times, got drunk. David's sisters told Mama, much later, that they had prepared a beautiful Hope Chest for her with linens and kitchen items. Mama always felt that she got cheated out of all that but she wouldn't marry David because of his drinking.

Granmaw, and later Great Aunt Bessie, described David as a little old scrawny man with a wisp of a beard and pock marks all over his face. Neither of them could figure out what she ever saw in him but figured that it might have been to get away from home because Granpaw was drinking heavily at that time.

Both Grandparents would find ways to get me alone to tell me these things because Mama stuck with me like a bee after honey because she didn't want me to say anything against the way their new Religion had upset my life.

GREAT AUNT BESSIE

I met Aunt Bessie in August 1983 in quite an unusual way the week after my husband, John, passed away.

My daughter, Vicki, had stayed over with me for a few days after John's funeral. While we were waiting for insurance settlements and paperwork, she suggested that we take a ride from Hiawassee to Tate City, Georgia, where my mother was born. It was about 27 miles away but I had never been there. My Uncle, Little Dock as he was called, had taken her there on one of her visits. I was quite surprised that Vicki knew how to find it but even more surprised when we got there. A sign by the road said Tate City - population 32.

There were no stores. Nothing except a church and quite a few very nice looking summer homes. One of them, across the creek, appeared to have been built on a huge flat rock. There was a swinging footbridge to the mailbox with a driveway across a homemade log bridge. It was very picturesque and I was glad I had my camera along.

We drove alongside a beautiful creek, later found out that it was the beginning of the Tallulah River, overhung by twenty foot tall wild rhododendron bushes, huge boulders in and on both sides of the creek, to an open field that looked like what had been described to us as the location where my Grandparents had once lived. I really thought it was a beautiful place, a valley with a bountiful stream of water running along one side and mountains surrounding it.

There was a Real Estate sign lying on the ground. I suspected that the property had been sold as Buyers sometimes lay the sign down until the Realtor picks it up.

While I was copying down the number to call about it, a car pulled up to one of the mailboxes across the road. I asked them if they knew any of the Nichols family in the area. The man threw back his head and laughed and then said, "everybody in this valley is related to you but me and I'm a Wilson". I was elated because I thought I had found someone related to me on my Dad's side. We compared families but couldn't make any connection between us.

He said "you've got kinfolks staying at their summer place and a cousin over the hill from my place". We followed him up his mountain driveway and came to a flat area where he had a house trailer. He hollered down the other side of the hill to Johnnie Ray who was at his trailer for that day only. What a miracle!

Johnnie remembered my mother and suggested that we go around the mountain and see his mother and two sisters and a brother-in-law that were staying at their old homestead for the summer.

I was absolutely thrilled to meet Johnnie's mother, who was my Great Aunt Bessie. She was ninety-three years old. I didn't remember ever hearing anything about her from my mother but I guess they had never had any contact with each other since my mother moved away as a young girl. Aunt Bessie had raised her family right there in that valley, called Tate City, until 1958.

Aunt Bessie, two of her daughters and a son-in-law were staying at the old house. It looked like a shack from the outside with a tin roof and a porch full-width of the house in front. There was an outside privy and a well in a big tile. The inside of the house was spacious and clean as a pin. There were beds everywhere and a nice bathroom complete with shower. An old wood range stove still stood at a back wall with a gas stove next to it. All of the beds had pretty hand-quilted covers on them and appeared to be ready for the many family members that Aunt Bessie said were regular visitors all summer long.

Vicki had a lengthy discussion with David, the son-in-law, about coon hunting and property that he owned, including the one that she had wanted me to buy across the road. He had just bought it. David was a big man, in excess of two hundred fifty pounds, with a big belly and a laugh that shook him all over. He was in his mid-seventies. I think that he enjoyed talking to Vicki as much as she did to him.

The two daughters reminded me of my Aunt Dallie who was about their age. They took us up the hill in back of the house to a small family cemetery. All the graves appeared to be well kept with small mounds of dirt raked to a peak in the center and full length of the graves. There weren't many markers but the women were sure that all of them were family. We had already been impressed by the vast numbers of our name that we had seen on Tombstones in the cemeteries and on the mailboxes on the way to this place.

Aunt Bessie had snow-white hair worn in a flat bun on top of her head. Her eyes were bright blue and her complexion was a beautiful rosy pink. I loved her from the moment I saw her.

Her two daughters, my second cousins, invited me to come to Belmont, North Carolina for Aunt Bessie's 94th birthday the next May.

When I saw her the next year at her birthday party, she told me of quite a different version of what my mother had told me of her first love. According to Aunt Bessie, Mama had run away from home when she was sixteen to marry an older man that Mama had described, to me, when I was a teenager, as "handsome and charming fellow". Aunt Bessie said that she "never could see what Evie saw in him.

He was bow-legged, scrawny and pimple-faced with a thin beard. Then aunt Bessie said, " Evie took her few clothes in a small valise and was going to meet him and marry him but he got drunk. She got mad and went home." We laughed about the two different descriptions, hers and Mama's. Aunt Bessie's story was almost exactly as Grandma Bettie had told me when I was twenty.

I had the profound feeling that I had been able to make my family acquainted with their ancestors in a memorable way. Had

9

I not had Vicki show me where Tate City was, Uncle Dock to show her, the coincidence of my cousin Johnnie being at his house trailer for that one particular day, and Aunt Bessie at what was now her summer home, this would have been a blank space in my life. I am forever thankful to have been able to meet and love these kinfolks.

This is about my mother. She was the oldest child of Erv and Bettie.

EVA MODENA

Eva Modena was born in September 1898 in Tate City, Georgia. She had auburn hair and mischievous, when she was happy, hazel eyes. She became a vivacious woman who married at seventeen, had eight children and "got religion" in her thirties in Lansing, Michigan.

Her religion consumed her whole life thereafter. She was a Missionary, at heart, without any training. She spent most of fifty years trying to convert everyone she met to her faith.

She was widowed twice. Her first husband, Henry who shared her faith, was the father of her six surviving children, including me. He died in September 1956.In February 1957 she married her second husband, Frank. She tried very hard to convert him but he wouldn't give up smoking until the week before he died. He was then accepted in the church.

She was a widow for several years and married her third husband, Bill, when she was eighty. He also shared her religion. He lived for about six months after she died in December 1983.

She was an interesting person often described as a "character". My daughter, Vicki, has said that she hopes that she will be remembered as a "character" as her Grandmother was.

ROLLING STORE

"Old Nick", my Uncle Ernest, owned the only Rolling Store in the foothills of North Georgia for over ten years during the late 1930s, through the 1940s and early 1950s. He was featured in a story, with pictures, in the Atlanta Journal and Constitution

Magazine on April 20, 1952. The story was by Wylly Folk St. John and the pictures by Carolyn Carter.

He built a shell over his truck chassis so that every item inside was protected from the weather, heat and cold. The inside was fitted with shelves to hold the variety of items he carried, rods between the two sides for hanging items and bins for goods sold by the pound. He would bring the yard goods that ladies ordered to make shirts, dresses or any sewing item they needed. He even picked the colors. Sometimes it was Medicines that they, or the Doctor, ordered and candies for the children.

He loaded his Rolling Store every morning and was on the road by 7:30 A.M. He had regular routes, on the same day each week, so the people knew that he would be blowing his horn to let them know he was near. Many of his routes included Sunnyside and Hog Creek, Bugscuffle and Fodder's Creek, Gumlog and Crooked Creek and Scataway. Most of his routes were in Towns County.

Scataway was an unusual name and since all roads had a reason for their name, Scataway did too. The story was told that during the Civil War some of the area men, fighting for the North, would sneak home for a few days. Before they came out of the woods their wives would wave their aprons if it was not safe for them to come in. If the men saw the aprons waving they would "scat" away.

The people would meet him at their mailbox bearing whatever they had to trade for their needs. He would pay 30 cents for a dozen hen eggs or twenty-five cents for pullet eggs. His customers often traded chickens or pigs with their legs tied together, sacks of corn, baskets of eggs, syrup in jugs, sassafras roots, maypops, bloodroot, ginseng or anything of value that Nick could sell from his warehouse on Tater Ridge in Hiawassee.

Sometimes he was the only person from outside the community that the mountaineers saw for weeks on end. Some of them bragged that they hadn't been to town in two years.

He had a gift of gab and a cheerful personality. He was a born salesman. One time he had the attention of a group of men who were watching his, almost like a sideshow, sorting of eggs.

11

He would pour the eggs from one container to another without breaking a single one.

Once, while we were visiting, my brother, Jim, went along on one of Uncle Earnest's routes. Jim listened and laughed as he heard him tell a lady that he had some Vick's salve that would help her headache. A man had a pain in his leg. Another bought a jar of Vick's salve to get rid of a cold. Jim never knew there were so many things that Vick's salve could cure.

He bought and sold over three thousand dollars worth of herbs in one year. He said' "there are over two hundred kinds of wild plants that medicine companies will buy". Ginseng root was a big sales item. He told us that the Chinese would pay a great deal for any Ginseng root that resembled any part of the human body, head, feet, hands or if a piece looked like a whole person it was worth a fortune. He kept sacks of herbs, roots, vines and pieces hung in his back-yard warehouse until he collected enough to make it worthwhile to ship it to his buyers.

His day usually ended by 6:30 P.M. but he had to sort and store everything he'd traded for. He was usually sold out of everything he started with by the time he got home. Some items, like the chickens and pigs, had to be delivered to his buyers the same day.

Many of the children who used to trade an egg for candy still live in Towns County and remember "Old Nick" fondly.

AUNT DALLIE

While I was living on Davis Island in Tampa, Florida, I invited Mama to come from Michigan and spend the winter with my husband, John, and me. Before she came she wrote to her sister, Aunt Dallie, and invited her too.

The pair were quite a handful. They talked, laughed and stayed awake until late at night not thinking that I had to get up and go to work the next day. They were seventy and seventy nine at the time. If they took a notion to have some buttermilk and cornbread during the night, they would get up and make themselves cornbread. It was quite a trying winter for my husband but he never said a word. He was glad when the five months were over.

Another time when I took Mama shopping to buy her a bathrobe for her birthday. She picked out the one she wanted and I started to pay for it. She said, "you've got to buy one for Dallie too, it's her birthday same as mine".

I was a little upset because I had let Mom pick out the most expensive robe the store had. I only had so much money to spend so I told Mama that I would let her pick cheaper robes for both of them or she could take the money, buy materiel and they could make themselves matching robes. Aunt Dallie was delighted. They made yellow quilted robes that they were very proud of. Lots of small memories bring them both back as they were then - full of life and having great fun being together. Aunt Dallie was born on Mama's ninth birthday.

PRESS AND DAVID

There are tales told by the Shooks and the Nichols abilities to fight. Of course, each one was tougher than the other and each time the story was told the participants grew even tougher.

One such incident took place in Tate City when the occasion arose that Great Uncle Press and Cousin David met, disagreed over something and proceeded to have a knife fight.

Darkness had fallen when the two had indulged in enough moonshine or had said enough to bring about the encounter. One of the sisters held the lantern as the men fought until each had been cut many times. Press had been cut several times but the worst one was over the top of his ear. It almost took the ear. David was also cut many times but his worst was across his stomach. This was deep enough for the fat to swell and roll out.

When the two men received the services of a doctor, some hours later, they questioned whether it was worth a fight.

The Doctor was upset over the needless injuries so he didn't use his kind healing hand. Press did get his ear sewed up but without anything to deaden the pain. David also got his stomach stitched together but first the swollen fat was sliced off. He too endured the needle without any painkiller. Maybe they didn't fight again for a few days.

13

COUSIN ODIE

Odie was the oldest of the three children when her mother died in childbirth. She was five at the time and remembers some of the hardships. Her father got drunk after her mother's funeral and went off and left the three small children for several days with no food or heat.

When the neighbors found out they separated the children by sending the three-year-old, to a family member in South Carolina. A woman in the family, who was already nursing her own child, was able take in and to wet-nurse the new baby boy. Odie was sent to her Grandparents, Tom and Sarah, who were my Great Grandparents.

I met Odie in Hiawassee when she was in her late eighties. She was a tiny woman with snow-white hair piled in curls on top of her head. She was wearing a stylish red coat and black knee boots. I was very impressed but didn't know that she was a distant cousin of mine.

Another cousin, Lena Belle, and Aunt Maude took me to meet her to get some more information about the family but she wasn't too much help. She was deaf as a post but she sure could talk.

She told us about the old man that was trying to court her. She said he would sit on her porch swing, look at the panoramic view of Lake Chatuge and say, "my new car'd sure look nice sittin' in your driveway".

She told him, "I got everything I want without no old man". Her daughter lived next door. Odie said, "even though I go there for most of my meals I do enjoy going out to dinner now and then and I love candy."

Several weeks after this visit, I took her some candy and tried to thank her for the information she had given me but I couldn't make her understand who I was.

FAMILY OF HENRY AND EVA

My father's name was Henry Jasper. Records, in the family,

14

show that he was born in Habersham County, Georgia in July 1895. He died in September 1957 in Toccoa, Georgia..

My mother's name was Eva Modena. She was born in Tate City, Georgia in what used to be Rabun County but is now Towns County. Her birth date was in September 1897. She died in December 1983 in Ludington, Michigan.

Beginning with me, I became the first one to start their family. They named me Etta Mae.

I was born on a farm called the 'Old York Place' in Hart County, Georgia in January 1917, near the home of my Grandparents on my father's side.

I had a lot of curly red hair. My mother described me as a plump, cheerful baby with cornflower blue eyes. She actually said that she could see little flowers in the iris (circle). Maybe that's why I've always loved flowers and want to see them all while I'm still living.

She and my Dad were both frightened one night when the pupils of my eyes dilated in the dark. They kept moving the kerosene lamp near and then way from me as the pupil enlarged or became smaller. They were new parents and too shy to tell anyone until Mama just had to write her mother about it. Granmaw Bettie was still laughing when she wrote back to tell them to move the lamp away and then back to each other and they would see that it was a normal reaction to light.

My birth certificate showed my name to be Etta Mae. It was filed in the Hart County, Georgia, courthouse where it was lost when the courthouse burned. Many years later I had to get verification, of my birth from some of my Aunts who were there when I was born, to get a replacement. What I got was a very informal paper just giving name, date and parents name. It has been sufficient for getting a Social Security number in 1936, my first official job, getting a passport and marriage licenses.

Eighteen months later along came my brother, Irving James, who was also born at the 'Old York Place', in July 1918. He had to get a birth certificate replacement when he took a job as bus driver near Chicago when he was in his early twenties. His was lost, as mine was, in the courthouse fire.

Mama described Jim as a scrawny, long-legged baby with a

shock of black hair. Because he wasn't nursing well, the old Doctor told Mama to boil white potatoes and give him the broth. He perked up so she gradually added the mashed potato and later the skins. It must have been what he needed because he outlived the five years the Doctor had predicted and grew to over six feet. At one time he weighed over three hundred pounds but is now eighty and still going after having a major heart attack about six years ago.

Mama believed the Old Wife's Tale that "if you kept nursing your baby you would not get in 'the family way' so soon. She found out that was not true.

The third child was William Ralph who was born in 1920 in Westminister, South Carolina. He was a lively child, had a beautiful smile and could dance before he could walk. Mama's brother, Clifford, used to bring his Fiddle to the house, stand 'Little Ralph' up beside a chair, and start the music. Ralph would dance as long as the music was played or until he would drop from exhaustion. He wore the heels and toes out of a little pair of high-top button shoes. He died in April 1921 about a month after his first birthday. I never knew that Mama had kept those little shoes until after she died, sixty-two years later. I have those shoes now.

Mom was pregnant for George when 'Little Ralph died.

George Dillard was born in September 1921 while our family lived on Burton Lake Road in Habersham County, Georgia after we had moved back from Westminister, S.C. George also had red hair, lighter than mine, and blue eyes. Everybody said, "he was too pretty to be a boy". His smile was infectious.

Next was Howard Ray. He was born in Hartwell County Georgia in April 1923. He weighed almost thirteen pounds and was a roly-poly baby who never really got over being chubby until he went into the Marine Corps at eighteen.

He was left out of a lot of Jim and George's skirmishes. Probably a good thing. He often had his feelings hurt and I can still see that lower lip squared away when he was really mad and cried. We nicknamed him 'Bulldog' because when he cried his face looked like a bulldog. He grew up to be a very handsome fellow with a deep dimple in each cheek. I used to say "the boys got all the good looks in our family". Sometimes my sister disputes that.

In August 1923, our family moved to Lansing, Michigan.

The twins, Leo Gene and Lela Dean, were born in June 1925 in Lansing on Thompson street between Melling Drop Forge and Motor Wheel Factory. Leo was born about ten minutes before Lela so has always claimed to be the oldest. They each weighed a little over six pounds.

Leo had big blue-grey eyes and blond hair. He had the bone structure and features of a regular husky little guy.

Lela had blond curly hair, blue eyes with long curly eyelashes. She was delicately formed and very feminine. A very pretty baby.

I was eight and a half at the time and absolutely knew nothing about babies. The only thing that was said in my presence was that the Doctor had told Mama that she had a big tumor and that she needed an operation. She didn't think so and just waited her time out.

Our neighbor girls, who were a little older, Jim and I hid under our back porch when we were banished from the house after the Doctor came.

Alice, the smart one, told me that babies were brought by the Doctor in his little black bag. When I saw how small that little black bag was, I knew that she didn't know what she was talking about. There was no way the Doctor could have brought both those babies in that little-bitty bag. The Doctor was somewhat red-faced when she had twins

When the twins were about three, Mama had a miscarriage because she had taken quinine and went into convulsions. I was eleven and didn't know what to do. I put a wash cloth in her mouth to keep her from swallowing her tongue, massaged her arms and legs. Neighbors called a Doctor who said that I had probably saved her life. It wasn't because of any skills that I knew but instinct told me she would choke. This was never discussed until many years later when she told me never to take quinine to keep from having a baby.

Eva Marie was born in April 1931. She got pneumonia and

17

only lived five weeks. She looked like a beautiful sleeping doll in her little white casket. She was buried in the Wacousta Cemetery on Wacousta Road a few miles from where we lived on what was called the "Martha Pullman Place".

Mama had one more pregnancy that I was aware of. That occurred while we lived on Vermont Street in Lansing, Michigan when I was seventeen. She was about three months pregnant. I remember Dad showing it, a boy, to Jim and me and saying, "you need to see this so you'll know what can happen". I remember being very upset about it.

As far as I know, Mama had eleven pregnancies. Three miscarriages, two died as infants and six lived to adulthood.

All six of us, my four brothers, my sister and I, retired from our jobs in the mid 1980's. All of us, including husbands and wives, except Howard's second wife, met at my house in Hiawassee, Georgia for a Family Retiree Get-Together. Just adults-no children! We had a great time looking up relatives, cooking, sightseeing and rehashing our childhood. We hadn't been together as a group, since our Dad died in 1957.

Jim, George, Leo, Lela and I have Diabetes. All of us developed Diabetes in our later years, sixties and seventies, except Leo and he has had it for over twenty years. Both our parents had Diabetes and our Dad had Heart problems too. So, we feel lucky to have made it this far considering our health problems. We attribute that to the fact that none of us drink excessively and don't smoke, Jim and Leo quit years ago and Lela, George and I never smoked. We have a positive outlook and are looking forward to many more years of good and interesting living.

HART COUNTY

There were the three of us, Jim, George and myself, when our family moved back to Hart County when my Grandpa Wilson died. He had a stroke at age fifty and left Grandma with ten children at home.

A Judge made Dad Administrator of the Estate so we had to live near Grandma. She could neither read nor write so had no way of keeping track of affairs.

Grandpa owned three farms at the time. Our family lived in what they called a 'tenant' house or 'sharecroppers' house. It had a big dirt yard, an unpainted house and a small barn. We had to carry water from Grandma's well.

Many problems arose as Dad tried to get the three older boys, Hamlin, Sanford and Leon to work. Elmer was a Mongoloid and a good worker but he required constant supervision. Evard was only six, ten months older than I.

Hamlin thought he should be Administrator as he was the oldest boy still living at home. He wouldn't take orders from Dad and they had serious problems.

Dad went to the Judge and asked to be relieved of his duties as Administrator. The Judge said, "the only way you could get out of it is to die or move out of the State".

During the summer that Grandpa died, I had Spinal Meningitis and George was sick. The fact that we were sick was mentioned in Grandpa's obituary.

Mom said that I would lie on the floor all curled up with my heels almost touching my head in back of me, they thought I was having temper tantrums, and that I ran a fever for three months. All my hair came out. It had been curly but my new hair was straight as a string.

I don't think that George had Meningitis unless it was a very mild case. He had none of the long lasting fever or hair loss and has never shown any results from it.

I can remember Dad making me walk the cracks in the floor to make me walk straight even after we had lived in Michigan two years. As far as anyone can tell, my walk is normal but I've had back problems all my life.

The Doctors in those days knew nothing of Spinal Meningitis and I didn't know that I had had it until I was in University Hospital in Ann Arbor, Michigan, during my mid-thirties, where they took spinal fluid for tests because of a back injury.

A year after Dad talked to the Judge, Dad decided that he had had enough of trying to run the affairs for his mother and decided to leave the State of Georgia.

That is when our family moved to Michigan.

19

CHAPTER 2

MY SIBLINGS

MY SIBLINGS

JIM

JIM'S STRAW HAT

We were all on the wagon ready to go to town, Hartwell, Georgia, when Jim's straw hat blew off and landed in the yard. He started hollering for Dad to stop the mules and let him down to get his hat. The mules were already in motion and Dad knew how hard it was to handle them so he just let them keep moving while Mama tried to convince Jim that his hat would still be there when we got back. Jim whimpered a little but soon settled down as we neared town.

A trip to town was always a treat for us kids. While Dad attended to replenishing the farm supplies, Mama would take us children to the General Store where she purchased sugar, salt, flour, and items that couldn't be grown or made at the farm. The clerk would give us children a small bag of candies when Dad paid the bill. This was a real treat for us because the only sweets we ever had at home were the occasional pie or cake that Mama made for us. Nobody made cookies in those days because they considered it a waste of sugar.

On the way home we filled ourselves with candy and usually were asleep in the wagon-bed when we got home. Not Jim. This time he was anxiously looking forward to getting his straw hat. This was the first time he'd gone anywhere without his hat since Uncle Ernest had brought it to him on his last trip down from the mountains. It was a child's size, made of straw with a band between the brim and the crown. It was made to last. We were back in our yard when Jim started yelling and trying to climb out of the wagon. He saw his precious hat, still on the ground, with one of our piglets standing on the brim and rooting in to the crown. The pig had his head inside the hat and was trying to get out by pushing into the crown.

The pig had torn the hat apart and was still trying to get through it to extricate himself when Jim pounced on him. It was too late. The brim was torn, the band was pulled apart and the crown was totally demolished. Jim couldn't be consoled and the tears flowed.

Mama got tired of hearing him cry and told him how he could get even with the pig. She said, "just sit on the bottom step of the porch and when the pig comes out from under the house, where he had run to get away from Jim, just grab him by the tail and bite it off. Jim was ready when the little pig came out from under the steps. He grabbed it by the tail.

Mama came running out to see what was making the pig squeal. She saw a cloud of red dust as Jim was hanging on and being dragged through the dust as he was trying to bite the pig's tail.

She laughed 'till she cried and tried to explain to Jim that she didn't really mean it. She was just trying to give him something to think about.

That little pig steered clear of our yard after that and grew up in the barnyard instead of roaming all over the place.

Jim was only three at the time and as far as I know he never had another straw hat until he was about fourteen. Somehow he got one which he wore to the Star School on U.S.16 near Wacousta, Michigan. The kids nicknamed him 'Farmer' which he was called until we moved into the city, Lansing, a few years later. He seems to always have a liking for straw hats. He had one that was flat, like an over sized mushroom. I guess it's worn out because I haven't seen him wearing it for a long time. I have one just like it but haven't worn it much. Maybe I'll dig it out and give it to him.

THE BARN

Mr. Dill owned the barn on the property behind the house that he had sold my Dad on Fredrick Street just north of Lansing.

He told Jim and George that they could have the lumber if they would tear down the horse stalls inside the barn.

They got some neighbor boys to help and had a great time wrecking those stalls. They used one of the longer boards to make a slide from the hayloft to a pile of straw below.

I remember a neighbor boy running to our house with about a four inch gash in his butt where they had missed pulling a nail. Mama put some Iodine on it and sent him home. She wouldn't let me see the wound but later said, "he came in a hair of being castrated".

Jim saw a big skunk in the hayloft and threw a pitchfork at it. He didn't kill it, just pinned it with its head in a hole to the lower level. He got the full benefit of the skunk's wrath. I don't know what happened to Jim's clothes but it was a long time, after several baths, before any of us wanted to be anywhere near him.

Not to be defeated, the boys decided to put their boards to good use. They built a boat that they intended to use on the ten-acre pond behind the barn. Warren, one of the bigger boys, got some tar from his father's garage and they smeared the boat and themselves.

Warren, the biggest of the neighbor boys, wanted someone to try it out with him but the only one game enough was George and he couldn't swim.

They got about half way across the pond when the boat started leaking. George bailed while Warren paddled furiously to get to the closest shore, which happened to be where people had been dumping trash. The boat sank. Warren and George walked to shore.

The boys salvaged some of the wood and built a raft. It was about six by eight feet.

Jim sent George to retrieve something he had seen in the water. George made good progress as he poled the raft about two hundred yards. Suddenly he was in deep trouble. The pole wouldn't reach bottom and the wind started blowing hard.

He tried to lift a small piece of a door, that had been left on the raft, for a sail. He had seen some of the older boys use boards and things for a sail on their makeshift rafts so he thought he could too.

The wind caught his sail and he couldn't hold the door upright. He managed to hang on to the raft until he could reach bottom with the pole.

Meanwhile Mama, several neighbors and I, stood on shore

screaming directions at George. The wind was howling so he couldn't hear a word.

George finally managed to get ashore. He got a whipping when Dad got home from work. I personally thought that the big boys should have gotten the punishment because they took advantage of their smaller brother.

Jim has led a very interesting life. Having dropped out of school at sixteen from Pattengill Junior High, he worked in a gas station for awhile. He drove city bus in Lansing for a few years before going to Chicago and driving bus there.

He was in his early twenties when he took Skinny Ennis and his band to Gary, Indiana and had a serious accident. A trolley power line had not been removed when the city was taking out the lines. It was not marked and, in the dark, Jim hit in the front center of the bus. The impact caught Jim's leg and broke it in three places. The accident was reported on the radio and in the newspaper. None of our family knew about it until about eleven days after the accident when a nurse got in touch with us.

Ray my husband, George my brother and I went down to Gary to see Jim. His leg was in a steel frame from his groin to his heel where a pin through the ankle helped to straighten his leg. When Ray asked Jim how they got the pin in, Jim told him, "they just took a hammer and pounded it right through". Ray turned green, slid down the wall and almost fainted.

Jim was in and out of the hospital for over two years. After all the treatment his leg is still an inch shorter than the other one. He wore a built-up shoe for years and decided that he didn't need it anymore. He later had to have back surgery and returned to wearing the built-up shoe. He also had injuries to his right arm. They didn't find that right away and the ends of the bones knubbed over but did not join and were wired together. About twenty five years later he lost the use of his right arm from the elbow down, including his hand.

Jim has accomplished much more than many college educated men. He took the settlement from the accident and started a storm window and door business in Toledo, Ohio. He was there from 1941 until 1946. He moved his business to Georgia in the late forties after he had married Peggy and had his first son, Rick.

Right after World War II in August 1946, while still living in Toledo, he decided to take a boat trip across Lake Erie to Detroit, up the Detroit River and along the western edge of Lake Huron to the Straits of Mackinaw.

He invited Ray and me to join him and Peggy on this Great Lakes Cruise. He had a twenty eight-foot cabin cruiser that was nicely fitted out with double bunks on each side and a small galley.

We hired someone to stay with our kids, packed a few things including our tent, and joined them at the dock in Toledo Harbor. They left Rick with our mother.

We were well on our way when Jim discovered that he had brought his aerial charts instead of his navigation charts.

When we arrived at Detroit, Jim told Ray to drop the anchor. He did... and it kept right on going. Jim had forgotten to tie the end of the rope to the boat. We made do with a cement block from there on.

At the next stop, up the Detroit River, we tied up to an old dock that had not been used for a long time. Gar Wood, the Boat race driver, and some of his buddies were racing up and down the river.

Peggy and I went shopping and bought about a case of toilet paper and stored it under the bunks. It had been so scarce during the war that this was a real luxury item. We had a great time shopping.

None of us paid any attention to the old drunk that tried to tell us that our boat had a leak. Something about old pilings under water and the boats racing up and down the river. He said he was called "Fat Ass Hamilton" and that he was "an engineer at building shit- houses". He staggered and fell in the river and was climbing out when we got back on our boat.

Peggy and I had bought ingredients for homemade vegetable soup for dinner. We had a big pot almost ready to eat when the kerosene lantern, hanging on a nail above, dropped into our soup. Sandwiches had to suffice.

In spite of our little incidents, we still were enjoying ourselves to the fullest when we went to bed that night. Jim and

Peggy had the lower two bunks, with a walkway between, while Ray and I had the upper two.

In the morning Jim woke up first and made such a roar that all of us came awake with a start. He had stretched his arms out and hit water! Inside the cabin! His shoes were floating and his pants were soaked where he had dropped them on the floor. Needless to say, our supply of toilet paper was totally ruined.

We all bailed water from there to Port Huron. The ferryboat Captain sent one of his men over with a bilge pump to help us out. He didn't want us to sink right there in the channel. The fellow said that he pumped about four thousand gallons of water out of our bilge.

Several people suggested that we try to make it up the Black River to an Airplane/Boat repair shop. By all of us bailing we made it to what looked like a makeshift ramp. The mechanic said that he had several ahead of us and we'd have to wait. We didn't have any choice. Jim and Peggy slept on the boat even though it was on an incline up the ramp. Ray and I pitched our tent. And then it rained for two days. The boat was finally fixed and we headed down river. We didn't get back to Port Huron when we ran into something in the river and had to go back to the mechanic. Another two days lost.

We just got back on Lake Erie when a big rain-wind storm came. We were traveling at night to make up for lost time. While looking to find a port where we could tie up for the night, we saw a lot of lights to the west of us.

There were dozens of people shouting and waving their arms. We couldn't hear what they were saying so Jim pulled in closer to shore and hit a sandbar. We were stopped dead in the water. That's what the people were trying to tell us.

The men got out in water that was up to their knees when the waves were out but over their heads when the waves came in. They pulled on ropes, when the waves came in and lifted the boat, until they gradually got it off the sandbar. We were all exhausted but our night was not over.

Ray and I sat on the bow, in the rain and darkness, guiding Jim through acres of old posts that were once part of a series of docks. We barely moved as we manually pushed our way through the maze. It was scary. More than once, I thought that I must be crazy to leave my three beautiful children for this nightmare.

We finally found a dock that looked safe and tied up to rest awhile. We were all sound asleep when we were wakened by the Coast Guard who had been out looking for us. We were docked at their pier.

It was a tired and bedraggled bunch that pulled into Toledo Harbor later that day. Jim and Peggy's friends were anxiously waiting for us, having feared the worst. We found out later that four people had been lost to the storm in Lake Erie.

Jim put his boat in dry-dock for repairs in August. It was the next June, 1947, before he got it out .

Rick was one-year old in June so they decided to take the boat on their first venture, after our eventful cruise, to an island in Toledo Harbor to celebrate Rick's birthday.

They had only gotten out about a quarter of a mile when the boat blew up. Peg was seated on a bench over the gas tank, Rick was in a Teeter Babe on the floor and Jim was steering the boat. He yelled for Peggy to jump but she was so dazed that she didn't respond. Jim grabbed Rick under his arm, got to Peggy and pushed her overboard and jumped with Rick in his arms.

Immediately there were boats to the rescue. When they pulled Peggy out of the water the skin came off her arms and legs. She was in the hospital for five weeks. The first time we saw her, in the hospital, she looked like a mummy except for the bridge of her nose which looked like a wiener split down the middle. I felt horrible because she was such a beautiful girl. Luckily she healed nicely and had no scars. Rick had a tiny tip taken off the end of his nose, which didn't leave a scar, and Jim had his eyebrows, hair on his head and arms singed but was otherwise alright.

Apparently the mechanics that fixed the boat didn't put in a new gas line from the intake to the tank and fumes spread below deck were ignited when the motor heated up. The insurance company would not pay because they said it was an "explosion" rather than a fire. The boat burned to the water line and sank. Jim had been offered four thousand dollars for the boat that morning.

In 1948, Jim moved his family to Albany, Georgia where he set up a business of re-modeling and selling awnings. He designed and patented a display sign for the top of his car advertising his business. That really worked but he found many flaws with the awnings he was handling so he designed machinery that would form the full width of the huge rolls of aluminum. He had dealers in nineteen states.

Jim was riding high when he bought his yacht, in Tampa, Florida, which he told Peggy was his "Canoe".

He called Peggy to tell her to get my kids and me and come to Tampa to see it. We drove his blue Cadillac with blue-walled tires.

I got the only speeding tickets I ever got in my life. The boys in the back seat didn't help when they told the policeman that I was doing seventy-five. I had to pay a thirty-dollar fine, half a month's rent, to a Justice of Peace to keep from going to jail for the weekend.

When we arrived Jim had food ready for us. We were overwhelmed by his forty two foot 'Shady Lady' as we stood in the galley, having a sandwich, talking about it.

Terry was sitting on a bunk across from us when he saw an old fashioned gun hanging on the wall. He reached over and said, "does this thing work?" as he pulled the trigger. The bullet lodged in the ceiling just above my head. I was so shocked that I fell to the floor. If either Jim or Peggy were standing where I was they would have been killed because both of them are taller than I am. Terry wasn't physically punished. The shock of almost killing his Mom did that.

Then, in the late fifties, Jim went into packaging awnings for standard windows that people could install themselves. They sold by the truckload. Then 'Boom'! The Government decided to regulate the truck lines so they could not make drop shipments. Dealers did not order by the truckload... theirs was mostly custom work. Jim's business was shot down.

A friend, that Jim had met in the aluminum business, from Houston, Texas invited him to come out there. He said, "Jim, move your business to Texas. It's centrally located and whatever it takes, even a million, I've got it so come into business with me. If you'll move out here, get set up and incorporate I'll take whatever I put into it in stock"

Jim took Rick with him on the 'Shady Lady' via the Intercoastal Waterways from Tampa to Houston while Peggy drove her station wagon taking the two younger kids, Jim and Kim and the dog. They ran into the rains from a Hurricane and had real problems on the road.

It took thirteen semi-trucks to move all of Jim's equipment. Mr. Coy advanced Jim fifty thousand dollars to move and set up. They were just about ready to get the business going when Mr. Coy dropped dead. No papers had been signed at that point … just a handshake.

There was a provision in Texas laws that protects the heirs in cases like this. Mr. Coy had appointed a Bank and a law firm as Trustees. They would not let Jim operate the business. They liquidated everything on the property, including all of Jim's equipment and his forty two-foot yacht, the Shady Lady. Jim lost everything.

He wound up in California working for an old friend, who was in the house remodeling business. That didn't last long and Jim went into the business of selling Convenient Foods franchises. He came to New York and convinced John and me that he could sell the canned foods on Long Island. John was not a salesman and there wasn't that much hunting in that part of the country. We lost over-three thousand dollars in a matter of weeks. Jim quit that business and went into another selling job. He was a born salesman.

Rick enlisted in the Marine Corps from Texas and Peggy took Young Jim and Kim to Pennsylvania for awhile.

From California, Jim went to Michigan while he was still selling franchises. Peggy and the children joined him there.

By then Jim was into the sign-making business. He redesigned the machinery for making the signs, plastic was pressed over forms while heated and then painted, and sold franchises for the machines.

While in Michigan his right arm, injured in the bus accident when he was in his twenties, began to give him trouble. The wires that held the bones together broke and caused a

Staphylococcus infection. That caused the Doctors to have to remove the small bone in his lower right arm. He lost the use and sense of all feeling in his hand. Cold weather caused it to freeze, without him knowing it, so he decided to move to a warmer climate.

He and his brother, Leo, went to Tampa, Florida in February 1972. Jim and Leo set up a location on North Nebraska Avenue for their headquarters for the sign-making and selling business. While there he heard that he could rent his motor home for four hundred dollars a week. He was on his way again. He bought a few more motor homes and went into the rental business.

Peggy, Jim and Kim came to Tampa when Jim made his first trip back to Michigan in August 1972.

A few years later, Jim bought a piece of land on Hillsborough Avenue and set up a Motor Home business. He sold new Jayco Motor Homes and handled resales of other brands. Rentals were a big part of the business.

In 1986 he decided to retire when he was sixty eight. He still owned the property on Hillsborough Avenue. He leased it with an option to buy but that fell through and he had to foreclose. He sold it again in 1992 and is holding the mortgage, which brings him a nice income.

Through the years, Jim has owned a succession of small planes, a twenty eight-foot cabin cruiser, a forty two-foot yacht and numerous Motor Homes.

Jim and Peggy have retired to Thonotosassa, Florida where they make their home base for the many Motor Home trips they make to Michigan, the Mountains and to Motor Home Owners club meetings. They have traveled extensively in Europe and all over the United States.

Jim and Peggy have had their ups and downs, financially and otherwise, but have stuck together through it all. They celebrated their Fiftieth Wedding Anniversary a couple years ago.

Jim dictated the following to Peggy who wrote it out for him. Since he lost the use of his right arm it's hard for him to write. I'm quoting: "After the Bull incident we moved into Lansing and I pitched baseball on the school team. People did not know my name but knew I came from the country, so they called me 'Farmer'.

Disney Dean, with the Detroit Tigers, lived close to us. He and I would play catch at the park. One day he said, "Hey, you are pretty good" and invited me to go to Detroit with him. They let me play with their farm team a few times".

Another of Jim's stories in the same letter is called 'The Hunting Trip" and again I quote: "Some friends and I were up north deer hunting. One of the fellows found where a bear had denned up. There has been the story that a bear sleeps with a paw in his mouth. We talked about it and decided to find out. I was chosen to check the bear. I crawled in the den, not knowing there were two bears. I stepped on one and they both woke up. One got hold of my arm and the other of my leg. I screamed as loud as I could but my buddies were in the next county by then. What happened???... They ate me up and I went back to sleep."

Jim told this story to my kids, Vicki, Lynn and Terry, while we lived on Norwood Drive when they were between thirteen and ten. After that, it was hard to convince them that he did tell true stories sometimes. He got a big kick out of having everyone's attention and then dropping one on them like the "Bear Story".

LITTLE RALPH

We lived in Westminster, South Carolina for a short time, where 'Little Ralph' was born. Ralph, to my knowledge he was always called 'Little Ralph' .I have no idea why. He was only a few months old when we moved to a place across the Creek from Granmaw and Granpaw Nichols in Habersham County, Georgia.

They always seemed to be glad to see us children when the folks, our parents, would take us by the hand and lead us across the foot log when the water was deep. I know there were times when we waded the Creek, walked through the red mud and onto Granmaw's porch. I can't remember her ever scolding us. She always had something for us to eat even if it was a piece of corn bread, which she called a "corn pone".

My memories of living there, on Burton Lake Road, were happy times until Little Ralph died.

33

He had been a healthy happy baby and would dance, even before he could walk, by holding onto a chair as Uncle Clifford, Mama's brother, played the fiddle. He danced the toes and heels out of his little leather button-up shoes. Mama had a little button hook that she used to put them on him.

Mama said that he died of Collar 'n Fanum. He was sick for several days, went into convulsions and died in Mama's arms. No Doctor that I have asked, in all these years, knew what Collar 'n Fanum was. I read that one of Rose Kennedy's children died of Cholera Infantum. Their Doctors diagnosed it because of seizures caused by high fever and diarrhea. I can only assume that is what Ralph died of.

Ralph was put in the little casket, which was set up across the backs of two chairs in our house. We all cried and cried even though we children had no idea as to what had happened. He was buried at Providence Church cemetery. When somebody threw dirt on the casket we all left and the men covered the little grave. This was in May a month or so after Little Ralph's first birthday.

A few days later my Uncle, 'Little Doc', came across the Creek and said we should play 'dead'. "

He was the smaller version of his 'Uncle Doc', who was about three years older than I, four at the time, and Jim who was eighteen months younger.

Jim and I helped him dig a hole in the sand close to the Creek. Little Doc climbed in the hole. We covered him up with sand and went on playing. I found some wild flowers and put them on the top of the dirt.

Minutes later Mama came out to see what we were doing. She asked where Little Doc was and we told her "he's dead and we buried him".

She was frantic as she dug a mad and sputtering Little Doc out. In another few minutes he would have suffocated. Mama nearly had a miscarriage. She was pregnant with George who was born in September.

GEORGE

34

George was born in Habersham County, Georgia in September 1921. He had red curly red hair and mischievous blue eyes. He was a happy child who often followed in his big brother's, Jim, footsteps who occasionally got them both in trouble.

COLT IN WATERHOLE

We only lived on the Wells Farm, north and west of Wacousta, for a few months but our family had several unusual experiences during that summer.

The family moved there from Fredrick Street a few weeks before school was out for the summer and moved again before school started in the fall. Because I stood to suffer most from missing school my parents let me stay with the Dill family for six weeks to finish fifth grade.

As a farmer from Georgia, Dad didn't understand any of the different methods used in Michigan so soon found out that the Wells Farm was not for us.

There was a mare, Dolly, who wouldn't work - wouldn't pull a plow, a wagon or buggy. Mr. Dill, owner of Wells Farm , tried to hook her up to his buggy but she wouldn't cooperate. He beat her with a stick. This was not Dad's way of handling animals and they exchanged a few heated words. Dad put her out to pasture after Mr. Dill left.

One day when George was seven years old, and I was eleven we were back in the pasture near the spring, a water hole that Dad had built a frame around, we heard strange noises.

Dolly had just had a colt and it was in the water hole. She was running around, snorting and pawing at the ground. The colt was too weak to pull itself out and was about to drown.

We got its head out of the water and I held it up while George ran to get Dad.

Meanwhile the mare was frantic, snorting and running in circles.

When Dad rescued the heavy colt, it quickly found its mother and started nursing. It survived the ordeal and was soon running around the pasture.

35

After the birth of the colt, Dolly willingly resumed her duties as a Buggy Horse.

THE BULL STORY

My brother, George narrated this story to me on a Sunday in September 1995. It happened while we lived at the Martha Pullman Place on Wacousta Road in mid-nineteen thirties..

The house had a wood burning pot-bellied stove for heat and a wood burning range for cooking so we had to have lots of wood for all year. Dad made arrangements with a nearby farmer to cut firewood on his farm on a fifty-fifty agreement.

Dad would chop down the trees and trim the branches off with an ax. Then he would put Jim and George to work sawing the logs with a crosscut saw. Each boy would alternate pulling the saw blade across the log until they had it cut into sizes that were about two feet long. The handles on the saw were almost too big for boys twelve and nine years old.

Dad then used a wedge and split the logs into stove-size pieces. While Dad was doing that the boys would drag the limbs to a big brush pile where Dad used a buzz saw to cut them into firewood sizes. Then they would stack the wood on a sleigh, drawn by a pair of horses, also borrowed from the neighbor who owned the trees, and haul them to the house a half mile away.

This work had been going on for several weeks. They were nearly through cutting the trees. It took a lot to supply two households.

George and Jim had worked alone all morning while Dad had some other chores he had to do. They walked home for dinner at noon and Dad went back with them for the afternoon. Most Southerners say they have "dinner " at noon and "supper " in the evening.

Just inside the woods they came upon a big Holstein bull. Jim bent down to be sure it was a bull. It was. It had jumped the fence from the second farm away. The bull snorted and pawed the ground as he lowered his horns to attack. Dad yelled for the boys to climb a tree.

George ran so hard that when he looked back, to see if the

bull was coming, he ran smack into a tree that knocked him flat. He got up and climbed that tree which was eight to ten inches in diameter. The first limb was seven or eight feet off the ground. He climbed a little higher where he was safe and able to observe all of the action from his perch.

Jim ran to a bigger tree, almost too big to climb. It was a rough bark Sugar Maple. He had just gotten out of reach of the bull when it started butting the tree. Jim cried, "there's no limbs", but Dad told him to keep climbing.

Dad picked up some cut tree limbs and began beating the bull across the nose.

When Jim finally reached a limb, Dad decided he'd better look after himself. He turned and ran to the woodpile where he had left the ax.

George watched in horror as he saw that the bull was only a few feet behind Dad, with his head lowered and snorting. He almost caught up with him when Dad suddenly stepped sideways into thick brush.

The bull plunged forward several yards before he realized that Dad was gone. He smelled around, like a dog, trying to locate Dad.

The bull was unable to find Dad. He went back to Jim's tree and started butting it ferociously.

Meanwhile, Dad had found a tree that was leaning so much he figured he could climb it if he had to. He was too heavy, at about two hundred and twenty pounds, to climb straight up.

It was a quirk of fate that a farmer came by with his team of horses and wagon in the next field. The bull lowered his head and charged through a split rail fence

Dad got his ax and came back to Jim's tree. It took most of the afternoon to talk Jim into coming down from the tree. When he finally did, the inside of both arms and legs were bloody raw from the rough bark. It took weeks to heal. He lost his appetite and the folks said "he didn't grow an inch for a whole year". For months he had nightmares where the bull was chasing him. For years he wouldn't go into a field where there were any cattle, cows or bulls.

When Dad and the boys got home and told their story to our

family, some of us had nightmares too. I know I did. I would see the bull coming after me with his eyes as big as saucers. Just before he was ready to pounce on me I'd wake up in a cold sweat.

The bull was later captured but our family never knew the details. Dad traced the owner of the bull down and insisted that the man put a ring in the bull's nose so it could be controlled. The farmer complied and apologized for the horrible experience his bull had put them through.

To this day, sixty-nine years later, both boys remember this experience as if it was yesterday.

This story was written, word for word, as George remembered it. It was a real nightmare for him and Jim.

George went up many stepping stones to become the fine person that he is today.

He spent his teen years growing up in Grand Ledge, Michigan where he graduated from High School. He was on the football team but had a hard time convincing Dad to attend a game. He finally did and felt proud when he saw Dad standing up and yelling at the top of his voice, "that's my boy", after he had made a touchdown.

He was drafted into the Army in September 1942 after he had been turned down by the Air Force because of his eyesight.

He had enrolled in Michigan State University and had purchased his books when the Draft Notice came from the Army.

He went from Basic Training to Officer Candidate School and was commissioned 2nd Lieutenant in May 1943.

Shipped overseas in April 1944, he spent several weeks in England, was sent to France in late June 1944 and assigned to the Fourth Division Infantry Division as Rifle Platoon Leader. He fought in France, Belgium, Luxembourg and Germany until wounded in action in February 1945.

At the end of World War II in Europe, he returned to the United States. Citations include Silver Star, Bronze Star with two clusters, Purple Heart with two clusters, five Major Campaign Ribbons, President's Unit Citation and French Unit Citation.

He married his high school sweetheart and worked for Dad

in the wholesale produce business. He bought the business when Dad moved South for his health.

George eventually sold the business and became an insurance Agent with Prudential Life Insurance Company of America where he attained many honors, among them "Man of the Year". The company did a "This is Your Life" show on screen, including his teen years as a salesman selling melons with Dad, which was shown at a Prudential convention in Lake of the Ozarks, Missouri. His brother, Jim, was invited to attend and was overwhelmed by the honors bestowed on his 'little brother'.

George wrote a book, over a period of about five years, about his experiences as a Lieutenant in the Army. He was to be promoted to Captain, but it was never official, when the war ended.

His book "IF YOU SURVIVE" was published in paperback in 1986 and is available to this day, October 1999, in Walden Book Stores in most major shopping Malls. He retired while still working on his book.

In July 1999 George was promoted to Captain in the Michigan National Guard by Governor Engler.

He and Florine moved to Thonotosassa, Florida where her parents, Florence and Hugh, moved in with them.

Florine's dad was in his early 90's and her mother in her late 80's when Florine moved back to Michigan, to take care of them, in 1992. They have both died since but Florine remained in Michigan near where her children live.

George recently moved back to Michigan where he and Florine have gotten their five children, several grandchildren and great grandchildren back together.

He is collecting materiel for his second book.

HOWARD

Howard was born in Hart County near our Grandmother Wilson's home. When he was three months old our parents took him, along with me and his brothers, Jim and George, to the home of their other Grandparents, Erv and Bettie Nichols. This was in preparation for Dad leaving to go north to look for work.

When he was four months old he was taken on a train ride that deposited him in Lansing, Michigan where his Dad had a job and an apartment ready for his family.

Howard was a chubby child with deep dimples and an infectious smile. Except, of course, when he was mad. Then his lower lip would square up and the tears would flow.

We called him our little "Bulldog".

He was usually a cheerful child until his bigger brothers would do something to hurt his feelings. Jim and George sometimes were merciless as they teased him or wouldn't let him go with them on some of their escapades. I thought that he was lucky not to be included in some of the things they did and were punished for.

He was a large teenager and ate ravenously. I thought he needed a lot to keep the big guy going but Dad was on his case about eating at almost every meal.

Sales seemed to be his calling and he did it well. He always sold more melons, or whatever produce Dad had, than either of the other boys. With his big blue eyes and his smile, he could talk almost anyone into buying whatever he was selling.

Howard graduated from Grand Ledge High School and joined the Marine Corps. in May 1942. He became a Staff Sergeant after going to Boot Camp in San Diego, California. He went from there to Hawaii and was in Guadalcanal by mid August 1942.

From there to New Hebrides in January of 1943 then to San Diego on furlough in May 1943.

I was working at Fisher Body in Lansing, Michigan on a World War II Contract when he came, in full uniform, to visit the War Plant. He was about the most handsome man I'd ever seen. I was very proud of him and the women absolutely went wild over him. He was there because the War Department thought that the sight of men in uniform would boost the morale of us War Workers. It did.

He was stationed in El Centro, California from May to August 1943 then shipped to Saipan-Guam. He was wounded on Tinian Island in July 1945. He finished his enlistment in Mojave

Desert in 1946 and was discharged at Chicago Great Lakes Naval-Marine Base in May 1946.

He and Betty were married shortly after he got out of service in 1946. After the ceremony they came out of the church to find that their car had not only been decorated but had been raised up and cement blocks had been placed under the axles. It made him so mad that he actually lifted the car off the first blocks. His brothers, and others, had done it again. Some of the other men helped get the rest of the blocks out and Howard and Betty were on their way. They had five children who are adults now.

For several years, after the War, Howard worked at Reo Motors when they were making fire engines, until they closed down, and then at Bishop's Furniture Store, until they closed.

He got into the Antique and Auctioning business. He and Betty owned an Antique store in Grand Ledge, Michigan for several years.

I attended one of Howard's estate sales during the early nineteen sixties, while I was on a visit from Bermuda, held at an abandoned Kroger store in Grand Ledge. It was very interesting to watch, and hear, him auction that particular sale. Tables covered with glass, china, rare glass, lamps, dolls, household goods and everything imaginable filled the entire store. The items being auctioned had belonged to an elderly lady who had been hit by a car as she was crossing the road near Mt. Hope Cemetery. She had no family and no means to pay for the Nursing Home where she had been taken. Some of her collections were wrapped in newspapers dating back to the 1920s. Her living conditions were sad but she would not sell any of her prize collections as long as she had control. The State took over and ordered the sale to pay her expenses in the Nursing Home..

Howard and Betty were divorced in 1967 but the family has kept in touch with the children and got reacquainted with Betty a few years ago.

He remarried and spent his retirement days managing his, and his new wife's, investments. He died in September 1990.

HOWARD'S ELECTRIC DANCE

"We were visiting Howard's parents, Henry and Evie, when they lived in Toccoa, Georgia. Their home was located on a small acreage outside of town in a large grove of pine trees.

On this particular morning, Howard was the last person in line for his morning shower. Earlier, the sky was beginning to darken with threatening clouds but no one paid any attention to the weather. By the time Howard got into the shower, a thunderstorm was beginning to develop.

The shower itself was an addition to the home. Concrete had been poured directly on the ground for the bathroom foundation.

By the time Howard had completely soaped his entire body and was starting to rinse off, lightening struck one of the pine trees nearby. It followed the root system into the ground under the shower.

Howard was screaming for help, hopping first on one foot and then the other, until I got there. What a sight that was. At first all I could do was laugh until I realized that he was experiencing electric shocks every time a wet foot touched the floor and then the other.

Finally I put a throw rug, with a rubber back, down for him to step on.

That broke contact and peace reigned. He was still soapy ".

LEO

Leo gave me this story on October 3, 1995 I have made changes to bring it up to date.
Here it is:

"I was thirteen years old when I became interested in music so went to the Band Room and for some reason I wanted to play the Tuba. Mary was the bandleader who handed me a book with notes and a fingering chart.

I wanted to play so bad that I would pack the Sousaphone in its case on Friday, take it outside, had to have help because it was so big and cumbersome, put it on a sled and pull it all the way home, over a mile. Then back to school on Monday.

Did pretty well, evidently, as I was sent to Interlochen National Music Summer School at age sixteen; went to Michigan State College, Summer School, in East Lansing, Michigan, when I was seventeen and was put on a scholarship list in 1942.

I enlisted in the Marine Corps in June 1943 but got an extension for six months so I could finish high school; went on active duty in January 1944 and was in combat on Guam and Okinawa; and was blown up in air by an Artillery Shell. No wounds but did get an injury from which I draw a Veteran's Disability Pension.

I was not auditioned for the band. They just looked at my jacket with the scholarships. I went to Naval School of Music in 1946, basic, and was promoted to S/Sgt. for meritorious service. In 1948 I was picked as one of the first fifteen Marines to go on Embassy Duty in London, England, said to be a very high honor, came back to the States in 1952 after traveling to thirty four different countries.

I played in parades and concerts for three Presidents of the United States, several Ambassadors and Princess Margaret of Great Britain. I have dined with Lords and Sirs.

I was invited and attended the Duchess of Kent's Ball; attended Ambassador's Garden Parties in England and Portugal and toured with the Marine Band in several states and Victoria, British Columbia.

Since my retirement I have been; an Automobile Salesman in California and Grand Ledge Michigan; General Sales Manager, Appliance Department with J.C. Penney in Clearwater, Florida; Store Manager and grocery clerk in Ludington, Michigan; a sign salesman for Jim Wilson and Manager of a Wall Paper Store in Tampa, Florida.

I have had many heart problems, having undergone over twenty Angioplastys, two Open Heart Surgeries, many Heart Catherizations and other problems caused by Diabetes.

Hiawassee, Georgia was my home for about ten years after I retired. While living there I took up square dancing which I enjoyed until my health failed. I must have watched hundreds of sports shows on my TV in my mobile home on Dogwood Trail. I had a nice little garden that produced quite a crop for my freezer and canning cabinet. When I could no longer live alone, I went to live with my son, Keith, and his wife, Tina Marie.

I now, March 1998, live in Linton, North Dakota with my son. I have two children, Keith and Lindsey Ann. I never remarried after my divorce in September, 1979

Note: Leo died of a stroke on March 15, 1999. His twin sister, Lela, lives in Lakeland, Florida.

LELA

Lela was always a dutiful daughter doing what her parents wanted.

Before finishing Senior High School in Grand Ledge, MI, she worked summers at Reo Motor Works, the Grand Ledge Chair Factory and Fisher Body. She earned enough money to attend Owosso Bible School to pursue a career in music. She graduated from Owosso in 1946.

She married Bud on August 30, 1947. Before they were to be married the preacher told them that he wanted to see them to go over the marriage manual to be sure that they understood their marriage commitments. Lela told him that they wanted a double ring ceremony.

He saw her engagement ring and told them that, "the Bible says you are not supposed to spend your money on anything but food and raiment because it is sinful. And, I won't marry you in a double ring ceremony".

Lela told him, " the ring is a promise between Bud and me that means we are dedicating our lives to each other". Lela and Bud were disappointed because they wanted to be married in their church in Grand Ledge, Michigan.

When they got home, they told Dad what the preacher had said. Dad was a Sunday School Superintendent and was a good friend of the District Superintendent. He got in touch with him and explained about the double ring ceremony. The Superintendent said he'd take care of that. He got in touch with the local preacher and told him that the recently retired preacher would do the ceremony. "Not in my church! If I have to do it, I'll just close my eyes." So, when they came to that part of the ceremony, he did.

Lela was brought up under the strict rules of our parents who had gotten Religion when she was five. Theirs was not a forgiving God. They threatened the wrath of God on everyone for the slightest infraction of the rules. Lela was never allowed to go to movies, wear make-up or jewelry or do anything that they considered sinful. Much of it was because of their interpretation of the Bible. All of us children knew that because the other parents were no where near as strict as ours were.

Lela lived in Lansing during her early years. The family moved to Grand Ledge when she was eleven. She lived on Jefferson Street until she and Bud married. They bought a cute little house where they lived until they divorced seven years later.

She took a lot of what I called "bossing around" by other people of the church who felt that it was their duty to keep her on the straight and narrow. Sometimes she resented it.

One time, while home from Bible School, she wore a pair of high-heeled sandals to Sunday School. The teacher took one look at her and said, "How can you wear those sandals, when they look so worldly, and call yourself a Christian?". Lela said, "I never saw a picture of Jesus when he wasn't wearing sandals"! The woman put her hand over her mouth and said, "I never thought of that". Lela made her point.

In June 1955, she came to my house, I lived in St. Johns at the time, carrying her suitcase. She had left Bud. She had many reasons to do so. I took her to my lawyer on the Saturday before I was leaving to move to Georgia on Monday. The lawyer told me not to let her go back to him under any circumstances.

She drove us, Vicki, Mother, an Aunt and I, south. She stayed with us about ten days, in Albany, Georgia, then drove Mother and the Aunt back to Lansing.

After that she lived in Lansing for twelve or thirteen years, during which time she met and married David and had her only child, Debra. Lela was married to Dave about two years when she divorced him. She had a dozen legal reasons.

After she married Ken, they bought a house and fourteen acres where they lived from 1970 to 1980.

Nobody should have to go through what Lela did with Ken. She finally divorced him and lived by herself for awhile. In the meantime, Debbie had gotten married and lived in New Hampshire.

Lela met Vern at a Singles Square Dance Club in Lansing in 1986. They were married in March 1987. In April, that same year, Debbie came back home to live with Lela and Vern.

Lela worked for thirty-four years for General Motors at Oldsmobile in Lansing. She started on the presses but was transferred to bumper plating, quality control, and stayed in that department for thirty-four years until she retired. Vern retired from Motor Wheel in Lansing. They both draw healthy pensions.

After living in Lansing a few years, they started going to Florida for the winter. They bought a trailer in Lansing where they hope to spend future summers. They spend their winters in Lakeland.

Debbie moved out, on her own, so Lela and Vern have had a few years for themselves playing card games, going out to eat and enjoying their lives together.

In January 1999, Vern had a cancerous right lung removed. Lela nearly lost him several times but he recuperated in a re-hab center and is back to his Poker games.

CHAPTER 3

MAMA

MAMA

MAMA AND FRANK

When Dad died, we children came from all over to be there for Mama. We took turns sitting, at the hospital, with Dad that week. We all had to get back to work. We planned on leaving on Tuesday morning. Dad died during the night, the day after Mama's 58th birthday.

He had Diabetes and heart trouble. He would go to church where the congregation would pray for him and tell him, "if you had the faith to be healed you would give up the Insulin". He did and had gradually been going blind for the last five years. He was declared to be ninety-five percent blind when he died.

I did my crying out behind the Hospital, the boys grieved silently but Lela couldn't stop crying and kept it up all during the funeral. Mama held up pretty well until the last viewing. She seemed to fall apart and two of the boys helped her to stand up as she looked at Dad for the last time.

Dad had loved the songs, "Amazing Grace" and "When the Roll Is Called Up Yonder, I'll Be There". Both are tearjerkers and I was relieved that the songs were sung by church members rather than playing a record of Dad singing them, as he had requested.

After Dad's funeral, we all went back to the church where a sumptuous meal was served to the family and congregation. Mama said there was about three hundred people including Dad's family, Mama's and ours along with a couple hundred from the church.

During the shaking of hands and condolences I saw a little short man hanging onto Mom's hand longer than the others. He put something in her hand. None of us knew who he was.

I stayed on with Mama a few days and so did Leo. We had decided that it would be good for her to get away for awhile as she had carried the heavy load of caring for Dad for so long.

One night after we, Mama, Leo and I, were all in bed, we were talking through the window openings of their house trailer, about how life had handed Dad such a bad blow. He was a good man and had provided for a large family all these years. He was a pillar of the church.

I was just dozing off when Leo, with his sex-minded way, asked Mama what they did about sex because he knew that was one of the things that Diabetes affected. She took a few minutes to answer and finally said, "Well it was kinda' like tryin' to put a wet washrag in a hole". Leo fell out of bed laughing. I was shocked that he would ask her something like that and surprised with her answer but we both got the message. We all laughed until we cried. Our tension of the last weeks was broken.

I thought Mama was overly anxious to go home with me, especially since the only transportation we had was her old Model A Ford. We drove it from Toccoa to Albany, Georgia in one day and I breathed a sigh of relief when we arrived.

We were in the house a matter of minutes and Mama was on the phone calling her "Church Children". She had left them behind when she and Dad moved to Toccoa about seven years ago. One call seemed to take longer than the others and naturally I was curious as to who it was.

She asked me if I knew the man that had put money in her hand, at Dad's funeral, in lieu of flowers. I didn't. She told me that his name was Frank. When she and Dad lived in Albany and were trying to raise money to build their little church he had been one of the biggest donors. He gave a cement block for every one the congregation paid for. His wife had gone to that church and had died three weeks before Dad.

Mama and Frank made arrangements to meet at the Wednesday Night Prayer Meeting. Whatever he promised her, I'll never know but she was like a schoolgirl with her first boyfriend. He did take her for long rides in his Cadillac and called her every day.

I asked her if she didn't think she was rushing things a bit as this appearance of a romance had shown up, really in a matter of days, too soon after she buried Dad. Her reply "I'm fifty eight years old and able to look after myself" left me with nothing to say. She seemed happier than I had seen her in years so why should I spoil her moment. Or so I thought...

She drove herself home about a month later and I was relieved that nothing had come of this little episode. I was wrong.

Within a few months, she wrote telling me that she and Frank had been talking on the phone, writing letters and making plans to get married. I was shocked when she said she'd come down a few days ahead of the day they planned on getting married, in February.

She had already sold her trailer and seven acres to her brother. They would make their home in one of the several little houses that Frank had built as a small-time contractor. She was in seventh heaven when he gave her his Cadillac as a wedding gift. I almost envied her the happiness that she was sharing with Frank.

So... when Ray came back from Michigan and said the only thing he wanted was to be with his family I was receptive and we remarried a few days after Mama and Frank married. She gave me her Model A Ford. It served us well as transportation to Lynn's work at the gas station.

In June 1957 Vicki married Dean, a Marine that I had met at a friend's wedding. Lynn enlisted in the Air Force in 1958 and Terry went to Michigan where he was going to enlist in 1961. He joined Michigan National Air Guard instead. My children all had a pattern to their lives. I was relieved.

Things had not gone too well with me. I had divorced Ray for the second time, after re-marrying him. Sometime later I started dating but was very lonely.

I had been divorced three years when I met and became engaged to Jack. Ten days before we were to be married, in October 1960, he was caught embezzling company funds and broke my heart.

Military friends encouraged me to go to Bermuda where they were sure I could find work, and start my life over.

I went to Bermuda in August 1961 and had worked there for four years when I went on a Christmas Cruise in December 1964. I met John from Seaford, New York at a Sadie Hawkins dance aboard ship the next day. John and I were married in March 1965. My world turned around.

51

Four years later, we were headed to Florida for retirement, after selling our house on Long Island, when I called Mama to tell her that we would stop on our way back to New York after we'd found something in Florida.

She could hardly talk but finally was able to answer my questions enough that I knew that she had had a stroke. Frank was away on one of his many fishing trips with his drinking buddies. Mama said that she knew Frank wasn't drinking but just went along to fish. She had tried desperately to get him to give up smoking too but he still wouldn't. Instead of going on to Florida we cut across the state from Savannah to Albany.

John and I decided to move to Albany rather than to Florida so we would be near if Mama needed us. John was a very compassionate man and treated Mama well. She often would tell people, " I love John even though he is Catholic".

It was a shock to see that her face had fallen and her speech was affected. She eventually got over it and three years later took care of Frank when he had lung cancer. The church finally admitted him as a member after he gave up smoking the week before he died.

During the week that Frank was dying Mama asked me to take her to the Court House so she could file Frank's Will. I told her that she couldn't file it until after he was dead but she insisted so I took her. She had never opened the envelope that Frank had put it in her hand and had told her to never let me see it or any of their personal papers. We found out why.

The woman at the Courthouse asked Mama if she wanted her to look at the Will. There might be some changes needed. It was too late. He was already in a coma.

Mama was shocked when the woman told her that Frank had left everything he owned to his children but she would have a Life Estate in the house.

Mama had bought that little the house from Frank when they were first married, seventeen years ago.

She had around eighteen hundred dollars left after paying for Dad's funeral and other expenses. She must have had more than that because she had made a donation to the church and would not tell how much. She gave the eighteen hundred to Frank as down payment. Then she rented the place out for seventy dollars per month while paying him fifty dollars in monthly payments. She thought the house still belonged to her but remembered that she had signed a paper so he could borrow some money using the house as collateral. He had also left the furniture and the Cadillac to his youngest daughter.

Mama was hurt beyond belief. The woman explained that a Life Estate meant that she could live there the rest of her life. Mom cried and said, "No wonder he didn't want Etta to see any papers".

Mama and Frank had lived in that little house for several years. He was generous enough that he told her she didn't have to pay him the fifty dollar monthly payment anymore. She thought she still owed him some money. Frank had lost every house he owned. There were three that I knew of. He had borrowed almost four thousand dollars from a Finance Company and was paying almost thirty percent interest to cover his personal expenses. He was broke although he bragged that he always carried at least five hundred dollars in his pocket for emergencies. The word was that he gambled but none of us ever found that to be true.

He had written the Will himself a few months earlier and had Mama take it to the Notary on Sylvester Road. He knew she wouldn't read it because he told her not to. The Notary signed it but Frank didn't sign it in front of him. The Will was invalid.

When the woman told Mama that "the Will isn't worth the paper it's written on", I knew that I had get Mama to my lawyer as soon as Frank died... which he did in a few days.

The next day after Frank's Funeral, I took Mama to see my lawyer. He read the piece of paper and said the same thing as the woman at the courthouse had. Mama started to cry and told the lawyer about Frank not wanting me to know any of their business.

The lawyer told her that he would do everything in his power to get everything for her. He filed for a Widow's Mite, legal support for a year for the wife in Georgia, and somehow got the Title to the car in her name. He just gave her the furniture with the house. I had to get five people to swear that Mama needed the Widow's Mite. My friends knew her circumstances and gladly signed for her.

The lawyer told Mama not to tell Frank's children anything so they were going along with her Life Estate figuring that when she died they would get it all.

In the meantime, one of the stepdaughters told Mama that she was sending her pregnant unmarried daughter to live with Mama. She called me. I called my lawyer. He said he would not allow it. Mama was relieved but uneasy. It was very hard for Mama not to tell any of her Church Family what was going on.

She, and her sister Dallie, went to Michigan for a visit that summer. Aunt Dallie pointed out a place, on my sister's property, where she would buy a trailer and put it under a little grove of trees out near the road.

That's when Mama decided to get away from all of Frank's family by selling her house and moving back to Michigan. She never said a word to me until...

On Christmas day, at the dinner table at my house, she informed all of us of her intentions. I couldn't believe that she had made all these plans without even dropping a hint. I asked her if Lela knew about this and she said, "well, she told me I was welcome at her house anytime".

I was pretty sure that Lela hadn't said anything about putting a trailer on her fourteen acres. I got Lela on the phone to be sure that she and Mama were in agreement on this. When I told her Mama's plans there was dead silence on the line for a few minutes. Lela said she would have to talk to her husband about this. After a short conference she came back on the phone and told Mama that she was welcome but they would have to see about a permit to put a trailer on their property. And nothing could be done about putting in water and sewer lines until April or May when the frozen ground could be dug. Shortly after Christmas we put Mama's house on the market.

I was a Realtor at the time, so my boss, the lawyer and I worked out a selling price and all of us told Mama that she was not to tell anybody because Frank's family would try to stop her. Within a very short time we had a cash buyer. It really was a cute house and Mama had flowers everywhere. I called it

'Mama's Doll House'.

She hated to part with it but it had lost its charm for her. We closed the sale and she moved in with John and me to wait until April. She was full of plans. She netted a little over eleven thousand dollars. She still had to pay off the Finance Company three-thousand –ninety dollars, including the thirty percent interest they were charging Frank.

Mama talked to her Church Family almost every day but I was surprised when I heard her say that the lawyer had said, "take your money and run".

What really had happened was that my boss had seen her downtown and thinking that she was supposed to go to Michigan, immediately after the closing of the sale, mentioned to the lawyer that Mama was still in town about three weeks after the closing.

He, in turn, called me and explained that if Frank's children heard about the closing they could contest it and take her to court and she would have to be in Albany for a hearing. She would either have to stay now or come back. I told Mom that the lawyer said that she should go to Michigan as soon as possible to avoid all that. She decided to run.

We all knew that Mama was waiting for a celebration at the Church when they would declare her as "The Mother of the Church". She had actually convinced enough people to come and form this church.

It was to be the highlight of her life but she did leave the next day and, to my knowledge, had not told any of her friends why she had to miss the celebration except that she had to, " get out of town in a hurry".

This is the reason that she wanted to move her Tombstone. She didn't want to be buried beside the little scoundrel.

THE TRAVELING TOMBSTONE

After reading the story, MAMA and FRANK, you will understand why Mama was determined not to be buried beside Frank. He turned out to be a selfish man and used her terribly. She had always defended him when people said that he drank and gambled. He used a lot of Sen-Sen and kept her in the dark as far as money was concerned. Now she knew him for what he was and she was hurt.

Frank didn't like her name, Eva Modena, nor 'Evie' as most people called her. So... he had a Tombstone engraved 'Modena'. He had it placed on the gravesite beside his own where he already had his first wife buried on of the other side. Frank liked to brag that he would be between his wives with one at each arm.

None of the family liked his dropping her first name because we figured that some day nobody would know who she was.

We were quite surprised when Mama called and asked John to take her to the cemetery to get her Tombstone. This was after she had sold her house. She decided to take her Tombstone with her to Michigan.

John objected, thinking this might be sacrilegious or that the manager of the cemetery would not let her have it. Besides it probably weighed two hundred pounds or more. It was rectangular shaped about three inches above the ground and several inches below ground. It was not something John wanted to do and he tried to talk her out of it.

That didn't stop her. She got two young men from her church to take her out to the cemetery in Albany, Georgia.

She went into the office and told the young girl what she wanted to do. She tried to convince Mama that "you just don't carry off Tombstones". Mama asked to see the Manager. He was quite shocked but he said, "Well, I reckon you can take it if you want to ...it's paid for and" ...

Mama was out the door and the Tombstone was dug up and loaded on a pickup truck before he knew what was happening.

When she called me to tell me that she had it, I asked her what she was going to do with it. She had that figured out before she got it. She had friends that were going to take an empty rental trailer to Michigan to bring back some furniture they had inherited. They would deliver the Tombstone, along with some other furniture, to my sister's house where Mama had decided to buy a trailer and put it on Lela's property.

Lela was unaware of all Mama's plans so was quite surprised when the Tombstone was delivered to her house before

Mama got there.

Lela couldn't stand having it sitting outside her side door so she had her husband put it in the basement in the laundry room. Even there it was not something she wanted to look at every time she did laundry. She had him put it in a closet where it stayed for several years after Mama made her move to Ludington.

When George, one of our brothers, told Mama about a new Senior Citizens Tower they were building in Ludington, Mama decided to move there. She got a nice one-bedroom apartment on the fifth floor. The Tombstone had to be moved again. George put it in his garage and figured it might be usable by adding "Eva" over the "Modena" when she was ready for it.

Time went by and Mama met Bill at a Senior Citizen's lunch in the building where she lived. A few months later she became a bride, for the third time, at eighty, and the Tombstone was moved again. This time it was put on the side of Bill's garage facing the neighbors. The neighbors complained so it was moved inside the garage.

When she died, in December 1983, our brother, Leo, took the Tombstone to get the name fixed. It couldn't be done so he bought her a new stone.

We don't know who wound up with the Traveling Tombstone but we hope it's 'lying at rest somewhere'.

WE REMEMBER MAMA

When the preacher said, "Brothers and Sisters, we are not here for a funeral, we are here for a celebration", I looked at my brothers and sister. They were as puzzled as I was. We were here in Ludington because our mother had died three days ago.

When I came from Florida, Lynn and Susan met me at the Lansing Airport near DeWitt. Lynn was embarrassed because I was wearing Jim's fur coat; he got it when he weighed about three hundred pounds, wrapped around me twice. I had Jim's fur hat on sideways to try to make it look a little more stylish. They rushed me to a shopping center so I could buy some boots. Lynn carried the coat while we were inside, then to Lela's where I could borrow a winter coat. Living in Florida for eleven years I

57

hadn't needed a winter coat.

Lela and I drove from Lansing as soon as we could get clearance from the State Police that Highway 10 was open from Clare to Ludington.

George and Leo lived right there in town. I had come from Tampa, Florida representing Jim and myself. Howard, nor any of his family, had come because of the terrible snowstorm that blocked miles of highway.

All of my children, Vicki, Lynn and Terry, along with their spouses, drove up just for the funeral. Almost all of the congregation from her church were present.

We were all grief stricken because Mama had left us quite suddenly after having been in a Nursing Home, from April to two days before Christmas 1983, after she had had more than one stroke.

The preacher began .... "We all knew and loved Sister Comstock and we'll miss her. We also know that she was looking forward to this day and wanted everybody to know that she was 'ready' and that she had reached her goal. She was happiest when she was doing something for some one else. She went out of her way to do things for others, especially those that she called her "shut-ins" who were mostly younger than she was".

All of us children knew that. She had left us to do the cleaning at home. She scrubbed floors, cleaned peoples houses and did whatever needed to be done to overcome excuses they gave her for not going to church. I deeply resented it as the major part of the work was left to me because I was the 'oldest' and 'a girl'.

The preacher knew her well as he said "Many of you were brought to this church because of her influence and"...as the preacher went on and on, my mind wandered backward over the years as I remembered the days before Mama was so involved with her church...

All of our lives had been affected since Mama and Dad 'had gotten religion', in August 1931, at a tent meeting. Dad had taken the family, except me, after hearing a quartet singing Gospel Songs outside Motor Wheel where he worked at the time.

The singing stirred his heart and he often told how he had thrown down his Pedro hand, while on his lunch hour, and went outside to hear the Southern men's quartet.

I was on a trip to Oklahoma helping some former neighbors take care of their two small boys - six months apart .Their mother didn't know she was three months pregnant when they adopted the first one. She needed help.

When I got home, changes had been made. All my little jewelry trinkets, which weren't much for a fourteen-year-old, my diary, my lip stick and all signs of 'worldliness' were gone. Dad had smashed his beer-making equipment and thrown away their cards. Every trace of sin was gone.

It took me some time to get used to the drastic changes. I eventually became involved with the young people of the Church but was never convinced that their new way of life was for me.

Further back in my memory I recalled the years before our family moved North and the changes that had made in our lives.

It was 1923 ... Mama was twenty-five and already had four living children. We had lost "Little Ralph" when he was just over one year old.

George was born in September 1921. "He was too pretty to be a boy", as Mama said. He wasn't quite two when Howard was born in April 1923.

In July that same year, Dad made a decision that changed our lives forever. He was twenty-eight. A big strapping man who weighed over two hundred pounds, stood just over six feet tall. A handsome man with bright blue eyes and a head of heavy dark hair. He had become the father of five, up to that time.

They made their first home at the Old York Place owned by Grandpa. Dad's family was not in favor of his marrying this seventeen-year-old from the mountains. They knew of her father's heavy drinking and thought Dad could have done better. Some of his sisters took an instant dislike for her and his mother did not treat her well. She was not trained to cook and keep house as they were. She had always had to help in the fields when her father was incapacitated, which was most of the time in those days.

A few years later many of the young Southern men were

going North to work in factories or whatever they could find to earn a living. Most of them left their families at home and sent money to them. Dad promised to send for Mama and us children as soon as he found a good job and a place for us to live.

He sold all his farm tools, his small interest in the farm and packed us in a wagon and took us to our other Grandparents, Granpaw Erv and Granmaw Bettie. They lived at the foot of the Blue Ridge Mountains near Clarksville, Georgia on the Old Lake Burton Road.

Dad took the train from Clarksville to North Carolina where he had kinfolk that he thought would give him a job. They took one look at him and said, "Big strappin' man like you ain't gonna last long in these cotton mills. Lungs'll fill up with this here cotton gin dust and you'll be dead in no time". They said, "you should never even think about working inside a factory".

With a heavy heart, he boarded another train going to Ohio where he'd been told men were finding jobs in all kinds of factories. Nothing there either. He was almost glad. It was so smoky in Cincinnati he could hardly see and the very air made him cough.

He met two men who were going to 'Deetroyt, Mitchigin', as they pronounced it, and joined them at the railroad station. He and his new acquaintances kept together and found a room, which they shared, and jobs within a day in Detroit.

In the meantime, Mama had not had an easy time of it while waiting the six weeks it took Dad to get settled on a job and a place for his family of six to live.

Granmaw and Granpaw didn't want their eldest "runnin' off up North whar he'd prob'ly be gone off someplace else by the time she got thar".

And "that's whar all them Catholics are too", they said, "ever-body knows them Catholics will steal yur young'uns and take 'em off to them Convent places and make Catholics outen 'em and you'll niver see 'em agin."

Granmaw tried to explain what Catholics looked like so Mama would be on guard. She said, "they wear long black dresses and cover up their heads 'cause they had all their hair shaved off. They wear long chains around their waists to tie up the young'uns. Women Catholics, they call 'em Nuns, are the ones that sweet-talk you while stealing the children and that's a fact", she continued.

Granmaw was very sure. "Catholic men always wear black suits with a white collar on backwards. They'll stand back and watch the women, as they try to get the young'uns. If there's one too big or ornery to handle they'll step in and hep em"." Granmaw warned Mama as best she could.

I knew that Granmaw was worried sick over us and really believed everything she had ever heard about Catholics. I looked at Granpaw for denial but he just shook his head and looked sad

Mama usually listened to her parents but she was determined to go where her man was. Even though she was worried about what she'd do if she saw a Catholic she was ready to go when he sent her the money.

I was only six and a half and couldn't understand why Dad had never warned Mama, in his letters, to watch out for these strange people. I knew that he would never let anything happen to us if he were there. We had a long train-ride before we would get to where he was.

I was scared and my stomach stayed upset. Granpaw begged Mama, to "give up this foolishness and stay home", all the way to the depot in Clarksville. He deliberately made the mules go slow, hoping we'd miss the train.

It was hot in August. The red dust picked up by the mule's hooves just made it hotter. I couldn't help wondering how it could be so hot here and so cold up North where Granmaw said "snow covered the ground and up to the roof tops in winter."

I had seen white frost come up out of the ground on very cold mornings around our house but it was always gone in a few hours. How it could get as high as rooftops was beyond my imagination.

We children, Jim was five, George was two, and I sat in the wagon bed while Mama held Howard who was only four months old. We were surrounded by everything our family had left in the world.

The lump in my throat and the knot in my stomach didn't show but my reddened eyes did. My nose was red, my eyes watered and swelled and I felt terrible. I was sad. Everybody cried, even Granpaw, when we got on the train.

He had a lonely trip back home with his mule team and his empty wagon. He was sure that he'd never see any of us again.

While Mama was waiting for Dad to send for us, he was having some rough times himself. He had taken a job at an ice-making plant in Detroit. It was July and his body wasn't used to the drastic change. Within a week he had pneumonia and came near dying. His new friends nursed him through it.

When he recovered they took the train headed for Grand Rapids, Michigan. The men had heard about jobs in furniture factories there and even though none of them had ever built anything, they were willing to learn.

They had to pass through Lansing, Michigan. Word had spread on the train that jobs were plentiful in the automobile factories. These were desperate men who were good workers and would work at anything for less money than some of the local men. Employers knew that and would hire a Southerner before a Northerner for that reason. This was causing trouble in some factories so jobs were not as available as they had heard.

However, Dad did finally get a job operating a streetcar. He had never seen one until he left Georgia. An instructor taught him what to do except when an automobile got stuck on the tracks, which was quite often. Within three weeks, Dad had demolished two model T's, that had stalled on the tracks, as the passengers jumped out and ran for their lives. That was too much for Dad. He just knew he'd kill somebody if it happened again so he tried to quit his job.

The manager offered him a job in the street-car-barn garage fixing the damaged ones. Dad figured that if any of the other drivers damaged them anywhere near like he had he'd have a job for awhile. He sent money for train tickets for Mama and us children.

Back to the train ... Most of the ladies were crying when it came time to board the train and say their final good byes. Some of them forgot their own tears as they helped Mama get all of us settled.

We had a huge leather suitcase, some pasteboard boxes and

several trunks. Granmaw had fixed us a basket of fried chicken, biscuits, tomatoes and huge slabs of cake to keep us from starving until we got to Michigan.

Within a short time, I was train sick. The rocking of the train and the telephone poles whizzing by were too much for me. A nice lady brought me something in a bottle and said it would settle my stomach. My first experience with Coca-Cola did just that.

Jim ran up and down the aisles trying to look out the windows. The conductor told Mama not to worry, he couldn't get off the train while it was moving. After he tried climbing over the seats, she tied his wrist to mine with one of Dad's big handkerchiefs. He had no choice but to thrash around on the seat because I wasn't going anywhere.

Our family had taken up two seats facing each other. Mama had arranged our things in neat piles and laid Howard on a quilt while she tried to hold a squirming George.

I was still queasy as we went around curves in the mountains, alongside rivers and crossed roads where people with horses and buggies seemed to be standing still as we left them behind. We saw the backsides of every little town where the train stopped to let some people off and others on.

When we approached Cincinnati, black billows of smoke and soot from the factories greeted us. Mama could see why Dad hadn't wanted to settle there from the descriptions in his letters.

We had to get off and change trains. The conductor told Mama that "if'n you-all will wait, ah'l hep you with yer young'ns".

Jim cried and hollered when the conductor helped me down the steps with Jim bouncing and tumbling behind me. He didn't know that Jim was tied to my wrist. Mama untied Jim for awhile but had to tie him to me again when he was found almost under the train trying to see where the steam was coming from. She finally got us all settled and our belongings stacked on the platform.

Women in long fancy dresses, wearing beautiful hats decorated with feathers, flowers and lace absolutely fascinated me. They wanted to hold George but he would only stand still for a minute while they stroked his head. He strutted around in his pink checkered rompers smiling at everyone. Howard was a fat, happy baby as long as he was dry and fed.

Mama had never nursed him in public before. On the train she had managed to turn her back to the aisle but now there was nowhere to turn. She was embarrassed but knew it had to be done because he was hungry and screaming his lungs out. So, sitting on our trunks she draped herself and Howard's head with another of Dad's handkerchiefs and was nursing him when she happened to look across the platform.

Not thirty feet away were four, yes four, of those Catholic people. They were whispering and looking at us. Mama panicked and tried to turn away from them as the two women walked over to us. She was convinced that Granmaw was right when the women offered to help her with us children.

They certainly fit the description that Granmaw had so vividly portrayed. They wore black dresses, covered their heads, Mama couldn't see a wisp of hair, and had chains wrapped around their waists. The men wore black suits with white collars that were on backwards. Mama knew she was trapped when the women started patting George's head and speaking softly to her, asking if they could help with us children. I was speechless and couldn't move. Even Jim quieted down. We knew that they had come to take us away just as Granmaw had said they would. Mama pulled George to her as he began whimpering and Howard started to cry when he lost his nipple. She began hollering, "You-all git away from my young-uns, I kin take care of 'em mysef".

The Nuns immediately realized that we were from the South and probably had heard some of the rumors they knew were being told about them. They mumbled their apologies as they backed away. Everyone around us was shocked at Mama's outburst. Some snickered as they walked away.

The conductor came to our rescue and helped us on the train while a porter put our belongings in the baggage car. Both men were black. I had never seen a black person before but remembered that Mama had told me about one that she had seen, when she was sixteen, in the little town of Cleveland, Georgia.

The black woman carried a fancy umbrella to keep the sun off. She thought it funny because the woman couldn't get any more sunburned than she already was. I felt no fear of these different-colored people and was grateful that one of them had seen our problem and helped us get away from the Catholics.

Mama was still crying as we settled in on the train and I was beginning to worry about what we'd do if Daddy wasn't there when we got to Lansing. I was dreading the end of the trip because I was sure that she would be disappointed. Everything Granmaw and Granpaw had said had come true, so far.

We had been on the train three days and two nights when we pulled into the depot on Michigan Avenue in Lansing, Michigan.

I was reluctant to move. I sat at the window and looked out at the hundreds of people waiting for the passengers to get off.

The conductor told Mama that he would help her if she would wait until the other people got out of the way. As I saw other people greeting people with hugs and kisses I felt so sad I wanted to cry. There were no tears left.

Then I saw a big tall man holding three red apples up over his head. I looked closer. It was my Daddy! I squealed with surprise and tears of happiness came over me. The joy that burst over me caused Mama to look too. Her face was transformed.

Maybe you can imagine how pitiful we looked: Mama wore a white blouse and a gathered skirt of black calico print with little ribbons of white flowers running from waist to floor-length hem. Her high laced-up shoes and a fancy straw hat, that Granmaw gave her made her feel well dressed until she saw what other women were wearing. She had somehow managed to keep her little hat from getting crushed.

I was wearing a dress with a Peter Pan collar, cuffs and waistband in front with a sash in back. My shoes were called "slippers" because they had a strap instead of shoestrings. Mama had parted my red hair in a perfect circle on top of my head and tied it with a ribbon that had been retied many times during the trip.

Jim wore britches to below his knees with what had been a white shirt when we started out. George was dressed in his third change of pink checkered rompers with elastic at the bottom above each knee. Howard was in a dress, the last one of several, and booties. When he had to be changed, Mama just upended him right at her seat and the porter hurriedly carried the diaper rags away.

We were a tired, dirty and anxious family when Dad was finally able to claim us. He was wearing his only suit, black, with a black felt hat and a big grin with a hint of tears in his eyes.

We must have looked like a family of immigrants to the well-dressed passengers and their friends at the depot.

Soon Dad had George on one arm, Jim hanging onto his pant leg and me holding his hand. Mama was carrying Howard and trying to keep up with the baggage man that Dad had hired to push our worldly goods to our new home.

We walked around the corner from the depot to the corner of Shiawassee and Larch Streets. There stood a tall building, three stories high. When Dad said, "this is it" we craned our necks but couldn't see how we could get to the top floor where Dad said we'd live.

There was a tiny porch sticking out the side of the building but no stairs to get to it. Dad proudly led us to a door and inside to the front of first floor, then to stairs that seemed to go on forever.

There wasn't much furniture. Dad had bought beds, a table and six chairs and most important of all, a kerosene three-burner stove that was new. Mama thought she'd like it, especially since there wasn't any wood around to build a fire and no fireplace either. She heated water, from the strange looking pipe, faucet, over a wash basin, sink, in a smoky kettle. I helped her wash the little ones for bed. She had brought feather beds, sheets and pillows in the trunks. We all had clean beds our first night in Michigan.

We arrived in August 1923 on a Saturday. Dad was around the next day helping Mama get settled. Needless to say, she was not happy with all the dirt in the apartment and vowed to clean it next day.

Monday morning she cleaned everything but when she got to the floors they looked hopeless. Her floors at home had always been easy to clean with a bucket of suds and a broom. She decided that was the only way to do it here.

She sloshed her bucket of scalding suds all over the floor and grabbed her broom. Scouring with all her strength, she suddenly realized that there was no place to sweep the dirty water out. At home she swept it out the door, except for some that ran through the cracks. These floors were covered with something that Dad said was congoleum. There were no cracks. Well, the stairs were dirty so she decided to do them too.

Just as she swished a broom full of the dirty water she heard a blood-curdling scream. The lady from the second floor came running up the stairs just as Mama lifted her broom again. It was too late. She got her full length. The woman was screaming something about water coming through her ceiling light fixture over her dining room table. She came to a screeming halt when the water hit her in the face. .

Mama froze with her broom in mid-air wondering what to do. The woman kept yelling, "get your mop, you fool, get your mop". Mama looked around. She didn't know what a mop was.

The woman ran back downstairs and brought her mop, thrust it in Mama's hands and said, "now mop it up". She tried and began crying as she looked at the woman.

The woman sure looked funny with dripping hair and a soaked house-dress as she tried to tell Mama what to do with this stick with a rag on it.

She started laughing and the woman, finally seeing the picture, laughed too. Mama had made her first friend, Ruby .Her husband, Leo, became my next brother's namesake.

Jim and I were enrolled in school for the first time. Children didn't start school until they were seven in Georgia in those days.

That was quite an experience. Jim with his youth and me with my limited reading, taught by Dad from newspapers, were both put in kindergarten. Within a few days it was apparent that Jim was not ready for school but that I was able to handle first grade.

Jim got lost on the way home and was taken in by a lady who gave him cookies and milk. She tried to find out where he lived but he didn't know so she kept him with her until the police found him in their door-to-door search. She didn't have a telephone so just waited for someone to come for him. He wasn't afraid of the nice lady.

I remember well, the other children laughing at us as the teacher asked us to tell about raising cotton to the rest of the class. We had such a Southern accent that it was funny to them, including the teachers. Jim became reluctant to talk but I just stood up and told them about picking cotton and how we did things in the South, even though they laughed.

While we lived in the third floor apartment several incidents will always stand out in my memory bank.

Uncle Ernest, Mama's single brother, came to live with us to explore his chances of finding a job. He told me that he would buy me a doll if I would stop biting my fingernails.

The only doll I'd ever had was a rag doll that Granmaw had made for me. I quit immediately. He bought me the most beautiful doll I'd ever seen, except in the catalogs we got at home. She had eyes that opened and shut, long wrap-around-a-finger curls and a voice box that said "Mama" when you leaned her forward. I was absolutely thrilled. I never bit my fingernails again. I named her Hazel. She was the first thing I hugged when I got home from school even before my baby brother, Howard.

One day my brothers, mostly Jim with a little help from George, had taken Mama's scissors and given Hazel a hair cut. My heart was broken and I cried for days. It didn't help when my parents said, "boys will be boys" which became a familiar phrase as we grew up.

Going back to my memories of the doll, I wondered why this incident about the haircut came to mind when it did. Perhaps it was because of Mama's hair. Since she had gotten religion, some fifty-two years ago, she had not had her hair cut. She wore it close to her head with a slight wave over her forehead and a bun in back. She liked to brag about how few gray hairs she had. At night she wore it in a braid down her back.

When my sister, Lela, and I visited her in the hospital just before her eighty-fifth birthday, we didn't know her. She had had another stroke and her face had fallen on one side but the biggest

68

shock was that her hair had been cut and permed. It was thin and frizzy. It had been cut because the staff at the Nursing Home, where she had lived since April, said they couldn't keep it clean. My sister-in-law, Florine, who worked in the office at the Nursing Home, had suggested the permanent, thinking it would help.

Bringing my mind back to the Celebration... I sat wrapped in my own thoughts as the preacher rambled on and on about Mama. He was telling the congregation that we were all going to Hell if we didn't mend our ways.

I listened to him as he related one incident when Mama was a dinner guest in his home. What he didn't know was that she had her own way of asking the blessing. All of us knew that she would deliver her blessing-prayer and at the same time ask God to punish wayward people who she felt needed chastising. This time it was the preacher's teen-age son who had apparently been giving his parents a hard time. She asked, "God, make him behave and quit sassing his parents". Before it was over he had been thoroughly chastised and embarrassed. Mama said, "he had it coming". Everyone at the service laughed. Some of them had been the subject of her prayers, always out loud in the church, but they loved her anyway.

Mama had been in the hospital because she had Diabetes, didn't eat right and her electrolytes had gotten out of balance.

She often went on streaks of not taking her Insulin shot because some of her well-meaning church friends would pray for her; tell her that she was healed and that if she was a true believer she didn't have to take the Insulin. I, personally, heard her Doctor tell her while she still lived in Georgia, that "it is alright to pray, but do what I say or your prayers won't do you any good". She didn't listen to him or me.

In spite of the hospital stay, she was back at the Nursing Home for her birthday in September.

Our brothers, George and Leo, had told us about her elaborate plans for her eighty-fifth birthday. She told them that she ordered three-hundred cantaloupes and was going to have them cut in half and filled with ice cream. They had no idea who, or where, she had ordered them from and were worried about

69

what to do about it. I reasoned that, "anyone accepting an order of that size from a patient in a Nursing Home should have checked it out". We weren't sure that she actually had ordered them. None were ever delivered.

Back to a few more memories... While we lived in the third floor apartment, Mama left Uncle Ernest in charge of us children while she went across Grand River to do some shopping. He thought I was old enough, seven at the time, to look after the other children while he stepped out for awhile.

A new bridge was being built on Michigan Avenue across Grand River. To get down-town people had to walk a block to the Shiawassee Street bridge or take the swinging footbridge on Michigan Avenue. Mama was afraid of the long footbridge, which swayed as people walked across it, so had crossed on the other bridge and looked across the river to see where we lived.

To her horror, she saw smoke coming out of our building right over our apartment She forgot that she was afraid of the footbridge and was back in a few minutes, only to be held back by the firemen who were spraying water on the building. Uncle Ernest arrived a few minutes later. He was not allowed to enter the building either.

By that time I had all the children out on the little porch, balcony. We didn't know there was a fire but were scared by the noise from the fire trucks as they came to a screeching halt in front of our building. To this day, my heart beats faster when I hear a fire siren anywhere near.

Some of the people on the ground were screaming, "drop the little ones down and jump". They said they would catch us. The firemen were yelling "stay where you are". When the firemen finally got up the stairs they found a grease fire in the kitchen of the apartment across the hall from us.

Not long after the fire episode, Uncle Ernest went back to Georgia and married his sweetheart, Maude.

Soon after the fire scare, Dad got a job in the North end of Lansing and moved our family to Thompson Street between Melling Drop Forge Plant and Motor Wheel Corporation, the factory where he worked. Thompson Street is still there but I believe it dead-ends near the overpass on U.S. 27 North.

To go on...... We moved at lot but always to something bigger and better. Leslie Street was quite a change. Away from the smoke and the noise of the factories. We had a nice house that was adequate and very few neighbors.

The people next door, Mr. and Mrs. Hunter, were black. They were friendly and helpful to us. He was very black, a slight man, with an ear-to-ear grin every time he saw us. She wore a cloth on her head all the time and reminds me, now, of Aunt Jemima the pancake queen. I wished I had teeth as white as theirs.

The twins were ten months old when Mama got sick. She was nursing both of them when she got red measles. She was exhausted, the measles went in on her, they never broke out, and she had pneumonia.

The Doctor came but didn't go in her room. He just peeked in from the doorway and said, "I'll write up the papers to have her committed. She is a crazy woman". She was delirious. Dad ordered him out and got another Doctor who sent her to Neller's Hospital, which was on the opposite end of town where North Washington Avenue ended.

Mama was delirious from fever and imagined all kinds of demons coming after her to take her to Hell. She thought the chains rattling below the elevator were to bind her up. She was in the hospital seven weeks and weak and listless at home for a very long time afterwards.

Dad hired a neighbor woman to cook and look after the younger children until I got home from school when I took over. Mrs. Gardner made oatmeal, sometimes three times a day, and said it was good enough for us. It was slimy but mostly so hard that milk wouldn't soften it. None of us children would eat oatmeal for years.

Mrs. Hunter prepared many meals for us and we survived a long year while Mama slowly gained back her strength. All of us loved Mrs. Hunter except Howard. He thought her hands were dirty and wouldn't eat anything if he knew she had prepared it. She finally won him over by putting candy orange slices in a little dish on her porch then she'd go back in the house and call him. I can still hear her calling "How-wood". She chuckled when he sneaked over and got the candy.

Dad was working at Motor Wheel by then so he bought a new Ford car when we moved to Leslie Street. The saying during those years was that "you could have any color car you wanted as long as it was black". He had to have a car to get back and forth to work and later to visit Mama in the hospital.

The car had a fold-down top, running boards and a spare tire mounted on the back. The gas tank was located under the hood in front of the windshield, next to the motor.

After Mama got better, Dad would rush home, help get us ready and take us to the ballpark. He loved sports and took great pleasure in Mama and me preparing a basket lunch to eat as we watched the games.

Motorcycle hill-climbs were another sport that he liked to watch. I was always scared when the bikes headed up the hills, almost straight up, because many of them tipped over backwards and some of the riders were hurt badly.

Mama wasn't interested in any of this but she went along with it mostly to get out of the house.

Dad always bought the groceries and usually drove all the way to the North end of town to Dill's Grocery, where he had established credit while working at Motor Wheel.

He was in a hurry to get groceries one Saturday and get home to take us to the ball game. There were no stop signs back then. He was crossing Kalamazoo Street when a car hit his back bumper. The force of it tipped the car over into a ditch with Dad pinned underneath.

He thought the water from the radiator, that was dripping on him, was gasoline. Somehow he gathered enough strength to lift the car off himself while stunned bystanders just stood there. Most of them had never seen an automobile accident before.

He walked the few blocks home. He came in bleeding. Most cuts were on his arms. Mama cleaned the cuts, put iodine on them and while she was wrapping them began asking where the car was.

Dad shed tears as he tried to explain what had happened. He didn't see the car coming because there was a small building too close to the street to see around it. The car was still upside down in the ditch.

Dad got Mr. Hunter to tow the demolished car with his truck. We had lots of vegetables and watermelon delivered from his farm on his truck but were really surprised when he pulled in our driveway hauling a totally smashed car.

Not long after that, Dad sold the car to Mr. Hunter for fifty dollars. There was no insurance in those days so Dad suffered a complete loss.

Mr. Hunter pulled the car to his farm and worked on it for weeks. Proudly, he drove it back to our house, with all the dents removed, a few broken parts replaced and a new paint job. He offered to sell it back to Dad.

In the meantime, Dad had bought a bigger car. It was still a touring car but it would hold the whole family comfortably. Those were good times. The children were all fine and Dad had a new car...

The service for Mama was over and everyone headed for the Church Hall where food had been prepared for all the people.

As I walked away from the casket the last time, I couldn't help thinking, she showed her spunk until the very end. She was determined 'not to go until she was good and ready'. She had just closed her eyes and gone to sleep and now she was Celebrating ... and we, for her. We love you Mama!

Because of the deep snow, the frozen ground and not being able to dig the grave, Mama wasn't buried for several weeks. We all knew that wouldn't have bothered her. She was where she wanted to be.

"We Remember Mom" is dedicated to Our Mama.

Note: As the reader can well imagine not all of the above was remembered during the hour-long service. Much of it came to me while writing the high lights of the particular years from 1923 to 1926.

CHAPTER 4

MANY MANY MOVES

MANY MANY MOVES

Our family moved more than any other family I ever heard of. It seems like, now, that Dad was always finding a bigger or better place. Of course, other reasons sometimes entered into the picture - like to get closer to work, to church, because of The Great Depression or an increase in the family.

PRIOR TO 1920

Beginning with when I was born in January , 1917, Mama and Dad, Henry and 'Evie', lived at the Old York Place in Hart County, Georgia.

I'll try to get it right as to when and where we lived, according to Mama, up until I was about six and from my own recollections after that.

(1)   The Old York Place was near my Grandpa and Grandma, 'Jim', and Rachel's farm, where my Dad brought his bride from where she lived on Lake Burton Road, now known as Ga., Hwy. 192, in Habersham County, Georgia. Mama told me most of what I am writing about that place.

It was an old house, two stories tall, had never been painted and had a Holly tree in the front yard which was bare of grass.

~~~~~~

Nobody had lawns in those days and kept the yard clean by sweeping it with a broom, hand-made of broom-straw which grew to about three feet tall.

Mama would cut the straws as close to the ground as she could and tie them together so their feathery tips did a good job of sweeping the yard. I do remember some of it. Maybe because Mama described it so well that I had a mental picture of it at a very early age.

There was a little Branch, small creek, where Mama did our washing. She boiled the clothes in a huge iron pot, then dipped them out with a smooth hickory stick, it had to be stout enough to lift those scalding hot clothes, and laid them out over big smooth surfaced stones, then scrubbed them with lye soap and beat the dirt out with a smooth paddle that Dad had made for her. She had to be careful not to hit the buttons or overall fasteners. She then rinsed them in the branch and hung them on the fence or bushes to dry. Her hands would always be bloody-raw from the lye soap. Sometimes they would heal before the next wash day. She made the soap herself from hog fat, ashes and lye in a big iron pot over a wood fire out by the branch. She knew just the right proportions so it became a thick jelly-like substance which she poured in pans, let it cool and cut it into bars of soap.

The branch had blue and red clay along the sides. I gathered some and made marbles that I put on top of fence posts to dry. They always dried with a flat side as nobody ever told me to keep turning them so they would be round when they dried.

The branch also served as our refrigerator. The water was real cold and Dad had dug a little hole on one side and lined it with stones. Mama would put her milk, and whatever she knew would keep a few days, in glass jars and submerge them in the water. We always had good cold buttermilk and sometimes a watermelon in the summer.

I don't remember anything about when Jim was born in July 1918 at home. I was only eighteen months old at the time.

~~~~~~

Years later, Uncle Evard took me to the old York Place to see it for the last time before the area was to be covered by Lake Hartwell, the lake formed by the TVA Dam, Tennessee Valley Authority. Part of Uncle Evard's property was later covered by the lake.

I was thrilled, but saddened, to see the old Holly tree which was now about forty feet tall with a trunk about eighteen inches through. It would be gone. I picked up a stone that was filled with small pieces of Mica that sparkled in the sun. We used to call Mica 'Isinglass'. Sometimes it could be found in good sized sheets and was once used instead of glass in small windows in the old fashioned pot-bellied stoves. It was very brittle and broke easily. I kept that stone, about a foot round and quite flat, on the ground at the foot of a dogwood tree in front of my home in Hiawassee, Georgia for years until somebody carried it away.

(2)   We lived in Westminster, South Carolina, for a short time. William Ralph was born while we lived there. I was about three and have no recollection of that place at all.

(3)   Right after that we lived in one of Grandpa's tenant houses. It was during that period that the Snake Stories and Jim's Straw Hat occurred.

SNAKE STORY

This is about the right place to tell the Snake Stories which my Dad was famous for.

He could make you see, almost feel the slimy creatures, with his vivid descriptions.

I was a little over three years old and Jim was eighteen months old when this episode Happened...

I was standing in our clean-swept front yard screaming and crying so hard that Mama came out on the porch to see what was wrong. Jim was sitting on the edge of the porch with his feet hanging off. She told me to "Hush up" or she would "whope me". I kept screaming she came out and paddled me and started back to the house when she saw what I was screaming about. The house was close to three feet off the ground, as all country houses were in the South in those days.

Jim was sitting on the edge of the porch swinging his foot back and forth at a rattlesnake that was swinging its head in rhythm. Mama ran as fast as she could. Uncle Ernest, one of Mama's brothers, who had come down to help Dad for a few weeks in the spring, came running with his shotgun. All of the men carried a gun with them to work in the fields and to the barns or anywhere there might be a rabbit or a snake. He shot the snake's head off. Uncle Ernest and Dad said it was still over six feet long.

They hung it over the fence so all the neighbors could see it when they drove by in their wagons or buggies. That was the custom. Everyone hung the snakes in rows on their fences so neighbors could see and compare them to the snakes they had killed.

Of course, all of this made a big impression on me, as a three-year-old, and left me with a fear of snakes that I never outgrew.

THE BIGGEST SNAKE IN HART COUNTY

When I was little we had no television, radio, telephones, electricity or any of the conveniences we take for granted now. Many times our bedtime stories consisted of very scary things like snakes, wild animals and the dark. Sometimes the neighbors joined our family and gathered around the fireplace to contribute their own stories or add to the one being told. Sometimes I was too scared to go to bed.

Of course, many of the stories were exaggerated, like fish stories, but just the plain truth was more often than not the most interesting.

Dad told this story many times and it was always the same. He swore it was the truth and neighbors verified it.

As Dad described it: he was plowing fresh rows for planting cotton when he came to a place in the terrace that looked strange. The land was so hilly that terraces of extra dirt were piled up in rows several feet apart making a half circle of a hillside to keep the rains from making gullies and washing the dirt away from the cotton crops. It looked like someone had dragged a log, about a foot thick, down the hill breaking the terraces as it went

After inspecting the path the log had made, breaking down several terraces, the hair on back of his head stood up. Suddenly he realized that there were no footprints, of man or animal, on either side of this path and knew that nothing could leave a trail like that except a snake. A big one.

He grabbed his gun and started to follow the path. When he stopped to think, he realized that this thing was too big for him to handle alone.

He gathered a few neighbors who made a posse. They walked alongside cautiously while trying to guess what it might be.

Several of the men had lost piglets and chickens recently. They decided that this thing was probably a snake that had swallowed something big enough to cause the wide path. When they got close to the swamp, they all decided that was as far as they would go.

Someone went to town for the Sheriff. When he finally came, the stories had multiplied several times. The Sheriff knew about the snake but hadn't told anyone because he knew that the whole countryside would panic.

He said that it was "right about thirty feet long" and "it escaped from a Carnival in Hartwell a few weeks ago". Nobody saw it, including the Sheriff, so he was using information that the Carnival people had given him.

To Dad's knowledge, no one ever caught the snake. People kept a close watch over their small children, piglets, dogs, cats and chickens for years. Our family moved to Habersham County not long after that. To this day, seventy nine years later, my heart seems to stop when I see a snake.

~~~~~~

Dad thought my fears were put-on until we lived in Lansing, Michigan many years later. I was about nine when one of our neighbor girls, Agnes-I'll never forget her, brought a little green snake to our house. It was made of wood, painted green with joints that made it wiggle as she chased me all over the house with it.

Dad made her give it to him and had me hold out my hands. When he laid the snake in my hands, I fainted

He ordered her to take the snake home and never bring it

81

back. I had played at her house a few times before that but never went there again. My brothers, all four, often chased me with little green garter snakes but when Dad heard me screaming my "snake scream" he made them stop.

~~~~~~

(4)   From there, we moved to a house on Burton Lake Road in Habersham County, Georgia, across the creek from Granmaw Bettie and Granpaw Erv when Ralph was a baby. He died while we lived at that place.

1920 - 1930

George was born, in September 1921 and Howard was born in April 1923, while we lived there.

(5)   When Howard was about four months old, we moved to Lansing, Michigan and lived in an apartment on the third floor of a building on the corner of Shiawassee and Cedar Streets. I was six years and eight months old at the time.

(6)   For a very short time, we lived in a little house a little farther north on Cedar Street. People used to look at Mama real funny when she told them "we live in the back-house".

Our house was behind another one that faced the street. There was another house, partially built, behind us. The City had stopped the owner when they found out that he was building a third house on one narrow lot.

SWEET PEAS

Jim and I were playing in that unfinished house when I spotted some Sweet Pea flowers growing on the fence next door. Jim and I sneaked over and stole a handful. We knew couldn't take them in the house. We found a tin can, put some water in it and looked for a place to hide them. There was a flat place above one of the windows so we pulled cement blocks over to it but Jim was too short to reach. We added another block on top and Jim climbed up.

He placed the flowers up there and while I was admiring them he fell on the cement blocks and got a deep cut in his eyebrow. Blood was streaming everywhere. There was no hiding what we had done. A Doctor came to the house and straddled Jim on the bed while Mama and I held his arms and legs. The Doctor sewed him up without anything to deaden the pain. I got a whipping and Jim will wear that scar until he dies

~~~~~~

(7)   We lived on Thompson Street in north Lansing when Leo and Lela were born in June,1925. The noise from Melling Drop Forge was a big factor in causing us to move from there.

(8)   The twins were just a few months old when we moved to a tiny house on North Street.

The only thing I remember that happened there was when George got mad one day and threw a carrot through a window. Of course, he got the usual spanking.

I still have a picture of Leo and Lela sitting in a rocking chair on the porch wearing little helmet-type hats that Mama had crocheted. She continued to make those and little sweater sets for all the new babies, Grandchildren and Great Grandchildren, as long as she lived.

(9)   Next was a small house on Leslie Street at the south end of Lansing. That is where we lived when Dad wrecked his new car and Mama had a nervous breakdown.

(10)   From there we moved to South Hayford Street . While we lived in the big three story house Mama's brother and sister and their families moved in with us. There was

Uncle Collie and Aunt Althea, and their two children, Pauline and Vaughn; Aunt Dallie and Uncle Tal, and their two children, Billie and Bobbie; Edgar and Eller and their little girl, Inez.

After they moved back to Georgia, Aunt Dallie eventually had a total of nine children and Uncle Collie had five.

I was the oldest, at nine, of all those children including my own four brothers and sister. There was a lot of work for me and I became run-down.

~~~~~~

The women were having a great time being together and with so many of them their housework was minimal. The four of them tried new hair-dos, experimenting with Rats, (buns made of their own hair), and placed over their ears with their hair stylishly draped over them. Somebody got the notion to cut their hair, outrageously brazen in the twenties, so they cut each other's hair. Some of the husbands did a lot of blasting them for it but Mama kept her hair cut until she got Religion in 1931. I deeply resented having so many children to look after and peeling, it seemed like tons, of potatoes

LYDIA PINKHAM

The women decided that I needed a tonic to make me eat better and put on a little weight. They bought me a bottle of Lydia Pinkham.

I had taken quite a bit of it before I read the claim on the bottle. It said that, "there is a baby at the bottom of every bottle". Two tablespoonfuls a day were supposed to make a woman healthy enough to have a baby.

From then on I poured two tablespoonfuls down the toilet every day. I figured that we didn't need any more babies around for me to take care of.

It was a bottle and a half later before they caught me.

~~~~~~

Eventually all the relatives either found themselves a job and a home or went back to Georgia.

Needless to say, I was relieved but this meant that we would move again. We didn't need such a big house and Dad had his first chance to buy a house, rather than rent.

(11)   That house was an old farmhouse at Lansing's northern city limits on Fredrick Street. It needed lots of work and Dad was not a handy-man. He did the best he could to make this house our home.

The man who sold us the house owned the grocery store where Dad had a charge account for years. He felt sorry for us when the Depression hit and we lost the house. Mr. Dill owned a farm about eleven miles away just north of Wacousta. He offered it to Dad with condition that he farm the land on shares. Dad had no choice so took him up on his offer.

(12)   So...we moved to what was called the Wells Farm. There had been an old man living in the house who kept his pet lamb inside. Mama and I had lots of cleaning to do to make the place livable.

APPENDICITIS

Mama knew that I wasn't just faking it to get out of housework, which I hated, at the house on the Wells Farm.

We had moved there after Dad lost his job and our house during the depression. The house was old and run-down. The old man who lived there before us had a pet lamb, that grew up to be a big sheep, that he kept in the house. I cleaned up sheep pellets by the bucketful and scrubbed floors along with Mama who was pregnant again.

I was vomiting more than she was and had a slight fever that she determined by placing her hand on my forehead. I had the worst pain I'd ever felt in my lower right side.

She told me to take a quilt and lay out on the front porch in the sun. Maybe I'd feel better. I lay there wondering what was wrong when our neighbor, Charlie, came over from his place across the road. He started teasing me and trying to make me get up.

I started to cry and he thought he would stop me by pulling the quilt out from under me. The more I hollered the more he pulled until he got me to the edge of the porch. He swore later that he thought I'd jump up and start pounding his chest as I usually did when he teased me. I fell about four feet to the ground and passed out.

He was beside himself with anxiety as he carried me around the house to the back door where Mama was. After I came to she sent me upstairs to bed where I lay in confusion as to what had happened.

Five years later, on the first day of school at Eastern High School in Lansing, I had my appendix removed. The Doctor said there was old scar tissue that showed that it had been ruptured before. I spent three weeks in Neller Hospital and another two weeks at friends from the church while I recovered from that ordeal.

We only lived there a few months when Dad and Mr. Dill had a misunderstanding about how to raise and divide some crops. We had to move in time to get enrolled in school.

(13)   This time… it was to a house on Wacousta Road about a mile north of U.S. 16. Again, it was an old house but there was a chicken coop where Mama could raise chickens and ten acres where Dad could raise food for our family.

It was here that Mama and Dad got Religion and Aunt Martha, not a relative, moved in with us. That, 'the Martha Pullman Place', was her property and she had been ordered out of her son's home so she had no place else to go. She was a cranky old lady and we soon found out why nobody could live with her. She bossed us children around, threatened us with her cane, had Mama in tears most of the time but was so nice to Dad that he had a hard time believing she was such a monster when he was gone.

(14)   I knew that the folks were looking for someplace nearer the church so when one became vacant about a half a block away from it they moved immediately. I thought this had to be it! North Street in Lansing again!

Everybody was having a hard time feeding their families so when the city offered our family 'free milk' if they could use our front porch as a pick-up center for poor families to come get their milk, Dad agreed immediately.

Not for long. From there we moved to North Highmont Street. I don't know the reason why except that we had some next door neighbors who hated my parents newly adopted religion. Their children would yell obscenities at us and the man would curse Mama. Rather than fight him or put up with these people we moved.

RAILROAD BUMS

(15)   So, here we go, moving again. This time it's to North Highmont Street right next to the Railroad Wheelhouse. There was a big circle of Railroad tracks, at the end of the line, where train engines would pull in, the wheel would turn and the engine would be headed back from the way it came. We kids loved to watch it, from a distance.

We had lots of bums come to our back door begging for food. The Depression was still on for our family but Mama always gave them something. Usually beans and cornbread, which we ate a lot. We later found out that our house was marked so the hobos knew before they knocked on the door that our house was good for a handout.

We probably had more fun while we lived in that house, by the railroad tracks, than anywhere else. There was a pond behind a nearby Fertilizer Plant where we went ice-skating. One of my boyfriends would bring his tiny hand-operated victrola and we'd skate to the music. If our parents had heard it they would have stopped it right away. It was too close to being sinful, like dancing. I loved it!

Lots of boys came to our house, on the pretense of seeing my

87

brothers, and somehow wound up walking me to church or taking me to some Youth Group activity.

One of my boyfriends, Jon, came to see me quite often but my parents wouldn't let me go anywhere with him except to church. Even if we were just going for a walk, we had to take my sister. I was sixteen and she was eight. A real pain in the neck because she told everything we said to my parents.

On one of those walks, we were walking along the railroad tracks when Jon got the brilliant idea of walking on top of the parked boxcars. Of course, we had to take Lela. She was scared but she wouldn't wait for us so we helped her up. She gripped my hand and walked in front of me. I was in the middle with Jon holding my hand.

He loved to tell scary stories and proceeded to tell one of his scariest. Lela kept turning around to look at him and walked right off the end of the boxcar. She was still gripping my hand, hanging in mid-air and screaming. Jon rushed down the ladder and caught her from below. We made her promise never to tell and she didn't. Mama couldn't understand why she didn't want to go with us after that.

Smoke and noise plus the long distance for Jim, to Pattengill Junior High School, and I, to Eastern High School, that we were having to walk made the next move inevitable.

(16)   The place on Cady Court, on an alley, was alright but the downstairs bedroom was too small for Mama and Dad. Lela and I got that room. A bum tried to get into our window one night. That was it. We moved again but not before I graduated from Eastern High School in 1936.

(17)   Vermont Street was just North of Grand River Avenue and close enough that the family could walk seven blocks to church.

We had been there a little over a year, in 1937, when Mama and I got into a big argument about my wearing some of Jim's pants to go target practicing with some young people from the church. Dad stepped in and threatened to hit me. I told him to go ahead but he backed off. I left home that day.

AND MORE MOVES

1930 – 1940

After I left home I moved many more times and will try to put those moves in the order they were made.

(18)   The first place was temporary for just a few months. I lived with Harold and Pauline and their mother but I can't remember the address. Their mother was a widow and knew some of the circumstances of my home life. She had told me that I was welcome to live with them if I couldn't take it at home anymore. Hers was the only place I could think of as I sat crying

(19)   From there I got a room next door, for about six months, but that didn't work out because the landlady was too nosy and got into my personal things.

(20)   Next would be apartment with Dorothy and Lester across the street from the Church on North High Street.

(21)   From there, the three of us moved to the South end of Lansing where we encountered a new experience at "The Whorehouse".

(22)   Then my little one bedroom apartment downtown, on an alley, where Jim moved in with me and where we were living when I married Ray.

(23)   We, Ray, Jim, Helen and I shared an apartment on Knollwood Avenue until we moved to

(24)   The small house, on Grand River Avenue, that Ray and I

shared with Dorothy and Lester and where we were living when Vicki Anne was born.

(25)   Then we spent six months living with Ray's parents, Leslie and Corneilia, on Ash Street until we were able to go to a house on our own.

(26)   It was a two story house on Larch Street about a block from Ray's parents. Jim blew up a can of pork n' beans while we lived there.

1940 - 1950

(27)   Before Lynn was born, we moved to a cute little house on Knollwood. We fixed the place up real nice and the landlord asked us to move so his daughter could move in.

(28)   From there we found a stone house on South Turner road off Jolly Road. We lived there when Terry was born.

(29)   Again, we fixed the house real nice and had to move when the owner sold it to a man who was going to War and wanted a nice place to leave his family while he was gone.

(30)   Viking Road was next. We bought a Redi-Bilt house and had it put up on our lot. in 1942. We lived there until 1950 when we had to sell the house because of hospital bills and lack of work.

1950 - 1960

(31)   Norwood Drive was our home from 1950 to 1954 when we sold it and moved to St. Johns.

(32)   We lived in a converted car-dealers' building from June to November 1954 when we had to move again.

(33)   We found an old house in St. Johns on Clinton Street which we hated.

(34)   From there, we moved to a house on Residence Avenue in Albany, Georgia. We were living there when Ray and I separated the first time.

(35)   The kids and I moved to a duplex on Cleveland Street. We lived there for several months when the place was condemned by the Fire Department and we had to move.

(36)   The kids had the place on Gordon Avenue all settled when I got back from my Dad's funeral. Next was supposed to be a good move for us, but wasn't, when we rented a duplex that belonged to my step-father, Frank.

(37)   I bought a house trailer where Terry and I lived until I fell into a hole at the Air Force Base where I worked. I had to sell the trailer.

(38)   I leased a stone house with my fiancée, we were supposed to get married, on Society Avenue across the street from the Albany High School Stadium.

1960 - 1970

(39)   When the marriage didn't go through, I moved to Hamilton, Bermuda to live with my friends, Will and Peggy .

(40)   After several months, I moved to an efficiency apartment by myself just a few doors from the hospital.

(41)   Living alone didn't work out so I rented a big house, 'Overlook', on Harbour Road in Bermuda and shared it with two other women.

(42)   When one left to go around the world and the other to get married, I moved across the street to a little cottage on the water called 'Brinkedge'.

(43)   The house was too damp for me so I moved to an efficiency on Queen Street in the city of Hamilton. That's where I lived when I went on a Christmas Cruise and met John, my second husband.

(44)   I left Bermuda for a split level house at 1830 Seaman Neck Road in Seaford, New York.

(45)   After John retired, we moved to a nice little brick house on Cascade Lane in Albany, Georgia to be near my mother. She had had a stroke and we thought she needed us.

1970 - 1980

(46)   Mom recovered and moved to Michigan so we retired to a little house on Columbia Drive on Davis Island, Tampa, Florida.

(47)   Because I was still working and having to drive a long seven mile bridge, with its many hang-ups, we moved to a condominium near Largo, Florida.

(48)   We lived, for about a year, in condominiums where I was Sales Manager in Tampa and leased our condo in Largo.

1980 - 1990

(49)   After John died, I moved to my little cottage on Dogwood Trail near Hiawassee, Georgia where I lived for ten years.

(50)   My third husband, Ben, and I lived my condominium at Place One on 56th Street in Tampa for two winters before we found a nice manufactured home in Lakeland, Florida.

1990 - 1999

(51)   We loved our place on Forest Lake Drive in Lakeside Hills Estates in Lakeland. I remained there after Ben died until I met and married Harry .

(52)   Harry and I bought a manufactured home on Linc Lane, Forest Hills, together. It was our permanent home at the time even though we spent our first summer in Michigan.

(53)   We lived at Harry's barn/residence on W. 14 Road, Mesick, Michigan the summer of 1996 and the spring of 1997 until we bought a condominium together.

(54)   Our present home is the condominium on Courtney Place, Traverse Hills, Traverse City, Michigan.

We hope to spend the rest of our lives in Traverse Hills at Traverse City, Michigan. We are both weary of moving and happen to really like it in this area .

CHAPTER 5

MY STORY

ABOUT ME

In order to pull all these stories together I guess I have to tell my part in them. Everything I have written about has had some influence on me and the person I have turned out to be.

Many people have told me, through the years, that I should write a book. They have not experienced many of the joys and sorrows, and in between, that I have and find it fascinating that one person could have such a varied life.

It started in January 1917 at the York place, a farm owned by my Grandpa Jim. I was a true red-head with cornflower blue eyes, my mother's description. I weighed over nine pounds at birth and weighed one hundred and eleven the first time I was married. I have added a few pounds since.

When I was about five, I ran a temperature for three months, caused by Spinal Meningitis. My hair all came out. When it came back, it was straight as a string but still red.

I have had back problems all my life but have learned to live with it.

Readers may get the impression that I am a crippled-up little old lady but I assure you that I am not. I don't let my back problems stand in the way of enjoying life at the fullest. There is no noticeable physical evidence, only a Milogram in 1954 in University Hospital in Ann Arbor and another at Emory Hospital in Atlanta in 1955 proved it. I am very lucky.

Even though I can't play golf, bowl or ride horses there are a million other things that I enjoy. Like: dancing, swimming, playing cards and other games, reading, embroidering, making flower arrangements, sewing... mostly for Vicki beginning from infancy through her wedding dress, painting, arts and crafts, flea markets, garage sales, home decorating, good conversation, telling and writing stories and the love of a good man .....one at a time.

Things I don't like are: meanness, gossip, indifference, laziness, selfishness, fowl language, loud and boisterous people, hurtful criticism, sloppy workmanship, snobbishness and people who constantly complain of all kinds of situations and especially of boredom.

The people that I enjoy most are: my children, grandchildren, husbands (four), family, friends and a few converted enemies. Especially great are people with a positive outlook and ambitions that they are striving for. I can relate to that.

Some of the things that I know about myself are: I have had to live down the old adage that 'redheads have a temper'. I think I won. I'm stubborn and opinionated, too sensitive, persistent and set in my ways as much as an eighty two year-old is allowed.

Now that my readers know what I think of myself, they can form their own opinions and we can get on with 'My Story'.

MY STORY

The move from Georgia to Michigan had a powerful impact on me. I was not prepared for the different kind of home; going to school for the first time at six years nine months. Children didn't start school until they were seven in Georgia at the time, learning to read, adjusting to winter and coping with mean boys, I had to beat up one big boy with my umbrella for taking our school lunches and hurting Jim.

Each move that we made had an effect on me as new friends had to be found, teachers understood and getting adjusted to new surroundings.

I had never seen a Negro before coming to Michigan and was curious about them. I asked my mother "what color is their blood"? She didn't know so gave me a flippant answer by saying "green".

"Green!!! What color green"?

"Green like what you see when you squash a caterpillar". She went on with her ironing. I accepted that, but was dubious. I didn't know any different. I vowed that if I ever had children and they asked me questions I couldn't answer I would tell them I didn't know, find out the truth and tell them what I had learned. Mama didn't realize how her lack of knowledge affected the lives of us children.

I was a pest, asking questions, curious about everything. My Dad would get annoyed too and usually answer with "because I

98

said so" when I asked him "why", "where" or "what for". For years he refused to accept the spelling of words in the dictionary as being correct. His attitude led to lots of disagreements.

'Old Man Tompkins', one of our neighbors, told my Dad that he should be glad that I had a curious mind. "Smart little girl, if you ask me" he said. Nobody asked him and the subject was dropped.

The twins were six when they started to Star School, with the rest of us, while we lived on Wacousta Road off U.S. 16. We walked the two miles each way. It was red brick with one-room where Mrs. Bottom taught all eight grades. Our family of six children brought the total enrollment to twenty-four.

We carried our lunches in gallon sized syrup buckets. After the paper was washed off, they were shiny and we took pride in keeping them that way.

~~~~~~

Our family ate lots of syrup, biscuits, beans, cornbread, sausage gravy and a variety of vegetables that my Dad grew where-ever we could have a garden. Mama canned, peaches, cherries, pears and vegetables of all kinds. She dried green beans, which became what we called 'leather britches'. She cooked them with a piece of salt pork or bacon. She also dried apples and peaches that she later cooked and made into 'fried pies'. Dried corn and peas made good soup. She dug dandelion greens, cut collard greens and went to the Looking Glass River banks', near Wacousta, to get 'poke salad', a type of greens which she loved. I never knew the real name but think that it was the very young greens of the pokeberry plant. We had rabbit and squirrel, I didn't like either, pheasant and chicken. Pork was a treat but beef was almost inedible because Mama didn't know how to cook it. She would completely ruin a good beef roast by boiling it instead of roasting it. Her excuse was that she had had to help clean too many beef carcasses when she was a child and couldn't stand the smell of it cooking. My Dad always requested that I fix him a beef roast when they came to my house after I was married.

~~~~~~

Back to my story... An older boy, Maynard, took delight in throwing stones at our lunch buckets which made dents and infuriated me. When it got to be too much, I pounded the daylights out of him with my bucket and left a bump on his head.

His Dad got with my Dad. They wound up having a good laugh about it and became friends. Maynard learned a lesson and eventually became an Army Major during World War II.

His parents invited my parents to join the neighborhood club where they met almost every week at someone's house to play cards, dance and have a good time. Dad had plenty of experience making 'corn likker' before we moved to Michigan and had gotten pretty good at making his own beer in our Michigan basement. He became very popular with his newfound friends.

Mrs. Bottom, our teacher, showed me how to shape the nail on my right forefinger that was badly deformed after I stuck it under the sewing machine needle, as Mama was sewing, when I was three. There was a ridge that stuck up, almost square on top. She told me to push down and rub sidewise. I did that for years until only a small scar alongside the nail is visible. She bought every child a comb and taught us how to comb our hair neatly.

Dad had always cut our hair but he wasn't good at making the boys keep it combed.

My hair was kept in a Dutch haircut until I was about twelve when Dad started layering it and it curled, slightly. He was proud of the way it looked.

We kept our bodies clean by daily sponge baths and a turn in the washtub on Saturday nights. Mama kept us as well dressed as possible in hand-me-downs that she remade, patched, washed and ironed until I was old enough to iron, about nine.

During my teen years, Mama turned the of ironing of shirts over to me. I got so I could do a pretty good job in seven minutes but I hated it, especially after our family started going to church making thirty white shirts a week a regular thing. They all had starched collars and cuffs.

In the spring of 1931, I had just turned fourteen in January , I met my first boyfriend, at a May Festival in Wacousta. When he asked if he could drive me home, in his Ford roadster, I was practically speechless. I told him to ask my Dad. I couldn't believe it when Dad said yes.

My brothers teased me unmercifully. One time, they persuaded me to sit on their go-cart and then wouldn't let me off as they pushed me around and around the house until Edward drove into the driveway and caught me being a child. I was mad at Jim and George for a long time.

That same year Dad bought me a beautiful blue coat with collar and cuffs of white curly imitation fur. He understood why I was objecting to wearing the one Mama had made into a botched up mess out of somebody's hand-me-down topcoat. She cried when I put it on.

We had a neighbor on the next hill from us on Wacousta Road who had a son that used to come to see his Dad quite often. The son, an old man of about thirty, Conrad, started coming to our house to play cards, have a few beers and talk to my Dad. He would bring a couple chickens and ask Mama to fix chicken dinner. The folks thought he was real nice but I stayed out of reach of his roving hands.

One Sunday, right after I got my new coat, Dad told me to put it on and show Conrad how pretty it was. I refused and went to my room crying. They had no idea what was wrong with me. Dad made me come out wearing the coat. Conrad complimented me endlessly and asked if he could take me for a ride ... to show off my new coat. I absolutely refused saying that I didn't feel well.

Not long after that we read in the Detroit News that he had been arrested for bootlegging and white slavery. He told the boys that the bullet holes in his car were from his being caught in crossfire on the streets of Detroit. Of course, they were glad to share his secret and never told Dad. I've thanked my stars many times that I followed my intuition that day.

That same summer I went to Oklahoma.

101

OKLAHOMA

I was allowed to start dating although I was only fourteen. That was before my parents got religion.

I had never been to a dance without my parents since I was about nine. There was a big dance hall built out over Round Lake near Lansing where my parents loved to go on a Sunday afternoon. I wanted to dance so badly that I would push a chair around, making believe that it was my partner, and watch the steps the grown-ups made and try to imitate them.

This was during the twenties so flappers were plentiful. I was absolutely fascinated by one lady who was wearing a blue chiffon dress with pointed scallops at the hem, which came to just above her knees. When the hem swished around, you could see that she had doll-faces painted on both knees. Other couples stopped to watch as she and her partner swung around the floor. I was impressed.

It was August 1931, while I was fourteen, when some of our neighbors from Fredrick Street, our old neighborhood, asked me to go with them to Oklahoma to help take care of their two little boys. They knew that I had lots of experience with my four brothers and a sister, all younger than I was, and a sickly mother.

We hadn't been on the road very long when a touring car filled with young black people, we called them 'niggers' in those days, passed us going very fast. There was a sharp curve that they didn't make. The whole car went right through a big sign at the elbow of the turn. The sign was advertising a Funeral Home.

Of course, we stopped. The car was upside down and the occupants were strewn over the field. One woman was reaching around trying to find her husband. A piece of her scalp covered her eyes so she couldn't see. He was several feet away from her, decapitated.

All I could think of was, 'their blood isn't green- it's red'. As a small child I had asked my mother what color their blood was and not knowing she said, "Prob'ly green - like them cat'rpillers when you squash 'em". I had never asked anyone else, just taken her word for it. She did get very tired of all my questions and just said whatever came into her mind.

A neighbor once told her and Dad that they should be glad that I had an inquiring mind but they thought that meant there was something wrong with me.

The rest of the trip going out was quite uneventful except when Mr. Rogers asked me to watch for "66" signs. I kept telling him every time I'd see a sign. I don't know how many times we had turned before he realized that we were not headed in the right direction. He wasn't mad, just upset, when he realized how much time we had lost because I had been having him turn at every "Phillips 66" sign. It was the first trip I had ever taken so he didn't blame me.

We finally arrived at Broken Arrow, Oklahoma and were greeted by many relatives who were looking forward to seeing the new babies. The Grandparents relieved me of my job.

They didn't have room for me so they sent me to stay on a farm, near Muscogee, with some cousins.

The Brown family had a daughter, about seventeen, and a son, who was nineteen. I do believe that he was the ugliest boy I've ever seen... all arms and legs, a long skinny face and no chin. He went out of his way to see that I enjoyed my week with his family. He took me, with his sister and her boyfriend, to the movies; a party held by the neighbors and sightseeing. We did have a good time even though one night we hit a heifer on the way to a show. It killed the heifer and smashed the front end of the car pretty bad. The boys pulled it off the road and when we got to town they told their friends that we hit the bridge. After the movie, some of the boys got into a fight using brass knucks. I'd never seen such rough fighting and so much blood.

The Brown family raised watermelon and peaches. I thought it was a real waste when we were told to eat only the heart of the watermelon and throw the rest to the pigs. They laughed when my eyes got so big after they sliced a whole peach that weighed a pound, with fresh cream, in a cereal bowl and told me to eat it. I did but my stomach hurt.

During that week a tornado hit and completely destroyed the Brown's barn while we young folks stood under the tin roofed peach shed and watched. They said we were just as safe there as any place. All we got was windblown and some dust. After the storm, we drove into Broken Arrow to see the damage. Many buildings were completely destroyed while others across the street were still standing.

One of their cousins, who worked for the Telephone Company, was up on a power pole when he touched a high voltage power line. It tossed him back and forth between two sets of wires before he was finally released and fell to the ground. He was badly burned all over his body, had several broken bones and lost most of his fingers. When we saw him in the hospital he was bandaged up like a mummy but he lived.

The daughter and I wrote back and forth for years until she wrote that she was going to Hollywood to be a dancer. I never heard from her again.

NEW FOUND RELIGION

I was wearing a pair of slacks, similar to blue jeans, and Mama was giving me a hard time about "wearing men's clothes". I thought it was better to cover my behind when climbing fences as Uncle Mutt showed us around the place.

Granpaw motioned for me to follow him out behind the barn. I thought he was really going to lecture me for upsetting Mama.

What he said was, "Etta Mae", he always called me by my full name, "your Granmaw and I are worried, I found out that they said 'worried' when they were concerned, about your Maw's goin' crazy over this 'ere religion thing. We niver brung her up thata way. We cain't see why she picks on you about yur hare and wearin', what she calls, men's clothes. We jest don't think she should keep tryin' to get you married off. It ain't like you cain't take care of yourself. You'all got a good job and you don't look like you're starving to death". That was a lot for Granpaw to say. I had observed him watching me and was wondering what he must think of me. Mama made me sound like a wayward girl.

I hugged Granpaw's neck and thanked him for understanding me. He couldn't see why Mama was blasting everyone who didn't see things her way. She had even been on Granmaw's neck for using snuff, which she had used since she was a little girl. It hurt her feelings but she wasn't about to give up her snuff. She showed me a corn cob pipe that she used sometimes. She grew her own tobacco and made her own plugs of tobacco.

Granmaw and Granpaw were conspirators when it came to doing something for a laugh. They encouraged me to model one of Granmaw's tobacco leaves as a bathing suit. It had the desired effect.

Mama thought I had nothing on underneath and began yelling for me to go in the house. "Not until we git a piture" they both said. Jim took the picture and carried one in his billfold for years. Of course, he never told anyone that it was his sister.

When I stripped off the tobacco leaf, showing my bathing suit underneath, they both laughed their heads off when they saw the expression on Mama's face. She still objected by saying, "you got no business going around half-naked in front of your Grandparents". It turned out to be quite practical when I helped Jim wash his car in the creek.

I explained the folk's newfound religion the best I could. Granpaw would shake his head and grin sometimes.

My interpretation was that, Mama and Dad had gotten this religion while I was on a trip to Oklahoma helping some former neighbors take care of their two small sons.

When I got home from the trip, my folks told me they had been 'Saved' at a church tent meeting. Dad had been playing Pedro with some of the men on their lunch break where all of them worked at Motor Wheel in north Lansing. He said, "I threw down my cards when I heard that Gospel Music and went outside to hear the quartet that were singing and inviting people to the tent meeting that night right down the street". He hurried home after work and took Mama and all the kids, Jim, George, Howard, Leo and Lela from Wacousta back to hear the music.

Brother Lambert, the preacher, gave a powerful sermon, then had an altar call. Both Mama and Dad went forward, prayed aloud for God to forgive their sins and Brother Lambert told them they were 'Saved'.

They were still going to tent meetings a week later when I got home. I was not happy about all this because Mama had already been in my room and taken all my personal things, my diary, my little pieces of jewelry, a lipstick and everything that she considered sinful. I was told that I would be going to church every Sunday and to prayer meetings on Wednesdays.

Worst of all was that I could not have Dad cut my hair again because all the women and girls in the church had long hair. Dad had cut it all my life but had been layering it for sometime and it curled slightly.

And my boyfriend, a nice farm boy named Edward, who was nineteen, could either go to church or I couldn't see him anymore. He tried going a couple times but when some women started jumping up and down and shouting he quit going to church but would drive in from Wacousta to drive me home. He came a few times but when the deacons of the church accused him of stealing tires in the parking lot he gave up. I never saw him again. I thought I had reason to be bitter about their new religion.

Granpaw seemed to understand my feelings about what I called their 'Overnight Religion'.

When I got home from that trip my folks had gotten what I always called 'Overnight Religion'. The change in them was unbelievable. Dad had smashed his still in the basement, gotten rid of his beer making ingredients and equipment, burned his playing cards and canceled all parties with their friends and neighbors.

Mama had decided to let her hair grow long. She never let Dad cut my hair again.

They had turned over a new leaf and we kids had no choice about anything. It upset me more than the boys. The twins were only five and never realized what had transpired in their lives.

We went to church twice on Sunday and a couple times a week from then on. Eventually we became used to it and made friends with the other kids. Some were going through the same upsetting, to me, conditions at home. We moved from Wacousta Road to Lansing to be closer to the church.

One of the pleasures we were allowed was ice-skating. A group of us from the church would go to Bancroft Park and nearby golf course and skate on the frozen streams. Sometimes we'd take a phonograph and skate in couples to the music. If our folks had known what we were doing, it was too much like dancing, it would have been stopped. We went to parties, always games and refreshments at somebody's house. We made our fun whenever and wherever we could. There was no drinking, smoking or necking. We were always chaperoned. My life was very ordinary, if you consider that the church is your whole life, between the ages of fourteen and eighteen.

In September 1933, I finally had my appendix out. They had ruptured and peritonitis had set in. I was in Neller Hospital for three weeks and recuperated at the Cole's, church members, for two more weeks.

They wanted to adopt me and be sure that "I was one of the Forty Thousand 'Chosen People' that they were sure would be called when the Pearly Gates opened. They had two daughters, younger than I, and a son who was about my age. I was a little afraid of them and thought that their religion was more narrow-minded and restrictive than my parents was even though they went to the same Church.

When I went back to school I had to take Gym and do a rocking motion lying on my stomach on the floor. I fainted. They excused me from Gym after they realized that the motion and strain had burst my incision, which was straight down the middle of my abdomen. Years later I had a lot of trouble with adhesions and when I was pregnant for my babies.

In the spring of 1934 my eyes started watering so badly that my folks got me glasses when I was seventeen. The next spring I realized that I needed more than glasses. My eyes would itch, turn red and water. The inside of my eyelid would peal from little circles that looked like ringworm. I could peal them out leaving the inside of my lid raw and hurting more than ever. After several Doctors, one of them decided to cauterize the spots. My eyelids would swell, water and itch within a week so he would do it again. This went on for one whole summer. Doctors said, "no swimming, no riding in open cars or reading which I loved. My church-boyfriend had an open roadster with a rumble seat. It was a miserable summer but my boyfriend, Clyde, stuck by me even though I looked like I was crying all the time. At the end of September they cleared up. The Doctors thought that I was cured of whatever it was.

The next year was almost as bad. It always seemed to start in April, but no more cauterizing. My eyelids were so thin the Doctor was afraid to do it. Then came ointments, pills and whatever anyone suggested.

My boss at Wolverine Insurance took a special interest in my case and brought me carrot, celery and mixed vegetable juices from his garden. I drank them every day in spite of the awful taste. Again I was declared cured at the end of the summer.

I was twenty-two, married and pregnant for Vicki when my Doctor recommended allergy tests. An Allergy Specialist, a new kind of Doctor, had suggested the tests to me before but at two hundred and fifty dollars that was impossible on twenty dollars per week salary. My Doctor ordered the tests and a chart from the drug store for twenty-five dollars. After Vicki was born, in April 1939, he tested me.

The little bumps that appeared from one drop of assorted well-known allergies soon confirmed that my Allergies were maple trees, plantain grass, ragweed, oranges, cantaloupes and a whole range of items.

My Doctor gave me shots in the summer, from April through September. I was fine as long as he was around and skipped 1940, while I was pregnant, until one week after Lynn was born in August 1940. I had the shots from then until I became pregnant for Terry. He was born in July 1942. Within a week the allergies were back.

The Doctor delivered Terry and left for the Navy shortly afterward. He turned my records over to another Doctor who wouldn't do anything for me without a new set of tests.

This one included four hundred items and had to be done by a specialist who almost went into shock when the tests showed allergies to one hundred thirteen items. The little drop on my right forearm swelled to half a baseball size. The specialist's eyes almost bugged out as he said, "Don't ever eat Crab Meat! You could be dead in forty-five minutes! You would swell inside and choke to death". He was sweating as he told me about a little eight year old girl that had died in Detroit, a few weeks earlier, after eating crabmeat. All seafood and fish tests had raised large bumps wherever they were tested on my forearms, backs of upper thighs and on my back but crabmeat was the worst.

Naturally, I have avoided seafood and fish but had quite an experience with scallops.

I was so naive that I didn't know that scallops were seafood until years later when John, my second husband, took me to visit his relatives, for the first time, after a wonderful dinner at a fabulous restaurant on Long Island.

Suddenly I became deathly ill and was lying on the floor in their bathroom when they decided I'd been gone too long. They were finally able to reach their druggist friend, at home on Sunday night, who opened his store and brought some liquid Benadryl. It was some time before I could keep enough down to help. I have kept Benadryl on hand, in various forms, ever since.

I've said, many times, "if I knew for sure what day I was going to die, I'd eat all the Lobster, Shrimp, Crab meat and all the seafood I could hold". Apparently, that wouldn't be much.

~~~~~~

Before I had my graduation picture made, I cut my hair. My mother cried and my Dad threatened to throw me out but I was tired of looking like an old lady. My hair was so long by then that I wore it in braids done in a double twist, like a figure eight, in back and absolutely hated it.

My opportunity came while I was baby-sitting for somebody. I tried to get my girlfriends to cut it, three of them had showed up to see this spectacle, but they were too scared of my Dad. I took the scissors and whacked it off, one side then the other doing the back last. One of the girls put it up on rollers and I thought it looked real good the next morning when I went to church. Mama was so ashamed that she made me wear a big floppy hat. One of the dear ladies at the church came up to me, peeked under the brim and said, "Etta, I do declare that you've lost the glory off your face!" I said, "You mean that I've cut my hair. I know that Elizabeth told you because she was there last night." She walked away without another word. When I told

Clyde, my boyfriend, what I was going to do he said, "you do and we're through". I offered to give him the two long braids after it was cut but he decided he liked me with my short hair.

I graduated from Eastern High School in 1936. During my high school years I was not allowed to go to any activities like football games, dances or any activity that my parents didn't approve of.

However, I was on the Debating Team and did very well and belonged to the Art Club. I loved my Art classes and took part in everything pertaining to them. I won a scholarship in Commercial Art at the Chicago Art Institute but my Dad refused to let me go after some literature, showing nudes, came in the mail. Even after Mr. Rich, the principal, came to the house to talk to Dad the answer was still "No". I didn't touch a paintbrush again until after I married John. I got an Artists' case complete with paints and brushes for Christmas. Since then my Artwork has been sporadic.

When I left home, at almost nineteen, I faced uncertainty and heartache because my parents had chosen their 'Newfound Religion' over their family and that was unforgivable to me.

TRIP TO GEORGIA

It was August 1937 when Mom, Jim, his first wife Helen and I began our much planned for trip to Georgia to see Jim's and my Grandparents that I hadn't seen since I was six.

Mom had been writing to Aunt Flora in Indianapolis and told her that we would visit her on our way south. We didn't know that one my cousins, Houston, was visiting Aunt Flora and wanted a ride home. He was anxious to get back to North Carolina after having no success finding a job in Indiana. His family lived just across the state line from Georgia where we were going. He was about my age. I was twenty.

We had just gotten started when Mama proceeded to lecture me about putting my bare feet out the window and not acting like a lady. Even though I was wearing pants, now called Jeans, and wasn't "showing everything" she kept reminding me. I could have been miserable the rest of the trip but because I was spending my own hard-earned money I was determined not to let her spoil it for me.

Houston was puzzled about the way Mama talked to me but he didn't know that her religion had taken over her life and greatly influenced our family since she had gotten 'saved' when I was fourteen and that it was the cause of my leaving home when I was nineteen.

Houston had never been out of the mountains before, he'd taken a train to Indianapolis, but was sure he could direct us to his home by car. We had no such thing as road maps; at least Jim didn't, in those days.

His directions led us along some very treacherous roads that the CCCs were building. Sometimes there would be a high bank on one side of us with a cliff several hundred feet deep on the other. The roads were very crooked, winding up and down and around lots of mountains. There were tunnels through solid rock while other areas would be through several inches of red mud but I loved the scenery in the mountains.

Jim was a good driver but when it became dark he was as worried as the rest of us.

During the daylight hours he thought he could cut across a curve, that had been filled in, even though it looked muddy. We sank to the hubcaps and had to climb out on the driver's side because of the drop-off on the passenger's side. It was a scary situation until an old man came along with a mule team and wagon. He looked the situation over and decided the only way to get us out was to use a block and tackle pulled around a big tree and hitched to his mules. He wouldn't charge us anything but asked us to help someone else who might need it.

Many hours later, during the pitch-black night, Jim was still driving with Houston telling him where to go. Many jagged rocks protruded from the roadbed. We hit one that put a hole in the gas tank. We could smell the gas and hear it running out of the tank. Mama wanted to light a match to see what the damage was. I nearly pushed her over the edge, in the dark, to keep her away from the car. I was petrified when we later learned that there was a five hundred foot drop within a few feet of where we were standing.

111

It didn't take Jim long to figure out that something had to be done. He borrowed my brown and white polka dot headscarf, wrapped it around a screwdriver and stuffed it in the hole. With Houston 's guidance and Mama's praying, out loud, we finally made our destination about 3:00 A.M.

Uncle Manual and his wife were not expecting us but quickly shifted the children to pallets on the floor to make room for us.

I was sitting in a small chair with my head in my hands, waiting for the sleeping arrangements to take place, when Uncle Manuel patted me on the head and said, "don't cry little boy, we'll find you a place to sleep". Mama couldn't help herself. She had been telling me for two years that since I had my hair cut short and had taken to wearing pants that everyone would think I was a boy. She started trying to explain to everyone that she didn't approve but by that time of night nobody cared and just wanted to get some sleep.

Jim went with Houston next morning to a nearby church and got some fellows to leave the service to help. They took the gas tank off, cleaned it, welded the hole and put it back on for two dollars.

Meanwhile I was still trying to figure out why Aunt Ila had white sand spread all over the floors when we got there.

When we arrived at Granmaw Bettie's I told her about the sand. She laughed as she slapped her hands on her knees. When she got over laughing she explained that the sand was put there to clean the floors. During the night it was supposed to absorb grease or whatever happened to be dropped during the day. It was Saturday night/Sunday morning when we arrived so Aunt Ila had swept the sand out the door, or through the cracks in the floor, first thing before anyone else got up. I could see that the floors were clean in the morning but I sure didn't understand how until Granmaw explained it to me.

THE WHOREHOUSE

This story keeps popping up in my in my mind so might as well write it down and get it over with.

My first husband used to love to tell people that he met me in a whorehouse. That was untrue, of course, but he thought it was funny. He didn't explain what he based his remarks on and a few people looked at me quizzically.. The truth was somewhat embarrassing but not because of anything I did.

I knew of such houses because before I was married our boyfriends, all members of my and my girl friends' church, favorite past-time on a Saturday night was driving down from Lansing to Jackson, Michigan and through the "Red Light" district. Girls hung out upstairs windows, scantily dressed, and called to the boys to come on up.

We girls were so naive that when the boys tried to explain their behavior to us they could only use Jezebel, in the Bible, as an example of a whore.

I've never understood why the boys didn't try to make passes at us on the way home, now that I think of it. I guess it was because we usually went by the carload and they were just too scared they'd have to face our wrath and our fathers. Which they would have.

Here is what actually happened...

I left my parent's home after a severe argument caused by my wanting to wear a pair of my brother's jeans to go target practicing.

I moved in with a married couple. Dorothy and Lester were from the same church where my family had gotten Religion a few years earlier.

We had sat together through many of Brother Lambert's 'Hellfire and Brimstone' sermons. We wondered where he had sampled all the 'sins of the flesh' that he preached about as he swept his finger over an audience of young people. We hated it when he aimed at us and then would say, "if you're guilty, you know who you are so get up here to this alter and ask God's forgiveness NOW!" I knew I wasn't guilty and refused to cringe. Some might have been but none of them ran to the altar.

After church Dorothy and I finally got to discussing what was uppermost in our minds. They were house/apartment hunting and so was I. My reason was because my landlady had snooped in my hope chest and told on herself when she mentioned something that I knew she couldn't have known about otherwise.

Dorothy asked if I would consider moving in with them if we could find a suitable place. That was fine with Lester because he was on a low paying job and Dorothy didn't work outside the home. It seemed like a good arrangement for all of us because I was only making fifteen dollars a week in 1936.

It so happened that a lady from the church had a vacant apartment upstairs in her house across the street. We all agreed that it would suit our needs. By bringing my studio couch that I had purchased for my one room studio, I could sleep in the living room, former upstairs bedroom. We had a small kitchen/dinette combination, a bedroom for Dorothy and Lester and bath, which we shared with the owner, Sister Lutz from the church, and her cousin Cliff, who lived downstairs.

We were cozy there...On the bus route for Lester and me and across the street from the Church where we were all members. My boyfriend, Clyde, was always welcome and we had several outings besides our church activities, which made it all very pleasant until---

Sister Lutz asked us to keep an eye on her apartment while she was away on business in Battle Creek the following weekend. She said that she had had silverware stolen before and all she wanted us to do was to make sure the downstairs door was kept locked at all times. That didn't seem like a lot so we agreed.

Before the weekend one of my best girlfriends, Lucille, died of cancer of the face. It was really sad as she was only nineteen and left a ten-month baby boy and her young husband.

Lucille and I had stayed over at each other's house many times as we used to put on Chalk Shows for young people at our church as well as going to other local churches to do the shows. She would play the guitar and sing and I would do the chalk drawings. One song she liked to sing was 'The Drunkard's Child', which she had learned from my mother. I drew a small blond-headed little girl with ragged clothes and torn shoes. Then I would draw a tall man with his hand on the child's head and fill in the features like Jesus. It was quite impressive because Lucille

114

could bring the tears as she mourned the child's fate... until Jesus came. A dear friend, from the church, borrowed the picture and never gave it back.

Lucille's snoring was so loud I had a hard time getting to sleep. Her mother said that she had been run over by a car and had severe damage done to her forehead and nose when she was five. That's where the cancer hit her. The family would not let anyone see her for the last few months. The last time I saw her head was completely bandaged but there appeared to be a baseball over one eye. Needless to say, I was heartbroken when she died.

The funeral was on Saturday. My face was swollen and my eyes were red and I just couldn't stop crying. I didn't want Clyde to see like that but he came over that night anyway. He took one look at me and suggested that we go for a ride in his roadster with the top down. He invited Dorothy and Lester to go with us. Lester didn't have a car so he was delighted to drive. Clyde and I sat in the rumble seat. There was a nice breeze but it played havoc with my hair. I must have been quite a sight with my swollen face, red eyes and windblown hair.

As soon as we got home, Dorothy rushed for the bedroom where she was taking off her girdle and Lester was removing his sox, when the doorbell rang. It was 11:20 PM. I remember it like it was yesterday. Dorothy asked me if I would go to the door, so with Clyde backing me up in case there was a problem, I did. No problem at all---it was Sister Lutz who had forgotten her key. I was quite surprised because she had said she wouldn't be back until Sunday night. I said something like, "oh, we didn't expect you". I let her in and went on back upstairs where Clyde and I listened to the radio a little while before he left.

I mentioned to Dorothy that Sister Lutz looked quizzically at me when I answered the door. We both thought that maybe she was expecting Lester to answer the door at that time of night. We dismissed it from our minds and went to bed.

Next morning at church my mother looked like she had been crying but she knew Lucille so I thought she was still thinking about the funeral. After getting a cool reception at the church for three weeks in a row, and tears every time she looked at me, I

115

decided that Mama was upset with me about something. I walked the seven blocks to my parent's home, after church, to see what was going on. We had long-since made up after my leaving home.

I followed my mother into the kitchen where she burst out crying and yelling at me. "How come you never told us that you and Clyde were married?" I was surprised and said, "what makes you think that we are married or that I wouldn't tell you."

"Then you shouldn't be sleeping with him if you're not." she replied.

This really surprised me because I had never slept with Clyde or any other boy. Nice girls just didn't sleep around in the thirties.

Of course, I was upset and asked her "where did you get that information?" She said that Sister Lutz had come home that Saturday night and caught Clyde and me in bed. She told her how embarrassed I was because my face was so red and my hair a mess. She had gotten up early Sunday morning and walked to their house to tell them what she had seen … with her own eyes.

It was hard to believe that dear Sister Lutz could have said such terrible things about me. She had told me several times that she just loved me and wished she had a daughter like me.

Mama said, "I know that Sister Lutz wouldn't lie, she's too good a Christian".

It was like a slap in the face…that my own mother would believe this woman who had so blatantly lied about me.

I was furious as I left the house, after telling her that I was going to make Sister Lutz admit that she was lying.

That seven blocks home was much shorter as my anger built every step of the way. Dorothy saw me coming from our upstairs window and was at the head of the stairs when I got there. She didn't say anything as I opened the downstairs apartment door and barged into Sister Lutz' apartment.

Naturally, she was shocked to see me and read the rage on my face. She rose from her chair as I kept walking toward her. She clutched her chest, started backing away from me and said, "I have a heart condition so please don't upset me".

"I don't care if you die right here, you're going to hear what

I have to say" and I proceeded to tell her what my mother had told me "the red face, the hair, my sleeping with Clyde" the whole bit.

By then I was yelling at her as she kept backing away from me until she fell over the end of her bed. I stood over her and screamed "you are going to apologize to my parents and tell them you were lying. You will also tell Grandma Hincher, the Coopers, and Brother Lambert and any others you told this to or I will sue you for slander".

I knew that she had told several others because I had heard many of them praying for me in church, out loud, and was wondering why so much interest in me all of a sudden.

The next day Sister Lutz contacted the people she had told this story to and added that I had "threatened to sue her if she didn't tell them it was untrue". Needless to say, there were some misguided people who preferred to believe her than a young woman who had left her parents home for reasons they didn't know and wouldn't have understood if they did.

Dorothy started looking for another apartment for the three of us on Monday. She found one immediately. It was on the opposite end of Lansing off South Washington Avenue just south of Grand River.

It was a rather unusual arrangement but we made it work out. The biggest drawback was that we had to share the bathroom with two other apartments; the landlady's and an efficiency on the first floor. Each apartment had a door to the bathroom, which we learned immediately to lock every time we went in. We did not like sharing a bathtub and commode but none of us could afford anything with a private bathroom.

We hadn't lived there very long when I had a chance to go to Georgia with my brother Jim, his first wife and Mama. We went to see our Grandparents that I hadn't seen since leaving there when I was six. It was a memorable trip.

While we were at Granpaw and Granmaw's place I made a decision that changed my future forever. I made up my mind to break my engagement to Clyde because I realized that I did not love him enough to spend the rest of my life with him. It took me six weeks after we got back to tell him. I felt like I was really

117

free... of my folks and him. I was really on my own.

Not long after I got home, Dorothy was in the basement doing our laundry when our landlady, Vi, came down to talk and get better acquainted with our trio. She was curious as to our living arrangements but Dorothy was very frank in telling her. We had nothing to hide.

The conversation led to where we had moved from, merely curious, Dorothy thought. Again, Dorothy was very open about it and told Vi about what Sister Lutz had done to me. Vi seemed very interested, wanting to know the address, who else lived in the house, where Sister Lutz went to church, what her first name was and every little detail. When Dorothy had answered all her questions, Vi started laughing. She laughed until she cried.

Dorothy didn't see anything funny about all that until Vi said, "her name is Helen, she operates two whorehouses in Battle Creek, the man living with her is not her cousin and she pays her tithes regularly to the Church ".

While Dorothy stood with her mouth open, Vi continued "I know because she's my sister. She tried to get me to go into the business with her after my husband died but I had two little kids. Anyway, I had found out that I could get money for it on my own so I quit giving it away. My kids are on their own now so I look after myself. I have a 'live-in' husband any time I want to ".

I'll never forget that night at dinner when Dorothy told us the shocking news. Vi seemed like such a nice person and would excuse herself if she told an off-color joke in my presence.

We talked it over and decided that as long as Vi's life-style didn't affect us we'd stay there. Her daughter and son visited quite often and they didn't seem to mind so why should we?

We thought it best not to tell anyone but had a good laugh when Sister Lutz found out where we were living. Brother Lambert announced several times that Sister Lutz had been very generous with her tithes lately. Her business must have been doing well. We still went to the same church but Sister Lutz never spoke to us again. We didn't wonder why.

The other tenants downstairs were a man and woman who were not married. We thought that was scandalous but still thought it didn't affect us and we were not in a position to turn around and move within a few weeks.

It was years later when I heard Ray joking about meeting me in a whorehouse. I had never thought of any of them, Sister Lutz, Vi or the girl downstairs that way.

THE COTTAGE

While I was still living with Dorothy and Lester at our last apartment, The Whorehouse, I met Ray when he came to see Lester about their plans for a trip to his sister's cottage on Diamond Lake that next weekend. Lester and Ray worked together on WPA. It was February and too cold for such a trip, or, so I thought.

I wound up in their foursome. They added another couple, Bud and Sally, before the week was out.

On arriving at the cottage we found knee deep snow outside and an icicle, a foot thick inside the house beside the fireplace chimney, from floor to the cathedral ceiling. Sleeping arrangements were a little strange.

This was before young unmarried people started sleeping together openly. Maybe some did but I didn't know anyone who had. I was very naive. I had never seen a naked man … only my brothers when they were very young.

Dorothy had it all figured out. We stacked six mattresses, double deck, on the floor in front of the fireplace. She put me on one end with herself next to me on my left and Lester next to her. Bud was beside Lester with his wife, Sally, next to him. That was fine with everybody but Ray. He wouldn't go to bed unless he could sleep beside me so he sat up all night and sang while we all begged him to stop. My favorite was, 'You're the One Rose That's Left in my Heart'. I fell in love with his voice that night. We all slept in our ski suits, or so I thought.

We dozed off but there must have been some action during the night because when I yanked the covers off of Bud, he wouldn't get up so we could move the mattresses and fix breakfast, there he lay, naked as a Jay Bird! He grabbed a quilt and disappeared before the others knew what happened.

After two more moves, while I lived with Dorothy and

Lester, I found a little studio apartment for myself. It was adequate after I bought a sofa-bed and re-upholstered an occasional chair. I was making seventeen fifty a week so rent of twenty dollars a month was stretching it a bit.

I was happy there until my sister-in-law, Jim's first wife, showed up crying. She had left Jim and wanted to move in with me. Another knock on the door and there stood Jim. She scurried to the bathroom and stayed there until he and I left to drive around and discuss his problems. He moved in with me and the landlady raised the rent five dollars

Because Ray was the only male working in his family. His Dad, Mother, three sisters, a crippled brother and his married brother with his wife were all living at home. He was giving most of his money to his mother, I didn't know that it was compulsory, I thought he was ambitious and admired him for providing for his family.

Ray had beautiful features, large hazel eyes, a nice nose, a firm chin and a sense of humor that was new to me. After we got home that weekend, I said to Dorothy "he's going to be the father of my children". She thought I was crazy but then she remembered how she had fallen in love with another redhead, she was redheaded too, and watched as the romance progressed.

We were married in August 1937 in Angola, Indiana while Jim was still living with me. Ray moved in too so the landlady raised the rent again ... another five dollars.

The three of us decided that we could find a better, bigger place for thirty dollars. We found a half of a house, now called duplexes, in North Lansing.

We were getting along fine, by this time I knew that I was pregnant for Vicki, when Jim brought his estranged wife home one night. That was a nightmare. She refused to cook because she got her meals at the Greek Restaurant where she worked. She wouldn't do any housework, left the bed unmade, smoked and read True Stories and cried the whole time. Ray and I moved out and left them in the apartment.

Dorothy and Lester had rented a small house on Grand River Avenue that was big enough for all four of us. Dorothy had already agreed to take care of my baby when it came.

Three months after Vicki was born her Dad was laid off from his, by then, Taxi-Driver job. We moved in with his parents on Ash Street and I went back to work at Wolverine Insurance Company.

Six months later we moved to a house on Larch Street where I became pregnant for Lynn and Jim moved in with us again.

I was in bed upstairs, on sick leave to keep from losing Lynn, when an explosion rocked the house. I ran downstairs, I thought the factory behind us had blown up.

I found Jim standing in the middle of the kitchen floor with beans dripping all over him. He had put an unopened number three can of Pork & Beans on the stove for his lunch, without opening it. I went back to bed while he cleaned beans off the ceiling, the walls, the stove, sink, floors and everything in the kitchen. He moved to Chicago shortly after that.

When we moved to a tiny house on Knollwood we were really on our own. Lynn was born in August 1940 while we lived there.

Many incidents related throughout this book will give some insight as to the way we lived during the years of raising the children.

Some of those incidents were interesting... some not. I will try to stick to the most interesting.

CHRISTMAS - 1942

We moved into our new Redi-Bilt house when Terry was three months old, Vicki was three and Lynn was two. It was a move of necessity, not choice, when our rented house was sold and we were given thirty days to move out by October.

A man who had seen the house several years earlier had bought it, without even coming inside, for his family to live in while he would be gone in the Army.

We were broken hearted but World War II was on so we could do nothing about keeping our little stone house on Turner Road, South of Lansing, which we had grown to love in the year and a half we were there.

We had no savings but had managed to scrape up three

hundred dollars. The first Realtor to show us houses treated us like dirt. The best house for us, according to him, was large enough but the family had five children and all of them wet the bed. You could smell it when you walked in the door. I gagged when he showed us the upstairs.

Without any way to raise more money we knew that we had a real problem.

When somebody told us about the Redi-Bilt house, that were built in sections and put together on your lot in one day, we didn't believe it. We pursued it and learned that it really was true but there were several drawbacks. You had to own your own lot, there was no plumbing, no bathroom fixtures, or kitchen sink. It did include the roof, walls and siding, studs for room partitions, wiring, sub-floor, pine flooring, trim and doors and a cement block foundation. It was truly a shell for a house.

The company suggested areas where we might find a lot to build on. Next, we were to find a Bank that would make us a loan for the balance of three thousand six hundred dollars.

We found a lot on Viking Road about a mile away. We had high hopes that were immediately dashed by the first three Banks. With only three hundred dollars to our name. It seemed impossible.

When the fourth loan officer learned that we had no money for insulation or walls, he loaned us back what had been our down payment. One of his stipulations was that the walls had to be up and plastered within a year. He had a heart. Our hopes were up. We were sure that we could do such a small thing.

We had forgotten that we had to have a chimney. There was no way of heating until we had one built. Ray tried but he gave up and hired a bricklayer who tore down the three feet of bricks that Ray had laid and started over again.

We were scared that we had taken on too much, especially after Pop, Ray's Dad said, "you'll never live long enough to pay for it".

We were determined to make the most of it even though we had no water in the house, couldn't buy pipe because of the War, no bathroom and it was impossible to buy plumbing fixtures.

Our next door neighbors, Blondie and Larry, saw the

dilemma we were in and offered to let us carry water from their well and to use their outside toilet. They had put water and a bathroom in their house recently and knew what we were facing. Wonderful people!

My Mother and Dad came over to see our new place. It was a long way from being a 'home'. They realized how cold it was and took our three children to their home, in Grand Ledge, until we could make the place livable.

Ray and I put in insulation, nailed up wallboard and laid floors. I didn't want pine floors. I wanted oak because I knew they would be bare. Everyone thought I was out of my mind when I called several lumber companies to see if they would trade me oak for pine flooring. I had read that there was a scarcity of pine because so many barracks had been built for the military. One company offered to trade me oak for pine, deliver and pick up and pay me thirty dollars to boot. We laid the oak flooring, rented a sander, polished, and varnished my beautiful oak floors.

We had worked with only a portable kerosene heater but knew we had to have more heat than that to bring our children home. My Dad found a pot-bellied stove somewhere for five dollars. We thought we had a miracle until we built a roaring fire and saw the crack completely around the belly of the stove. I slept in a chair by the stove many nights, with a fire extinguisher on my lap.

Fuel oil was rationed. Since we had never been a customer, no company would sell to us because of the War. Some one intervened for us, mainly because Ray was a War-Worker at Oldsmobile. That helped. We were finally able to buy a space heater and live quite comfortably even though the floors were cold.

We still had a big problem carrying water but we got by going to Ray's parents in Lansing for Saturday night baths. I sent the laundry out to a lady whose husband picked it up and delivered it after she had ironed and folded it.

Because of the War, we were unable to buy lumber to build an outside privy or plumbing to finish our inside needs. It was a rough winter but we worked hard every day after our regular

123

jobs.

I was a War-Worker on the Nacelle for the B-29 Bombers at Fisher Body and Ray worked at Oldsmobile on the 16 inch gun barrels used on Navy ships. We fell into bed so exhausted that we didn't worry about our situation.

Christmas was coming. I did what I could to decorate our little home which consisted of living room, kitchen/dinette combination and two bedrooms after we had put up the partitions, wallboard and laid the floors. We couldn't do anything to the bathroom area so we made it into a nursery for Terry. The two bedrooms upstairs and finishing the bathroom was done after the war.

Then it was Christmas Eve and all the family gathered at the homestead, on Ash Street in Lansing, for the big night. Our children were swamped with gifts from everyone. I knew that they all felt sorry for us having to live in such circumstances but we were surviving and I was thankful for that.

There was a chocolate candy box under the tree for Ray and me. It seemed ridiculous that any of the family would give us a box of chocolates when there were so many things we needed. The box was handed to me but I didn't want to open it.

I remembered the Christmas when we were first married. I had said all that I wanted was a watch. Ray gave me a beautiful Bulova watch box. I was elated. It turned out to be a dime-store watch, which was never replaced. That was the kind of humor the family enjoyed and most of them laughed when I cried. They said that I couldn't take a joke.

It was typical of his family to play jokes or tricks on each other so when Ray opened the box I didn't think it was unusual to see a note that said, "look under the porch swing". I was thinking 'snow shovel'. There was another box with a note that said, "go upstairs and look under Yoland's bed". By that time everyone was following us and urging us on to the next box. After several more boxes in unusual places, the final note said, " go out the grade door in the back of the basement". It opened from the outside through doors that lay on a slant above the steps. Pop had put up a second door that swung inward to keep out the cold.

124

When we opened that door there sat Bud, my brother-in-law, on one of the neatest two-holers I'd ever seen. One side was a little one for the kids. I don't know if I cried from the shock, the thoughtfulness of Pop or the grateful feeling of never having to go to the neighbors' privy again.

Pop had gone to a lumber company that had a big fire and scrounged through the charred wood to find enough boards and pieces, he had to cut the ends off, to build us a Pre-Fab privy.

He had built it in his basement and scrambled to hide it one day when I had gone to his workshop to ask him about an order of toy trucks that he was building. I was selling them at Fisher Body. He had retrieved a bushel basket of grommets from somewhere and got the idea to build little wooden trucks and cars, using the grommets as tires. I could get more orders, at five dollars each, than he could handle because it was difficult to buy either metal or wooden toys during the war. I thought that was why he was so busy in the basement. He thought I knew what he was doing but I didn't have an inkling.

Now we had the problem of getting the privy to our house, which was about eight miles at the opposite end of Lansing. The men borrowed a trailer and hoisted the outhouse on it. The women tied a huge red bow on top with wide strips of ribbons that went from the top to the bottom. When we drove through town, people started honking their horns, waving and laughing. They all knew what we got for Christmas.

It was sometime later that we were able to buy pipe to put in our own well and bring water into the house. What a blessing to turn on the faucet and get water. Now we could take our Saturday night baths at home, in the kitchen. We didn't finish the bathroom until the War ended and we could buy fixtures. Those were unforgettable years.

THE PREACHER

Several years after I was married, I went with two of my Uncles and their wives to an Aunt's funeral in South Carolina. They stayed on after the funeral, visiting relatives.

It seemed like a good idea, before going back to Michigan,

that I spend a few days with my mother and father in their trailer near Atlanta, Georgia.

Mama said that she was going to Tuesday Night Prayer Meeting at the nearby Church. She invited me to go with her.

I was reluctant but she promised that no one would approach me begging me to go to the altar to get 'Saved', as she called it.

I had had an experience with her church in Lansing when I was eighteen that turned me away from the Church forever.

Back then, she had instigated a prayer group to get me to the altar. They literally picked me up and carried me. They dropped me down in front of the altar and started pounding me in the back while hollering to God to 'Save' me. I was hurting and embarrassed. I wiggled my way out from under them and walked away. They were so caught up in what they were doing that they didn't know that I was gone for several minutes. I was on everybody's prayer list after that.

Now she was inviting me to go with her. It had been a long time, eighteen years. She said her Brothers and Sisters didn't go that far anymore. I thought I could handle it.

We got to the vestibule where she introduced me to her preacher, a 'Brother Somebody' by saying, " Brother, I've told you that I have two daughters" he nodded and she continued "well, this is the one that's a Sinner". I could have dropped in my tracks.

I was a good Presbyterian, at the time, and was deeply offended but decided to stay for the service. Partly because the 'Brother' had looked me up and down. I felt that he was undressing me with his eyes. I thought, 'this should be interesting'.

He preached to 'cigarette smoking, drinking women'. All eyes were on me as if I had a brand on my forehead. Nobody approached me as they sang the Altar Call but I was the only one that people turned around and looked at when they sang, 'Come All Ye Sinners'.

I waited at the back of the church until the preacher came to shake my hand, after the service. That was all I needed. I don't think anybody ever dared to speak to him the way I did that night. When I got through with him, he knew that I neither smoked nor drank and didn't consider myself a 'sinner'. I told him that if he cleaned out the hypocrites in his church he wouldn't have any congregation left.

Mama never invited me to her church again. Through the years I did have to go to attend my Dad's funeral, hers and a few weddings.

TRUCK DRIVER

Years later, during the time we lived on Norwood Drive, I went to the terminal to pick Ray up after one of his runs hauling cars.

I was on medical leave at the time because of back injuries and was wearing a back brace.

While I was waiting for him to take a road test, something new that ICC had come up with, I stood outside the big van taking notes.

The van had been outfitted with facsimiles showing all kinds of simulated road conditions like ice and snow, vehicles and children on bicycles running and turning in front of you and movies of accidents. Some very unusual tests were supposed to show the reflexes and skills the truck driver would use in avoiding these scenarios or anything that came up on the screen. Included was shifting, ten gears, and braking while adhering to rules of the road.

When he finished, the fellow in charge asked Ray if I was a reporter.

Ray said "No. She thinks she's writing a story".

The fellow asked, "why don't I give her the test? Then she'll really have something to write about."

They both laughed when I climbed into the van and took the set-up steering wheel. I'll admit that I was scared. I had learned to drive an old Model A stick shift that would only make right turns, and gone on to drive our Model A Ford then to an Oldsmobile and later to a Buick but I had never driven a truck! When the test was over, I had scored ninety-seven, two points higher than Ray did.

The instructor asked me if I'd like to attend a seminar for

Truck Drivers to be conducted at Michigan State College the next week.

He made the arrangements and I showed up in the classroom, along with twenty men in coveralls. I, in a business suit, notebook in hand, on a cold Monday morning in November 1952.

The men were surprised to see a woman in a class. They were attending this high-level training course so they could become Truck Driver Instructors for the various companies they worked for. Five were from Shell Oil. Others were from large trucking companies who had hired many men that needed training. The instructor introduced me and told them I would be sitting in for the day.

I knew that truck drivers had the reputation of being foul-mouthed and rowdy but I thought I could handle that to get a story. I preferred to think of them as "Gentlemen of the Highways' as I'd heard.

I was taking a night school course in Short Story Feature Article Writing and really wanted something special. The writing instructor said to "pick a subject that you absolutely know nothing about, research it, then write about it". I didn't know what 'the fascination' was for Ray and decided that his job would be a good one for me to research. It was a couple years later when I found out that 'the fascination' was a waitress who lived in Ohio.

When the eight hour class ended that first day, the Professor asked me if I'd like to come back Tuesday. I was delighted. He told me to wear coveralls, like the men in class. Luckily, Ray's uniforms fit me very well.

I was back next morning with my notebook and a short transcription of the notes I had taken the day before.

I went out to the practice field, set up on campus, and took my turn at everything the men did. Each driver had an instructor who taught us to park, back up to ramps, swerve around roadblocks, brake for objects in the road and re-act to emergencies. I just did what the instructor said and to my surprise it worked every time.

There was one little, cocky, fellow who resented having me

there and made a few remarks but the instructor stopped him by saying "you just do as well as she is and you'll be OK". The rest of the men were very respectful of 'the lady', as they called me.

After class on Tuesday, the Professor asked me if I'd like to complete the course. I said, "I certainly would". He then said that I would have to find a sponsor. This whole program was set-up by sponsors. I went home and excitedly told Ray. He said he'd ask his boss. It wasn't until Thursday that the boss said they didn't need the publicity and declined to pay the three hundred fifty dollars tuition.

The fellows had started to take up a collection to pay the tuition for me when the Professor told them that only companies could sponsor a driver. I was crushed but invited to finish the classes anyway. I just wouldn't get a Certificate of Completion for the course.

On Thursday we all went out to the practice field in trucks and watched as the College Fire Chief set up a demonstration for putting out fires. He had a big pan, about four feet square and a foot deep, filled with oil. He explained that he was going to set it on fire and show us how to put it out.

He gave quite a lecture about using the fire extinguisher for horseplay; I guess he thought some of the men might try it. He gave the example of fishermen using it to freeze fish solid until they could get them home from ice-fishing trips. It was dangerous unless handled properly.

He lit the oil and used a large CO_2 fire extinguisher as he went around the edges, making the fire less in size with each go-around, until he had it reduced to a small fire in the middle and then released a large amount of foam. The fire died.

Then he said, "Now, one of you is going to do what I just did" and handed me the fire extinguisher. My hands were, bare, in my pockets. I grabbed the extinguisher, with both hands, and proceeded to do what he had just done. I made a circle around the fire and zapped it in the middle. The fire was out! The men cheered.

When I started to hand the extinguisher back to the Fire Chief my hands stuck to it. My fingers were covered with the frozen fluid, they looked like the coils in an old-fashioned refrigerator when it needed defrosting, that had backfired into my hands. I started shaking and my fingers came free, with some skin missing, still covered with CO_2.

The Chief turned white and ordered the owner of the only car there to take me to the Infirmary, as quickly as possible.

The only person who seemed to know what had really happened was the little cocky guy. He wrapped his jacket around both my hands and said, "it's like a freezer burn".

We had all come to the field by truck but there was one car. It belonged to a cameraman, from Newsweek magazine, who had been taking pictures. He was looking through his camera but didn't see what had happened to me.

He was the only one who had driven a car. The rest of us had come by truck.

When the Chief yelled at him to get going, he quickly gathered his equipment and we headed for the Infirmary on campus at MSC in East Lansing. He thought I was a nurse and he was taking me back to work. He tried to start a conversation about how beautiful the Campus was. I realized that he didn't know why the Chief was so adamant. I showed him my hands. We practically flew the rest of the way. When we got to the Infirmary, they didn't know what to do for frostbite. We drove to Sparrow Hospital on Michigan Avenue. They sent me to St. Joseph Hospital on West Saginaw Street in Lansing. I came out with both hands wrapped to the size of footballs.

In the meantime, the Fire Chief was trying to find out where I was. By the time he had traced me to the third hospital I was gone.

He called Ray's boss and said, "this is the Fire Chief at MSC. We've had a little accident out here and we're trying to identify Mrs. Thayer". He realized his mistake and said, "I mean, we're trying to find her".

Ray's boss dropped the phone. He thought I had been killed. His immediate thought was for Ray. He had been in an accident, driving a truck, the night before in Muskegon where a man was killed when he ran a red blinker light. He was home trying to pull himself together to go back to work.

The Chief finally explained that I had just been hurt and sent

130

to the hospital. He had to have my full name, and so forth, so he could turn in the faulty fire extinguisher. It was brand new. A pin in the handle had fallen out and let the contents backfire into my bare hands.

I was in a state of shock, I guess. I don't know how I got from one hospital to the other or what ever happened to the little guy's jacket.

I walked in, at home, just as Ray was answering the phone about the accident. He couldn't believe what had happened.

The men were surprised when I showed up in class the next day for final tests.

Each man was alone in a truck. Among other things, he had to shift all ten gears and be able to stop the truck the instant the yellow chalk, fired from a pistol fastened to the front bumper and set on a timer, hit the pavement. I couldn't use my hands at all.

I was upset but the men were wonderful. They acted like they were more proud of me than they were of themselves.

A whole forty -hour week together and I had not heard one cussword, dirty joke or anything that would change my mind about the 'Gentlemen of the Highways'.

I got an A+ on my story and tried to sell it. Somehow, a large trucking firm got it and told me that they could not publish it in their 'House Organ', trucker's magazine, because I was not a Union member.

Newsweek never printed the pictures.

~~~~~~

Several things happened during the next four years: we moved from Norwood Street in Lansing to a gas station/garage in St. Johns, Michigan; from there to a house on Clinton Street and from there to Residence Avenue, in Albany, Georgia in June 1955.

I divorced Ray in 1956 the first time. Remarried him the next year and divorced him again. He did not pay the child support that the Judge ordered, seven dollars per week per child, for the first marriage and there were no children from the second marriage so he got off free. He went back to Michigan and lived with his mother and Max, his crippled brother, until they died.

CHANGES IN MY LIFE

During the fifties, right after my Dad died in September 1957, my brother, Jim, said that they needed the studio couch that I had borrowed.

I had been left without enough furniture for my living room when Ray and I separated. He took some pieces with him when he went back to Michigan. I had to call the furniture store, where we had bought living room furniture after moving to Georgia, and tell them to come and get it because I couldn't pay for it.

So, I was trying to figure out what to do when I saw an ad in the paper about a hide-a-bed sofa that someone had reupholstered. They were only asking sixty dollars, a whole months' rent then, because the customer decided they didn't want a black sofa after all.

I bought it even though black was not my idea of living room furniture. I got friends from the Marine Base to bring someone's pickup and haul it to our new residence on Gordon Avenue in Albany, Georgia.

During the transaction the woman, who did upholstering in her shop at home, and I got pretty well acquainted. Her name was Peggy. She was a very attractive woman with an hourglass figure so I was quite surprised when she confided in me that she was having problems with her husband. He was a Master Sergeant Marine stationed at Cherry Point, North Carolina and was coming home less and less on weekends and holidays.

Meanwhile, she was trying to keep the upholstery business going so that when he retired, within a couple years, they would have established a good business. It seemed to me that he was leaving it up to her to carry on while he had interests elsewhere. This went on for a couple years. As it turned out he did have other interests.

She divorced him and we became good friends. We both loved to dance but neither of us had ever taken lessons. A young Air Force Sergeant, Will, had tried to teach me to Cha Cha but I wasn't very adept at it. I told him that Peggy was anxious to

132

learn. He gave her lessons and they fell in love. They made such a great dance team that they gave exhibitions later on.

Then Will got orders to Bermuda. They decided to get married because she couldn't go with him except as his wife. I helped her with flower arrangements, hurry-up plans and a brief wedding ceremony. Peggy could not follow Will until after he found a place for her and her youngest son, Tim. Will found a two-bedroom apartment on Queen Street in Hamilton, Bermuda.

A year passed. I had occasional letters from Peggy. I wrote her telling her of my plans to marry Jack, Manager for five Southeastern States, with a Life Insurance company out of Jacksonville, Florida.

Jack was very loving and kind. He had been a former Methodist Minister for fifteen years, which endeared him to Mama. His former wife had demanded that he give up the ministry and get into a more lucrative field. He did and got into the insurance business. He was dedicated to his job.

He was so anxious for us to get married that we leased a house on Society Avenue, in Albany, and started refinishing it inside. Walls, floors, every inch of the large house were finished when I had to go to Michigan.

I had promised my son-in-law that I would go to Michigan to be with Vicki when she had my second grand child. I had waited to take time off from my job, at the Air Force Base, in Albany, Georgia, until Vicki was ready to come home so I could be of more help to her. I was gone ten days.

Jack had seen Mama at the bank two days before I was to get back from Michigan. He told her " I can't wait until she gets back so we can get married and set up housekeeping". He had called me every day while I was gone but I didn't hear from him after Mama saw him.

I was too busy to think much about that but when I got home I was expecting a message of some kind. We had planned on being married in late October 1960. Jack's sister was coming from Pensacola, Florida and bringing his Mother. His Aunt was coming from Alabama. I was only planning on Mama, Step-Father, Terry, who was back after spending the summer in Michigan with his Dad, and a few friends. We had talked to my

Minister, about the ceremony. Jack had written some very nice words that he wanted used and we had had our blood tests. Everything was set for the wedding when I got home, except... I couldn't find Jack.

I called his home office in Jacksonville. They said, "we don't know where he is". I thought that was very strange because he was in daily contact with them when I left. He usually stayed at the same motel when in Albany. Nobody there knew anything about his where-abouts. I was puzzled and anxious. When I called my Minister he said, "Etta, something must have happened to him because he told me how much he loved you and wanted to get married". Our Doctor even suggested that he may have been hurt or suffered amnesia. He seemed to have disappeared off the face of the earth.

I was crushed. I had allowed myself to care deeply for this man and was looking forward to many years of happiness with him.

I didn't hear from him but bill collectors starting appearing at my door. They wanted payments due on the new Buick he had bought, he put my name on the title with his, and some furniture that he had bought. I hadn't signed anything so I was hurt that he had done this without talking with me. There was nothing the collectors could do to me.

I went back to work with a heavy heart. Mama told people that I "had been jilted" which really hurt. What could I do? This man had been in my life for over a year and I thought I knew him well.

Terry felt badly and said, "maybe Jack doesn't like me and that is the reason he isn't going to marry you". Terry offered to leave, even though he was in his senior year, and go back to Michigan. I assured him that if I ever needed him it was then. He decided to stay with me.

I had already contacted the woman that Jack and I had leased the house from but she wouldn't release me from the lease, which had ten months to go. I was stuck.

I kept myself so busy that I would just drop in bed. My mind went wild just thinking of all the things that could have happened to Jack. It was a bad time in my life. I tried desperately to think of anything that I might have done to make this happen. Jack had assured me many times that I was just what he wanted in a wife even after I told him of my failed marriage. His first one had failed too and we had lots in common.

I invited Mama, my step-father, and my good friend, Sarah, for Thanksgiving dinner so Terry and I wouldn't be alone. I knew that it would tire me so much that maybe I wouldn't have such bad dreams for one night at least.

But I did. It was so real that I sat up in bed expecting to see Jack's mother standing at the foot of my bed. In my dream she said, "Etta, don't cry anymore. Jack is not sick". That shocked me and for some reason made me mad. I was so mad that he would do something like this to me that I determined to find out why and where he was. Six weeks was a long time for him to put me through this nightmare.

The next morning I went over the list of people that I had called before and saw one name that I hadn't been able to reach. In my confusion I had forgotten to call him again.

When I finally got him on the phone, he said, "Well, what a surprise! How are you doing?"

I said, "I'd do a lot better if I knew where Jack is. Do you know what happened to him?" He didn't know that I hadn't heard from him. He waited while I told him how long it had been, what had happened about the furniture and the car and about my dream last night.

He finally said, "I know this is not what you want to hear but Jack got himself into a lot of trouble and was nearly arrested".

I was thinking, 'not my Jack, he wouldn't do anything wrong'. He hated lawbreakers and had no sympathy for people who were troublemakers.

Larry said, "Well, I don't know how to say this but in plain truth he was picked up for embezzlement of company funds. He was taken to jail and his company contacted. They said that if he would pay the money back, in excess of thirty thousand dollars, they would not press charges but he was definitely out of a job".

He continued, "In order to keep from going to jail he contacted a former lady friend whose father had offered to set him up in business if he would marry his daughter".

Jack had told me about her but said that "she had two small children and he did not love her enough to take on that responsibility at his age", forty.

Larry continued, "The father paid the Life Insurance Company the money and Jack married the woman. I sure am sorry that he didn't tell you and left you in such a state".

This news did not make me feel better. I was hospitalized a few weeks later with a spastic colon, brought on by a traumatic experience according to the Doctors.

Five months later I got letters from his Mother and an Aunt. They both wanted to know, "if he divorced his wife, would you marry him". I certainly would not!

In the meantime, Peggy and Will were expecting Jack and me to come to Bermuda on our honeymoon as planned.

When I finally answered Peggy's letters, I told her what had happened. In her next letter she called him every kind of son-of-a-bitch she could think of and invited me to come to Bermuda. She was sure I could find a job as a teacher, nurse or secretary. I had no experience except secretarial so her offer only stirred a mild interest in me at first.

After a few more letters, I started making plans to go to Bermuda when my lease expired.

I had no ties in Albany, except my mother. She was totally wrapped up in her church and her second husband, Frank.

I took Peggy and Will up on their offer, sold some things, stored the rest in Mama's attic and was on my way.

BERMUDA STORY

I had a sinking feeling as I left Albany, Georgia in August 1961. I said 'Goodbye' to my brother Jim, my sister-in-law Peggy, my two best friends Sara and Vivian at the small airport in Albany.

I was embarking on a trip that was both daring and exciting for a woman, in her forties, who had just sold most of her possessions, given up her job and determined to make a new life for herself.

It was a challenge and I knew that it could be foolhardy. I

was leaving everything behind on the assumption that I could find employment and a place to live on a small island that I hadn't heard of until about a year ago.

So...here I was at the airport leaving everyone and everything in Albany, Georgia where my family had moved six years earlier.

I wrote to my daughter and told her of my plans to go to Bermuda. She was married to a Marine and had two little boys, Jeffrey and Randall. She thought it was a wonderful idea and encouraged me to do it.

Lynn, my oldest son, was stationed in Germany with the Air Force. He thought I deserved a change and wished me luck. He really didn't want to come back to Albany when his hitch was up because there were no jobs with a future in that area.

Terry had no plans to stay in Georgia either.

I felt that I had done a good job of raising them and had no further obligation to stay in Albany for my children. They were all on their own and I felt that they should get on with their lives.

I carried Peggy's little Chihuahua to them. It had been left with friends because it hadn't had the proper shots.

When I got to Jacksonville, Florida I was told that I could not take the dog with me because the cargo hold was not pressurized. To carry it from Jacksonville, hopscotching back and forth across the state, to Miami would mean certain death for the dog. I couldn't leave the little mouse-like dog so had to stay overnight in Jacksonville and wait for a larger plane the next day. I wasn't about to turn back. I had a job lined up at the Air Force Base.

Even though Will and Peggy knew that I didn't like animals at all, they had asked me to bring their dog with me and I was determined to do it.

Because of the dog, I was a day late in getting to Bermuda. Will and Peggy were anxiously waiting when the dog got through customs before I did. The customs agents finally accepted my story, for late arrival, when they saw the little dog with her family.

Just out of Miami, the dog was put in my lap right after we left Miami Airport. The man next to me showed immediate interest in the dog... and me. He was a handsome Cuban who had fled to the States in the late fifties and was now a salesman for a detergent company out of Detroit. He sold me on the idea that we would see Bermuda together for the ten days that he was going to be there.

We went to dinner and dancing every night. I thoroughly enjoyed dancing under the stars at the Eagles' Nest on a hilltop near Hamilton, nightspots at the Hotels, sail boat trips with picnic lunches and hiring a taxi driver who took great pride in showing us the beautiful island of Bermuda.

We took Peggy and Will out to dinner and dancing with us several times, on his extensive expense account. Will's military salary wasn't sufficient to allow them to go out, except to the AF base, so they were very grateful. We were all sorry to see him leave Bermuda but weren't surprised that I never heard from him again.

Will and Peggy made me feel very welcome and tried to make it up to me for all the problems the dog had caused. Like, getting a room where dogs were allowed and having to hide her in my carry-on luggage bag while I nervously ate dinner and breakfast the next morning. They were full of ideas of things to do and people they wanted me to meet. On the way into Hamilton we stopped at the Swizzle Inn and had Bermuda's famous drink, the Swizzle

Lucky for me, Bermuda is like a small town so everybody knows when somebody new stays over a couple weeks. Men were plentiful and more than willing to show-off Bermuda to an interested newcomer. I was absolutely fascinated.

Being one of two adult female redheads in town at the time, the other one was an anchor person on the local TV, I was noticed right away. The people were charming and everyone I met seemed happy except a few jealous wives. I ignored them because they had no reason to worry about me. I never, knowingly, dated a married man. When they realized that, some of them invited me to their homes and proudly included me in many of their social activities.

Home with Will and Peggy was a two-bedroom apartment on second floor of a flatiron building between Front and Queen

Streets in downtown Hamilton. There was a large living room, kitchen/dining area with windows facing both streets and a view down King Street from the end of the room. We had to go down a stairs from Queen Street to get to our second floor apartment. There was an upholstery business below us, facing Front Street, and an apartment above us that faced Queen Street. It was an odd arrangement but every inch of Bermuda is utilized, as I found out later, and done in an eye-pleasing way.

I shared a room with Tim, Peggy's fourteen-year-old son. It was not the best arrangement but it worked out. We both dressed and undressed in the bathroom.

Within a week, Will and Peggy took me to a house party that their Air Force friends planned to welcome me. I later learned that people had parties for just any reason they could think of.

I met the fellow Will and Peggy had lined up for me. All I could think of was 'Ichabod Crane'... all arms and legs that flew in every direction when he danced. He had a small head, a big Adam's apple and a long neck. Poor George! He thought he was God's gift to women. He 'turned me off' completely. I made up lots of excuses when he asked me to go out dancing with him.

The most interesting person I met at the party was Georgia, an Air Force wife, who taught dancing. She told me about a temporary job, as a secretary, that might fill in until I got a regular job.

I had already gone for an interview at Tindal Air Force Base pertaining to the job that I had lined up before I left the States. The base was near the end of the island, towards St. George. It looked exactly like Turner AFB in Albany, Georgia. I decided that if I was going to work in a foreign country I wanted something different than what I had just come from. I didn't like the fact that the base looked like all the buildings and offices had been picked up at the base in Albany and placed in Bermuda. Nothing was exciting or different except I would have to take a bus or taxi to work every day. The only bonus, as I saw it, was that I could look at the beautiful scenery on the way. I told the employment manager that I needed two weeks to get acclimated and settled in before going to work. He accepted my request.

When I went for the temporary job interview, I knew that I

was throwing caution to the winds but I had dreams of starting a new life... not continuing in the same old rut.

The temporary job was to work for the owner of Santa Maria Shipowning and Trading, Ltd., a firm that managed six ships out of Bermuda. None of them ever came there because they were cargo ships leased to haul grain and scrap metal. The job sounded fascinating to me so I took it figuring that I could try it for a week and if I didn't like it I could still go to the Air Force job.

I was to temporarily replace a woman who had been hired but chose to take a five-week holiday in Scotland before starting her new job.

Appealing to me was the offer that the owner made me. He said that I could go for interviews for a steady job on one condition. That was: that I bring all the information pertaining to salary, working conditions and benefits, before I made my decision, to him and let him help me in making the right choice. I was pleased with his 'big brother' concern.

I enjoyed the job from the first day. But, he turned down every job offer that I brought him so at the end of the five weeks I was without a job as of Friday. It was with a heavy heart that I started to thank him for the opportunity to work with him and learn so much in such a short time.

He said, "why don't you just stay on here and see what happens"? I was apprehensive because I knew the new hired woman would be in on Monday.

He and I had already had a couple of differences of opinion so I doubted that it would work but was willing to try.

One of those times he dictated some letters filled with filthy language. I didn't even know the shorthand for them and determined that I was not going to type those words even if I got fired. I looked up the correspondence that the former secretary had done. She used his language. I typed the letters, left a blank space (...........) for every filthy word and handed him the letters.

He blew his top, threw the letters toward me and started yelling more of the same expletives.

I told him, "I have never used that kind of language and I

140

don't plan on starting now". As I backed out of his office, I was sure that I would be fired, I added, "it seems to me that a man, as educated as you are, should be able to express himself in a more intelligent way".

He calmed down, started laughing and handed me the letters and said, "You know what I want to say… just do it". He never dictated a letter like that again.

Another time I told him that, "even though your Doctor told you that you should scream out your frustrations", he had an ulcer and that was supposed to help, "I did not cause your ulcers and you are not to scream at me". Why he didn't fire me I'll never know. I think I was the first secretary that had ever stood up to him.

I had my first paycheck converted to Sterling and determined that I would pay everything with it except my room and board to Will and Peggy.

I was glad that I had a little knowledge of what it was worth when I took over the accounting and had to learn the value of several kinds of foreign, to me, currency. I had to call the banks every time I paid the office bills, payroll for the ship's crews and all outgoing bills to foreign countries to get the rate for that day and transfer American money to the currency for whatever country we were dealing with. I kept a chart on Drachmas, Yen, Lira and Sterling (Pounds) to keep me generally informed but checked for exact amounts for each days' checks.

Mr. M and I became friends. He respected me and always treated me like a lady, more like a younger sister. He wanted to pass approval on my men friends but I drew the line on that.

The new secretary arrived and immediately took charge but had to ask me how to do most of the work. I was angered when she made it clear that she was 'boss'. She gave me the work that she didn't like, shouted orders, then would make an about face and ask me to show her how to do the few things that she decided she would do. She went home early every day leaving me with final cables to be sent and closing of the office for the day. After two weeks I was ready to quit.

Mr. M, as I always him, called me into his office and told me to fire her.

141

I said, "I didn't hire her and I'm not going to fire her".

He looked surprised and told me to, "write her a check for two weeks pay plus separation pay and send her in".

I could hear her cursing and shouting at him, threatening to have her husband come and throw him out the window, we were on the fourth floor of the Fire and Marine Building, and that she was going to get our work permits canceled.

He told her, very calmly for him, to "go ahead and try. All I have to tell them is that you are not qualified to handle the job and that you have not put in a full days work since you've been here".

I didn't know that he had been observing the whole scene until I heard him tell her some of the things she had refused to do and had turned over to me. She never reported us.

I thought that Mr. T, the head of accounting until he turned it over to me, was a very intelligent man. Not only did he know all the kinds of currency we had to deal with but several languages. He was often called to the hospital to translate for sailors who had been left there, by their ship's Captain, if they were sick or injured.

None of them had previous experience riding the little MoPeds, that they rented for transportation, so it was almost a certainty that one or more would be injured. After recovery, I had to make arrangements to notify their Captains who would make arrangements for them to fly home or rejoin their ship somewhere.

But, my personal regard for Mr.T dropped considerably before he left for his 'two months vacation'.

He made the statement that he "never washed or changed his Bermuda, knee-socks for a year". I could smell him before I got to his office but just assumed that he had a very bad case of body odor.

I asked Mr. M. if there wasn't something he could do about it. He handled it by taking Mr. T fishing in the Harbour in his small wooden boat. He knew that Mr. T couldn't swim so he managed to swing the boat around so fast that Mr. T fell out. Mr. M threw him a bar of Ivory soap and told him to use it or he wouldn't let him back in the boat. Mr. T would announce, quite regularly after that, that his wife had washed his socks. He still needed baths but Mr. M could never get him to go fishing again.

Within a few months Mr. T asked Mr. M for passage on one of his ships for himself, his wife and baby to Denmark for a Holiday.

I didn't realize that Mr. T had been training me to take his place while he was gone. I enjoyed the work and was pleased to put names and places on the spreadsheets instead of numbers and items that had no identity for me. Mr. T had been teaching me in what he called, 'a code'. It was more like an assignment and none of it was the method he used. I wasn't too happy with his set-up but was learning a lot so went along with it.

Not long after he left, I ran into problems with the method of accounting that he was using. I finally asked Mr. M if he could explain it to me. He couldn't understand it either so hired and auditor from Canada to go over the records. It took months before he gave his version of what happened.

Mr. T had devised a method where he could hide some of the money until just before he left for his trip. He should have been charged with embezzlement but he had disappeared, having left his wife and child in Denmark. She was contacted but didn't know where he was.

Mr. M told the auditor to write it off, thousands of dollars, as a bad debt and to set up a new system that we could understand.

Many exciting and interesting things happened at the office after Mr. M made me Office Manager.

We kept track of the ships by cable, from the Captains, daily. Sometimes hourly if there were problems. I learned to place the little metal ships, about a half inch long, at the proper place on the magnetized world map and to be able to tell at a glance their position and estimated time of arrival, determined by charts, at their next port.

I went to the office every day, except Sunday and then too if Mr. M was away, to collect the cables and relay them to him wherever he was and knew, if he called me at home, approximately where each ship was every day. It was fascinating and interesting.

One of the ships, an old World War II Liberty ship, broke in half near Midway while on its way to Japan loaded with scrap metal. The two halves floated until they were picked up by scavenge hunters - always the first scavenger at the scene after they heard the SOS Mr. M made a deal with them that if they would deliver the cargo to its destination, he wouldn't fight them for the ship's hull. Such events were interesting to me. It was almost like watching, by phone and cable, Pirates taking over a helpless ship. Some of the scavengers were merciless but Mr. M always was able to make a deal with them that allowed the crews passage to the next port.

Another time a ship lost its screw, propeller, off Manila. A screw was brought to the floundering ship and scuba divers put it in place. Hadn't that been done, the ship would have wound up in the scavengers' hands. The ship proceeded and delivered its load of grain.

It wasn't unusual to have a strike at the docks, which made it impossible to get a ship unloaded. Mr. M was very savvy as to what was happening in the shipping world and usually had insurance on the ships that might be docking in England, where most of the strikes occurred, or anywhere there might be trouble. He did get stuck a few times with huge penalties of up to two-thousand dollars per day for a ship that was port bound. He did a lot of screaming on the phone on those days.

The first time he left me in charge of the office while he went to Spain, where he was having two ships built, a cable came from a Captain on a ship at Duluth, Minnesota. I was quite surprised because the ship was supposed to have left there a couple days earlier. The cable was in Greek. I couldn't read a word of it.

I called Mr. M's son, Stacey who was fourteen, and asked him to come to the office. He could only make out two words, "Ice" and " Bound".

I panicked because I knew what that meant from all the years I lived in Michigan and had crossed the straits on a boat following an Ice Breaker in the 1950s.

I didn't have the authority to order an Ice Breaker so called Mr. M in Spain and read the cable to him, Greek letter by Greek letter. He took care of it and fined the Captain two months pay.

Two thousand dollars a month was a lot but he did keep his job. There hadn't been a strike. Just a slow-down in loading the ship.

Mr. M used to say that we ran the office around my Social Calendar. He always let me off work when I needed to do something during the day because he knew that I would more than make it up.

I took off a few hours when President Kennedy came to Bermuda for the 'Big Three' meeting. I was only able to see his head, from about two hundred feet away, so was disappointed.

I was invited to Garden Parties, family occasions, Guy Falk's Day, Boxing Day, swimming parties, picnics, boat trips and many of the wonderful things to do there.

One was to a Garden Party that was called the 'Governor's Tea'. I was quite surprised when I got a formal invitation. It was held at the Governor's mansion.

All the ladies were dressed in beautiful spring dresses, small hats, tiny purses to match and wore white gloves. I felt 'Hoity-Toity' for a few hours. Guy Falk's Day was held at many homes, all over the island, in November. It was strictly a British tradition and was done in remembrance of the occasion when Guy Falks tried to blow up the House of Parliament in England in the seventeen hundreds. An effigy of him was made of straw stuffed into men's clothing and at a given time it was hanged and set on fire. Fireworks went off in every direction. You could see the effigies burning at parties all over the island.

My first Christmas was spent with Will, Peggy and my Air Force friend, Bill, on a picnic at Horse Shoe Bay beach. I got caught in the undertow and would have drowned but Bill and was able to pull me out.

Boxing Day had nothing to do with Boxing. It was held the day after Christmas. Families would invite their friends and neighbors to come and eat some of the many special foods they had prepared for the holiday. Usually a group of us would go to several of these before the day was out. Boxing Day was originally set up as a day for the wealthy to Box food and take it to the poor people in England. .

I even got a special delivery Invitation to attend the funeral for the mother of one of the men, Johnny, that I was dating at the time. Printed invitations were necessary because there were so many relatives that you couldn't get into the church without one.

I later learned that burial plots are so scarce that whole families are buried on top of each other. In this case, the father died first; then a child. It's casket was dug up temporarily, the mother's casket placed on top of the father and the child on top of his mother. Even then, many lots were several feet above sea level.

Johnny owned a grocery store and kept Peggy, Will, Tim and me supplied with groceries for several months while I was dating him. He'd just send his delivery truck with several big boxes of food that he knew Will and Peggy couldn't afford. We also took them to many 'first-niters' and shows, usually by Americans, at the various hotels.

I rented an efficiency apartment a few months after I realized that my job was quite secure. It was furnished with two hide-a-beds, that became chairs in the daytime, tables and lamps for the combination living/sleeping and eating areas with a cute kitchen and bathroom with shower.

I sent for my personal items that I had stored at my mother's. She completely ignored my list of sixteen small electrical appliances.

Duty on new appliances was extreme and way above my budget. It took about five weeks for my possessions to arrive.

When the Harbour Master called I was elated until he said, "Miss you will need to hire a lorry". I thought he was trying to trick me into spending extra money for a truck. I figured that I would just take a taxi to the dock, unload everything right there and be on my way.

What a shock! The toaster, iron, midget Singer sewing machine, miscellaneous items totaling sixteen was packed in a Household Goods box, made of 4' by 8' foot sheets of plywood, like those used to move Military families. I was in tears as I showed him a copy of the list I had sent to my mother.

He had his men use one of their lorries, to deliver the huge box to my tiny apartment. He came with them and told them to unload everything but he didn't want to see anything but those on my list.

My embarrassment mounted as they carried my ironing board, boxes of books, drapes and bedspreads that I couldn't use, and the unbelievable array of housekeeping items that I had saved. The men were getting quite a kick out of it but they howled when I opened three boxes of empty peanut butter jars that I had saved to use, someday, when I made jams and jellies.

I was only charged a small duty on my 'used' electrical items but the freight was several hundred dollars. I had no money for tips but gave each man something for his wife. They were delighted. The Harbour Master said he'd never had an experience like that in his forty years at the docks.

When I moved out, the groceries at Will and Peggy's house stopped. Johnny was out of the picture for me soon after that. He drank too much.

Invitations to picnics, boat rides at the Yacht Club and private parties were received every few days. No reason at all except that someone felt like throwing a party. Dining out and dancing invitations were so often that many times it was difficult to choose which to accept.

While I was still living with Will, Peggy, her son, Tim, and I would drive around sightseeing. Bermuda is a beautiful place with flowers everywhere.

The pretty pastel colored houses all had white roofs; made of coral slabs about eighteen inches long, ten inches high and almost two inches thick. They were built of coral blocks, cut from the island itself, slightly larger than cement blocks. Many of the houses had coral block walls around them. Every house had a garden of flowers that bloomed profusely. They looked like something you might find on a postcard.

The water changed colors with the weather but was always a beautiful shade of blue or green. Sometimes the sun cast millions of tiny diamonds over the water that could turn into a silver sheath at night. You could look in any direction and see something beautiful.

Ferns were pocketed in crevices in palm trees that swayed in the breeze, orchids attached themselves to several kinds of trees, vines festooned walls and every kind of blossom was there at some time of year. The Poinsettias were as large as dinner plates.

Poinciana trees were hung with huge clusters of red-orange blossoms and wild Philodendron with leaves, as big as my head, grew in profusion on vacant hillsides.

If that wasn't enough flowers, you could always walk in the Botanical Gardens or Parlieville Park above and behind the downtown post office.

I tried very hard to learn to ride a Mo-Ped, motor bike, but just never got the hang of it even after my next door neighbors guided me until I got started. When they released me I would immediately lose my balance and crash. I drove through a three-foot wide hedge twice and tipped over at Botanical Gardens.

Mr. M offered to give me his wife's bike, after he bought her a car. My neighbors went with me to test drive it. One of them started down the winding hill from the M's house but the brakes didn't hold and he hit one of the many coral-made fences. Sharp stalks of trimmed shrubbery cut him badly. One took his wristwatch right off his arm and another jabbed one lens out of his glasses. He was lucky.

I never learned but carried a scab on my knee for a year after I tipped over in the park. I figured that I could take a taxi hundreds of times for what it would cost me to be hospitalized once. Mr.M dumped the bike in the sea.

In April a huge parade, where every float had to be made completely of flowers or real foliage, was held in downtown Hamilton. One winning entry was a butterfly, as big as a small car, hovering over a flower. There was a fire engine with snow-white horses. A dinosaur was made of white Lilies with a row of red Amaryllis lilies from head to the end of the tail. The men who made that one were all dressed in coconut bark, palm tree leaves and wore wigs of moss to imitate cave men. When they turned the corner to get in line for the parade, their forty-foot dinosaur hit a building and broke its neck and head off. It was funny, but sad, to see the cave men beating the poor thing with their clubs. They might have won but they were eliminated before the parade started.

I was fascinated by some of the facts that were relayed to me and a little turned off by some. I learned that every house had a cistern under it, to catch rain from the painted white coral roofs, the only source of water, and that goldfish were kept in them to eat bugs which kept the tanks clean. I had no choice but to forget about the goldfish and learn to conserve water because if it didn't rain enough they had to have water brought in by ships from Canada.

BETA SIGMA PHI

I was invited to join Beta Sigma Phi, a sorority for business women, and spent many happy hours in activities with the group of about thirty women. They were Canadian, English, Indian (India), Swedish and American but mostly Bermudian.

The Sorority held a Ceremony every year and crowned the Queen for that year. The first ceremony that I attended was at one of the women's homes. The President simply walked over to the girl, who didn't know that she had been selected, and placed a tiny rhinestone crown on her head. I thought that was quite a let-down for all the accomplishments she had made to earn it.

The next year, I was President and suggested that we glamorize the event and make it a formal affair with a big dance, our money making project, and a proper ceremony. Everyone agreed and the committees started planning.

I wasn't sure how we'd present the Queen herself but took that as my responsibility while the others worked on getting a place for the Ball. They got the Bermudiana ballroom and the Hotel orchestra in return for bar receipts. They found donors for tickets, door prizes, entertainment and whatever it would take to make people want to buy tickets for five pounds sterling, about fourteen dollars at the time. The group worked together fantastically well.

I designed an eight-foot heart made of chicken wire over a bamboo frame. We tied it, in the shape of a heart, while it was still wet after some of my friends cut it for me. The center was red tissue paper with white Kleenex, five large boxes, tucked into the chicken wire to make a ruffle. Across the center was a huge white ribbon bow that, when snapped, popped out and there stood the Queen. It was quite sensational and I was very proud of my ingenuity.

149

One of the women who was a dancer got a friend to be choreographer to teach us a dance routine and to mime 'Guys and Dolls".

'Guys and Dolls' was a roaring success with the audience screaming for more as the 'girls' pealed off their gloves; long white ones bought in New York; their 'poils' ,long ropes of dime store variety;, their 'minks' ,yards and yards of pink net - several inches wide and gathered and their chartreuse 'gowns'. They had been designed by a volunteer dressmaker to be removable by snaps along the sides.

I refused to shed my gown, being the oldest of the 'girls'. I turned my back, removed and threw my weighted garter into the crowd. It turned out to be quite sensational. People were clamoring to buy tickets for the next year that very night.

When John came into my life he donated a nine-inch tiara of flashing rhinestones that he bought at a costume store in New York. It was fit for a Queen.

The Valentine Ball was one of the biggest Social Events of the year after that. I was Mistress of Ceremonies until I left Bermuda. I loved the involvement.

~~~~~~

To continue...I stayed with the Ms children, Stacey and Deppie, many times during my years there and almost felt like one of the family. Even their customs and home life were very different from anything I had ever known but I adjusted quite well.

Mr. M and his wife traveled extensively while he was having four more ships built. Two in Japan and two in Spain. The children and I had a cook, maid, gardener and chauffeur while they were gone. Staying with them did affect my social life but I often had friends come to their house. It was always a treat for those of us who were not used to such expensive, and expansive, surroundings.

The Ms have kept in touch with me since I left Bermuda in 1965. They invited Harry and me to their condo in North Palm Beach, Florida for the weekend in 1996 and have given me many invitations before that I was not able to accept.

As I mentioned before, I shared a room, while living with Will and Peggy, with her fourteen year old son. That was not a satisfactory arrangement for me so I made plans to find a place of my own.

In 1962 I lived in an efficiency apartment for about five months, then found a house that I shared with two other women. One was a retired Army Major who left to make a trip around the world. The other stayed with me until I introduced her to George, Ichabod Crane. She married him and left for the States when he got transferred. About that time I got notice that the owner of the house had died and left it to a Girl's School.

I moved across the street to, 'Brinkedge', a little cottage right on the water. I had already found out that I couldn't live alone. It was too expensive, so one or two girls shared the cottage with me while I lived there.

The cottage actually was built on coral that was part of the harbor wall. It was so damp that you could put your hand on the wall and get it wet. I used and electric sheet to dry my bed every night but always made sure it was turned off when I climbed in. The sheet was made of seersucker with tiny wires running through it.

None of the houses in Bermuda have house numbers, only names. The place where I lived with Will and Peggy was the 'Triangle', in the triangle of Front and Queen Streets, the efficiency was 'Banana Tree', a lone banana/strawberry flavored tree stood in the backyard. The house on the hill was 'Overlook' with a panoramic view of Hamilton Harbor on Harbour Road. There was always something about the house that made the name seem appropriate. If you knew the name of the house, the taxi driver could take you straight to it. It was amazing.

The two girls who shared my cottage worked together at a hotel on the beach and had been living in quarters furnished for them. It was like a dorm with several girls sharing a big room so my place looked good to them.

My cottage, 'Brinkedge', on the very edge of the Harbour had been converted from a carriage house where the groom and maid lived…hence two bathrooms.

151

The land-lady was the eighty five year old widow of a Sea Captain who had such grandiose ideas for living that he left her practically penniless when he died. She had put two apartments in her big house besides what she reserved for her own living quarters and our separate cottage.

I admired her for her spunk and always invited her to my parties. She loved wine and had to be helped home many times. My 'Hangover' parties were very popular, absolutely no alcohol, especially on New Year's Day or anytime after a big party celebrating the many special occasions.

One time she charged me five pounds sterling, about fourteen dollars at the time, for a truckload, two thousand gallons, of water. She said that we had 'wantonly' used, only to find out later that a tree root had grown into the wall of our cistern and caused the water to leak out. She didn't give us our money back.

I had my own bedroom. Edwina and Caroline shared the other one and a bathroom on the street level floor. The hall and stairwell were large, opening into the downstairs living room, a second bath, kitchen/dining area with a deck outside over the water. We could hang our feet off the deck into the water when the tide was in. I caught several fish with string, a safety pin and a piece of bacon. There were seven built-in bookcases. The landlady explained to me that she had just put shelves in the spaces where the walls had been blown out during hurricanes.

~~~~~~

Hurricane 'Arlene' made an 'eye' over Bermuda on August 9th, 1963 after storming around the Atlantic for eleven days.

I stayed in my office. It turned out that I was the only person in the Fire and Marine Insurance Building through the first half of the Hurricane.

I watched as water-spray went over the top of my little cottage across the Harbour. Boats, below my fourth floor windows, were yanked from their moorings and smashed in a big heap in the corner of the Marina. The wind sent missiles through the air of anything that was left outside the building.

152

Mrs. M had driven their tiny car, a four passenger with no room for me, to take Mr. M, a Sea Captain that was working in the office at the time, and their two teenage children home. The Secretary and the Accountant left at the first warnings.

The wind and rain died down so I decided to get out of the huge four-story building that faced the Harbour. I didn't know that when Hurricanes die down a bit they are reversing themselves for another assault.

I headed for my friend's apartment about a block away. I had barely gotten to the street when the wind and rain pelted me to the skin. I hung onto walls and buildings to get to her place. Luckily, her clothes fit me. We dried mine and waited the storm out. When it was finally over, everyone was out looking at the damage. Hundreds of boats, mostly small individually owned, along with sailboats that had been in the Newport-Bermuda yacht races, lay piled on top of each other. Millions of dollars were lost in boats alone.

Damages to the stores, buildings and houses were minimal because everyone had put storm shutters, which were kept from storm to storm, on their windows. A few shingles, made of two inch coral slabs, were blown off and lots of trees were down but not one single injury was reported. I, in my ignorance, could have been the only casualty.

I was afraid to go to my cottage. I just knew that all my possessions were ruined, especially when I saw the huge tree toppled over at one end of the house and a second one lying on top of a little English Ford. It was smashed to about eighteen inches high. I was amazed that nothing inside the house was even wet and there was no place to put the eighth bookcase!

Having survived the Hurricane, I felt good about myself, my life in Bermuda and was determined to make the most of everything that came my way. I had many men friends, had a full social life and could visit my children in the States at least once a year.

~~~~~~

When I met a blond, blue-eyed Italian in the grocery store, I was in for a new experience. He offered to cook the eggplant that I was looking at and wondering what to do with it. He invited another couple and cooked a delicious Italian dinner.

He loved redheads and proceeded to take me places in his tiny Carmen Gia, to nightclub shows, dinner and dancing. He showered me with gifts and flowers.

I didn't realize that he was getting serious until he started talking about wanting a son. I told him that it was too late for me but he had a suggestion.

He wanted to marry me and have a child by a Surrogate Mother. I had never heard of such a thing. That cooled any feelings that I might have had for him. I tried to quit seeing him. He wanted to pursue the issue and said the he was flying in the woman that would be the Surrogate Mother. I told him to "go ahead, I'm still not interested".

I went on a dinner date that night and when I got home there was a box of a dozen long-stemmed roses leaning against my door. Each rose had a note attached to it giving a reason why I should go along with his idea. I finally had to tell him that I had found someone else.

~~~~~~

My favorite man-friend was Raymon. He was Portuguese, six foot three, a widower with three kids. His mother was determined to make me the stepmother of his children. He owned the only car dealership on the Island at the time, was fun to be with but he was not ready to settle down to one woman. I was not ready to take on the raising of a family again. We have remained friends through the years and I see him when I go to Bermuda.

~~~~~~

I had finally settled down to one man, after giving up on Raymon, Ed from Toronto, Canada. He owned a rendering business with forty trucks that picked up butcher's scraps for making soap. He had been coming to Bermuda to play golf for

154

some time before he spotted me on the dance floor at the Princess Hotel.

He became a regular fixture in my plans for fourteen months, 1963-1964. He scheduled his ten days a month of golfing around what I had to do. He always stayed at the Bermudiana Hotel so quite a lot of our time was spent having lunch and dinner there. He played golf in the morning, took me to lunch, spent the afternoon golfing and took me to dinner and dancing or some other kind of entertainment that he'd heard about at the Golf Club. We went sailing in the moonlight, took dinner cruises across the Harbour, always something different and interesting. Everything we did cost money but I didn't feel guilty about what he was spending on me after he told me that he allowed himself two thousand dollars a week for recreation and wanted me to help him spend it.

~~~~~~

In June 1964 I had to go to New York for what the two Bermudian Doctors had diagnosed as a possible brain tumor. I was going for another opinion when Mr. M got back from one of his extended trips. When he saw how bad I looked, he called a Greek Doctor friend in New York and told him I'd be in New York next day.

He gave me the key to his apartment in the Picasso Building on 52nd Street, an airline ticket and some money and practically pushed me out the door.

When I started working for Mr. M he refused to give me the benefits I wanted but said, "if you have to go to the Doctor, in the Hospital or whatever, I'm a gambler and if I lose I'll pay for it".

The next morning when I opened the door at the apartment on 52nd Street there stood Ed. My friend had called him in Toronto and told him what the Doctors thought and where I was. He didn't want me to go through that alone.

He went with me to the Doctor and listened too while the Doctor called Mr. M. We heard him say, "she's got an abscess on the top of her Eustachian Tube and it will take six weeks of treatments, once a week, to clear it up".

We didn't know what Mr. M said but the Doctor was yelling, "well, I'm not Jesus Christ and I can't heal her in one day". They decided that I should stay in New York a week and have a treatment every day, after the abscess had been opened by going through my nose and sinus, if I could stand it.

Ed took me to the Doctor's office every morning and to the Mets ball game every afternoon. After dinner and a full day I'd collapse at the apartment and Ed would go back to the Waldorf for the night. On Saturday I headed back to Bermuda and Ed went to Toronto.

THE CRUISE

A few months later, when Mr. M got home from a three months absence, by this time I had been office manager for about three years, he decided that I needed a rest.

He had me call his friends at the Greek Lines in New York for literature about Christmas cruises. I objected by saying, "I don't have that kind of money" but he countered with, "you've got two weeks pay and a Christmas bonus coming and I want you out of here for awhile".

I wanted to go home and see my kids but he said, "let them come see you, you are going on this cruise to get some rest".

He had already expressed his feelings about Ed, calling him "a Goddam English Jew", and didn't want me to stick around waiting for him to come back to Bermuda after Christmas.

I never heard from the Greek Lines but a travel agent friend booked me for fourteen days on the Ocean Monarch, which left New York and came by way of Bermuda on its way to the Caribbean. She advised me to take all my party clothes, formals and sport clothes. I objected by saying, " all I need is to get away from the office, and Ed, and get some rest".

Ed had become quite possessive and expected me to stay home and wait for him to come, for ten days of every month, with nothing to do but my Sorority activities. He came for ten days just before the cruise. He couldn't come down or go with me right at the time because of his business, so he proceeded to

156

tell me what to do-not do during the cruise.

He told me that I could spend my 'on shore' time looking for Golf Courses where he could play at a later date.

He had my whole cruise planned, verbally, when I told him during lunch at the Bermudiana Hotel, "I don't see any rings on my fingers and until I do, I'll do whatever I want to".

He said, "I know you're holding out for marriage but I'm just not ready yet". We were both in our mid-forties. I could see why he was trying to enjoy himself so much because he had taken care of his parents for the last twenty-five years and felt that he deserved some time for himself. I was feeling very bound to his wishes without any commitment from him

By the time of my "Bon Voyage" party on board the ship, I was ready to enjoy my first cruise.

On the second day out the ladies were all given a Dance Card, which we were supposed to get filled by that night for the Sadie Hawkins dance. I had no trouble filling mine by asking other ladies to let me borrow their husband for just one dance. We were to go to their table, buy him a drink, light his cigarette and claim him for that dance. There were only three men that I would have given a second look.

When it came to my seventh partner, he was nowhere to be found. While I was looking for him I saw the tall white-haired, handsome fellow; I'd seen him earlier with a willowy blond on his arm. She was protecting him from all the other women. Single women outnumbered the men six to one. He was watching me. He called over and asked if he could help me. I guess it was evident that I was looking for someone. He said he'd be glad to fill in…. and he did for the rest of the cruise.

His name was John, had been a widower for five years with no children, and was on this cruise to get away from Seaford, Long Island, New York for the holidays.

I figured that if he really was what he said he was, we could have a good time and if he wasn't I would treasure some good memories anyway.

After being divorced for eight years and going through the trauma of losing my fiancé, Jack, four years earlier I didn't trust any man.

157

We toured and shopped the Caribbean Islands every day in port and danced the evenings away in the Ballroom on board the ship at night. From the first day he wouldn't let me spend a dime of my own money. We made friends with other couples who were watching what they called the "Shipboard Romance". It was a glamorous, exciting and fun time in my life that I would never have dreamed of in a million years.

One of the first things our shipmates wanted to know was 'what do you for a living?' He told them that he sold caskets...ahead of time. He had quite a line. Customers could pick the casket they wanted and the lining. The caskets were designed so they could be used as coffee tables, grandfather clock cabinets, gun cabinets or whatever the buyer wanted to use them for until they needed them. One lady wanted to order hers with a mink lining; another wanted a telephone installed in hers; while one of the men wanted his casket lined with pockets so 'he could take it with him'. Everyone got quite a kick out of John's bizarre business. He even had business cards and stationery printed that said, "ask about our lay-away plan".

Of course, nobody believed him but a few offered to make deposits so they could see his catalog when we got back to New York.

I enjoyed the jokes people made about the caskets but was positive that none of it was true until I got a letter from him on his printed stationery. I had some second thoughts.

DOWN TO EARTH

When we landed at the pier in New York, for the turn-around back to Bermuda and the weekly runs between, John's bother and sister-in-law greeted us.

We spent the day at the Ambassador Hotel, mostly to keep me from freezing to death, I didn't have any winter clothes with me, getting acquainted.

I didn't know that John had written to them, from one of the islands, and told them he had met someone he wanted them to meet. They seemed quite concerned that I was divorced. I found out later how complicated that was.

The seas were very rough on the way back to Bermuda, from a big storm that caused the piano to break its chains and slide across the ballroom, dishes and bottles to break and a lot of sea sickness.

When I left the ship in Bermuda, in January 1965, I immediately walked to my office where a corsage of Gardenias was waiting for me. How nice! He'd remembered my birthday. He called that night to see if I'd gotten the flowers; the next day to see if I'd gotten his letter; and for just no reason for several days. I told him he could visit me for all the money he was spending on phone calls.

I invited him down for a visit. He brought me a beautiful Amethyst ring that matched perfectly the formal I'd worn on New Year's Eve aboard ship. He stayed for a week and went home for a week. He was back and forth so many times that my landlady kept a room for him. By February he had asked me to marry him but I was still skeptical of all men.

Poor John. He was trying to prove to me that he wasn't like the others.

Mr. M suggested that I accept John's invitation to New York so he could prove that he wasn't lying about his big house, his Cadillac and his friends. I went for a week. Everything he had told me was true.

After he proposed, I wrote to my mother in Albany, Georgia telling her all about John. She wrote back that she hoped I didn't have to do what her preacher said I would and that was, "She'll have to sleep with the priest the night before the wedding to get 'purified' before she can marry a Catholic man".

John was with me when I read the letter. I was furious that she would believe such hogwash! We called Mama and John talked to her telling that he had never heard of such a thing and even if it was true, he knew it wasn't, he wouldn't permit it. The way he spoke to her pacified her and he was calling her 'Mama' before the conversation was over.

We left Bermuda on St. Patrick's Day in 1965 to get married in New York. Because John was Catholic and I was divorced we could not be married in the church in Bermuda.

It didn't work out in New York either so, we were married

by a Justice of Peace in March, 1965. We went on a month long honeymoon all through the South so John and Mama finally met in Georgia.

We lived in John's big split-level house on Seaman's Neck Road in Seaford from March 1965 until August, 1969.

After 'living in sin' for twenty three months, we got a Dispensation from the Pope. According to the Catholic Church my first marriage was dissolved. I knew that it was just a formality but Terry, my youngest son, was bitter about it.

In the meantime, I had to get letters confirming that I had never been baptized in any church.

Later, Mama tried to take back her confirmation after her preacher told her that she was "sending me straight to hell'". After she saw how John treated me she relented some. I heard her tell someone that she "loved him even though he was Catholic".

When we got married the second time, in February, 1967, we went to Bermuda on our real honeymoon. The M family were away and loaned us their house, and all the hired help, for two weeks.

John retired from his job as a Professional Tile Setter in 1965.

By the second year I discovered that we could not live on John's retirement because he was a big spender and his savings were dwindling fast. My solution was for me to go to work doing something I really wanted to do to supplement his income. I realized my life-long dream of selling Real Estate.

~~~~~~

Twenty years earlier, I had wanted to get into Real Estate Sales but my first husband said, "what makes you think you can sell anything?". I was crushed and vowed that someday I would show him! Especially after he said, "just because you've sold a few Stanley Home Products and some brushes doesn't make you a salesman".

I had to leave that business after he had been off work a year and we had to sell our house to pay his hospital bills. I had to have a permanent income and even though, as Unit Manager, my group had out-sold every dealer in the state of Michigan, I was not able to continue to guide my seventeen dealers as I had been before his illness.

I got my initial training in Real Estate by going to the office of Cruise and Smith on Sunrise Highway, in Seaford, and took the test in November. I was fifty. My bosses were very impressed when I sold six houses before Christmas and two more between then and the New Year. I learned, very early, that a good sales person has to be 'sold' on his/her product. I retired from Real Estate in Hiawassee, Georgia when I was seventy.

~~~~~~

Our house was burglarized in December 1968 while we were out, for two hours, finishing our Christmas shopping. The police estimated that we lost thousands of dollars in jewelry and miscellaneous items. We thought it was much more because John had a pinkie ring with three separate diamond karats and a three karat ring that had belonged to his mother that he had given to me. The insurance company paid us three thousand six hundred dollars. We decided to go on another cruise. Nobody could take that away from us.

That house was never the same after the burglary so it wasn't hard to make the decision to move to Florida. I was doing quite well in Real Estate and had passed my first Broker's Exam but I was ready to head for Florida.

Several other reasons helped us to decide. One: the Oyster Bay Expressway, six lanes, was being built one hundred and forty feet from our front door. Two: Our taxes were over three hundred dollars a month and rising and Three: our neighborhood was going black. This was in the late sixties when there was a drive to 'get a black in every block'. We had three in our block after we sold to the Vice President of Chemical Bank where John's brother was President. We took a loss of ten thousand dollars. Five thousand for the expressway and another five for the neighborhood.

161

RETIREMENT
WITH JOHN

We headed for Georgia, after giving up on Florida, when we learned that my mother had had a stroke and needed us. We were interrupted by Hurricane 'Camile' in August 1969. We had minimal damage to our furniture because the truck driver listened to the weather reports and zigzagged out of its path.

We settled in a nice three-bedroom two bath brick house in Albany. I got my Real Estate license in Georgia and went to work for Tift & Westbrook Realty. I had lived in Albany for six years before going to Bermuda and three more years after Mama's stroke. After Mama's second husband, Frank, died we pursued our plans for retirement in Florida.

We settled in a two-bedroom house on Davis Island in Tampa where I, again, got a Real Estate License and went to work for Yates Real Estate with offices on the main street of Davis Island. By this time I had passed the Broker's exam in New York and Florida. I flunked the only exam of my life when I took the Broker's exam in Atlanta the week after my mother's husband died.

Eventually, I went to work for James Burt Realty and from there into Condominium sales in Zepherhills, St. Petersburg, Clearwater , Tampa and back to St. Petersburg.

In the meantime, John had to spend a lot of time alone but he knew that we absolutely had to have more income. We could not live on his Social Security and a small pension.

He read very little, watched television, sat by the windows looking out over the Hillsborough River where the big ships came in turned around and headed back into the Gulf, and he shopped the Malls… anything to kill time.

He loved to shop better than any man I ever knew and spent money like it was flowing from an everlasting well. He often said, "I would be the happiest man in the world if I just had all the money I could spend". However, he did continue to spend long after he had spent what he brought into the marriage. I brought nothing in the way of money but I did my best and earned what would have been adequate for most couples our age.

I was forty-eight and he was fifty-eight when we married.

He was a compulsive spender and just couldn't seem to help himself. Like the time in New York when I took a bad fall. I had tried to jump the brook in our backyard, about six feet. I landed on the cement retaining wall that John had built. It left me with extreme pain in my left rib cage from November 1965 until February 1966. Because thirteen Doctors had not determined what was wrong by Christmas he bought me a Mink coat. He thought it would make me feel better. I had to have major surgery the very day that he had booked us for a twenty-six day Mediterranean cruise.

Another time was when he tried to get me to decide which purse, at fifty dollars, I would rather have. I thought I'd put him off by saying, "I can't decide whether I'd like the white or the black". The next day I had both.

John didn't play golf, play cards or drink. He didn't like to read and wasn't interested in hobbies of any kind. His whole life centered around me. I felt imprisoned.

After we moved from Albany, Georgia to Tampa, Florida, in August 1972, things didn't get any better, financially, for awhile. It was a year; you had to be a resident a year before applying, until I got my Real Estate license. John was very pessimistic and worried that we'd starve to death.

We still had money left from the sale of our house in Albany and even after we put several thousand dollars into remodeling the little house on Davis Island, we were a long ways from starving. There just wasn't any spending money. I finally got my license and worked hard to get the commissions rolling in again.

Every morning John would send me off with the warning, "if I'm gone, meaning…if I'm dead, when you get home you know where the insurance policies are…". I got so tired of hearing that. I had to go out and show the public a smiling face, a good attitude and try to sell them a house. It wasn't the way I thought it should be. So, one morning, after such a dour prediction, I went back inside the house, back to the beautiful family room that we had created, sat down across from him and said, "if it's going to be today I'll just wait". For a few moments I think he was stunned. Then he laughed and said "It won't happen again"

163

and it didn't.

For years he had kept up the 'up today-down tomorrow' attitude. This was so different from the fun-loving man I'd met on the cruise that I didn't know how to handle it. I spoke to the Priest about it and he said, "that's just the Irish in him. Don't worry about him, he'll be alright". Most of the time he was but his not working, sometimes no money coming in or just about anything depressing would get him down for days. Other days, he was on top of the world and wanted the world to share his happiness.

Through it all I still loved him and knew that he loved me. His moods were my cross to bear.

~~~~~~

I'd been doing exceptionally well in Real Estate when I realized that I had absolutely nothing to show for my years of work, but our house, a good car and the Ability To Sell. It was nineteen seventy seven . I was sixty years old and I was scared.

I started talking about building a place in the mountains of North Georgia as a retirement home and for security, thinking that we could get along on a lot less. This was not John's idea of security at all.

During the years between 1975 - 1985 I made more money than I ever had but it was being spent almost as fast as I could bring it home.

We had visited my relatives in Hiawassee many times and when we found a lot, in May 1980, on a seven thousand-acre lake with a view of the mountains, I thought I had found my dream. John humored me and said, "If that's what you want it's alright with me". I didn't find out until much later that he really didn't expect me to earn enough money to have a house built on that lot.

I had always loved the mountains where my Grandparents, Erv and Bettie had lived out their lives and where some Aunts, Uncles and Cousins still lived. I'd been telling them for years that "someday I'm going to live here". Of course, most of them thought it was a pipe dream. It was real to me.

164

My relatives encouraged me to join them and share in what I thought it was 'Heaven on Earth'. John went along with what I wanted to do. He just wouldn't have any part of it. He wasn't interested in the plans but didn't do anything to stop me.

My cousin, Frank, agreed to build the house from the plans I had drawn up and had an architect refine. I wanted the finished house to look like the one my Granpaw and Granmaw, Erv and Bettie, lived on Fodder Creek Road. It did except there was another level below that you couldn't see from the road.

I paid cash for everything as it was built. When it was finished, I furnished it in Country furniture that I bought in North Carolina. It was perfect as far as I was concerned but John kept telling people that it was our 'Summer Home". He had no idea of ever living there permanently. I put his name on the deed even though he had not contributed one dime until he realized that I wasn't planning on screening the big porch facing the lake. He sold his 1959 Cadillac and paid to have the porch screened. He spent most of his time on that porch every time we could get there.

We spent as much time as possible there after it was finished in 1981. My children from Michigan visited us as often as they could. We all thought that 'Hiawassee Haven' would be our gathering place from then on.

~~~~~~

While we lived on Davis Island I worked across the Bay from Tampa and had to cross a seven-mile bridge with all its traffic hang-ups every day. We eventually bought a Condominium in Largo. It was beautiful but miles from grocery stores or any kind of activities except what there was at the Clubhouse. John liked condominium living. He did his shopping in Largo, Clearwater or St. Petersburg wherever and whenever he felt like it . It was quite different when I had to cut down on expenses because of commitments to the cottage but he still found things to do as I kept working every day.

I was Sales Director for the years of 1977 through 1981, selling Condominiums when most of the money was coming in.

By the time the place in the mountains was finished I had spent thousands of dollars, including furniture, in cash. I was quite proud of myself. I had learned that if I took part of my earnings, bought one or two Condos on each project, rented and resold them later, I could provide a good living for about ten years.

My first job selling Condominiums was in Zepherhills, where I bought one; then to 'Williamsburg' and 'Jamestown' in St. Petersburg, where I bought two at each place; from there to Clearwater, where I bought two more at 'Fountain Square' and two more at 'Place One' in Tampa, then back to St. Petersburg at 'Le Chateau' where I didn't buy any. A final one was in Largo.

Sales of Condos started dropping everywhere. They had run their course and were over-built by eighty thousand in Florida alone. My bosses sold the business and I was out of a job when the new owner said, "we are trying to project a youthful image". The average age of the buyers at Le Chateau was seventy three. I could have sued for discrimination but I had no witnesses. The new company hired two 'young things', paid each half of the five hundred a week that I was getting, plus my commissions, and thought that a 'youthful image' would create sales. It didn't. Eventually prices dropped ten thousand before the last ones were sold. I was out of a job at sixty-five.

This gave me more time to spend with John. I was still managing the rental of about twenty Condos that I had sold to other people besides the ones of my own that I hadn't sold so money was no problem for awhile.

We went to the mountains for most of the summer of 1982. My kids and their families visited, some more than once and it was great.

John got sick on the way back to Largo. I had no idea that he had a sore throat because he had let me enjoy my family and never said a word. Before we got home he became so violently ill that I took him straight to the hospital.

He was there ten days and wasn't getting any better. I finally caught the Doctor in the hall and asked him why. He said that John had Septicemia. They couldn't find its source until I told them about his sore throat.

John hadn't told him about his throat. He said, "they're

166

Doctors, they shouldn't have to be told". I wasn't aware at the time that he thought he had cancer. He had smoked for sixty years, and didn't want to face it.

The Doctor told me that one of his tonsils was the problem. John didn't believe it because he had had his tonsils out three times. The Doctor showed us a cut-out picture of the throat. There were six tiny tonsils, three on each side, about as big as a flat match head unless infected. One of them was. They took it out the next day, which caused the Septicemia to spread.

He proceeded to deteriorate until twenty-two Doctors gave up on him. They told me that he didn't have the 'Will to Live' and there was nothing they could do about it. The twenty-third Doctor was a Psychiatrist who recommended that I take John to the mountains where it was cooler. That was in June 1983. The Psychiatrist said, "John thinks that he has cancer and that nobody will tell him. He has a 'death wish' and all the Doctors in the world can't help him get over that".

We left within a few days and I thought I might be able to convince John that he didn't have cancer. Within days he was in the Hospital in Hiawassee with breathing problems. He was there about a week and back home again. He lost control of all his bodily functions, he couldn't stand up without getting me to stand in front of him with his arms, and a lot of his weight, leaning on my shoulders. I wheeled him into and out of the bathroom and to the table but he couldn't eat. By the time he was in the Hospital for the third time I was completely exhausted.

I was staying alone when Jim, my brother, called from Tampa wanting me to go with him to Indianapolis to pick up a motor home that he had ordered for his Motor Home business. He knew that John was sick but didn't realize that I couldn't leave

I was quite surprised when he showed up that Friday evening. He said he just felt the urge to see me. I slept like a log for the first time in weeks so didn't hear the phone until the last ring. I heard someone say, "I guess she's not home". I called the hospital. They had been trying to reach me to tell me that John had "taken a turn for the worse".

Jim and I jumped in our clothes and sped to the hospital. The

Doctor met me at the door. He said "John passed away at six thirty A.M." Only minutes before we got there.

It had been fourteen months since he got sick, six weeks since we went to the mountains and had been hospitalized ten times altogether. My mother and a step-grandson also died that year.

When I asked the Doctor what actually killed him he said, "Heart failure". That made me furious. I said, "Everybody that dies has heart failure". After the Doctor had studied John's records he wrote 'Toxemia' as the cause of death.

I had to get help in finding a place to bury him because the Baptist or Methodist churches preferred not to have a Catholic buried in their cemetery. The undertaker finally told me about Laurel Hills on highway 17 at the state line between Georgia and North Carolina ... only seven miles away.

I couldn't get the Priest from Hayesville, North Carolina, where we'd been going to church, to do the funeral because it was out of his parish. A substitute Priest came from Blairsville, Georgia. Tom, John's brother who came from New York, was pleased that I had seen to it that John had a Catholic funeral.

I went to the church in Blairsville once, gave them a generous donation and have never gone to a Catholic Church since.

HIAWASSEE HAVEN

The condo in Largo seemed forlorn so I decided to go back to the mountains to see if I could handle the winters enough to move there. I went to 'Hiawassee Haven' for January, February and March, typically the worst months, and decided I liked it.

Vicki and Ridge came to Florida and helped me move. I immediately went to work selling Time-Share Condos in Helen, Georgia while studying for my second Georgia Real Estate license. There were no reciprocal laws between Florida and Georgia. I didn't like Time-Share Sales so went to work for a Real Estate broker in Hiawassee as soon as I got my license. A year later, I passed the Broker's test.

For something to do, other than work work all the time, I got involved with Recycling and was chairperson for the Litter and Solid Waste Control Recycling Committee for five years. Besides working with the County Commissioner, Truman. I kept him informed as to what was going on in the 'like-new world' of Recycling and wrote an informative article for the Towns County Herald newspaper every week.

As part of my committee-chair job, I appointed two of my friends as co-chairs to make a scrapbook of the committee's activities. The entire committee contributed to making a beautiful scrapbook by donating Artwork needed and giving of their time.

The scrapbook was entered in a contest between several counties who vied for first place. Ours won among the Counties and first place in the State. The whole LSWC committee was invited to Washington, D.C. as one of the top contenders for National Recognition. Six of us went in Truman's van after we had collected donations to cover our expenses for the trip. We watched as President George Bush, in person, lauded us with praise for the outstanding work we had done in cleaning up our county and starting a Recycling Program that was the pattern for surrounding counties. The Commissioner received an Award, on our behalf, for our accomplishments.

I spent many hours volunteering, and coaxing others to join me, in getting our county roads cleaned up and starting the Recycling Program at the Towns County Landfill. Our second scrapbook won first place in the State too but we were not invited to Washington. I wrote and received Grants for money to build storage buildings for newspapers and a machine for crushing aluminum cans and got local businesses to donate old dumpsters for glass. All those things had to be sold and buyers were not that easy to find. Through the joint efforts of many people, I had no connections at first but one led to another, and the coordinating of buyers it worked out that we made a profit. I made arrangements for a local junk car dealer to haul old cars away, at no expense to owner, so many areas were relieved of eyesores that they had no way of removing.

It was a rewarding time for me even though it took a year for the new Commissioner, Dayton, to accept what I was doing. He was so rude to me about it that one day I went into his office talk to him after he made the remark, "you know I'm in charge here and I can put a stop to all this Recycling stuff just by my say so".

I had never interfered with any of his plans to clean up the county. He didn't have any. I knew that he was feeling the importance of his new job, and himself, when I told him "what our committee is doing will benefit your political career". He changed his mind and cooperated with us completely. Years later, he invited me into his office and said, "Etta, what you have done for this county can never be repaid, we are all better off for it andwe're sorry you moved away". All of my involvement with the Recycling Program was after John had been dead a year.

THE MOTOR HOME

Jim took me, several times, with him to pick up Motor Homes that he had bought from Jayco at their plant in Indiana. Some of those trips are unforgettable.

Like the very first time when he picked me up in Hiawassee in his small car that he intended to pull behind the Motor Home. We attended a three-day Motor Home Show where several hundred were displayed for sale.

There was such a terrific discount that Jim bought seven. He had to hire a man to drive each one to Tampa where he had his business. He was short one man so I agreed to drive the smallest one. What he didn't tell me was that I'd be towing his small car behind it. It was too late to back out.

The show was over and we had to get out of the huge building before dark. It was pouring rain. We got gas, only three gallons was allowed inside the building so the lines were long, and Jim took the lead.

After a short distance I noticed that all the road signs were indicating that we were going North. I knew we were supposed to be going South. I called Jim on the CB. He soon saw that we were headed in the wrong direction and told me to get off at the next exit. He didn't know that I was a couple exits behind him. I got off and wound up in a seedy part of Indianapolis. I was too scared to stop and ask for directions so just kept heading South.

It took me awhile to find an entrance back onto the expressway but after stopping by a police car for directions I was able to relax a little when a voice came on the CB calling my name. I was outside Jim's five-mile limit and the voice wasn't his. It upset me because I thought some truck driver had heard Jim calling me and was just being cute. He finally said, "Etta, your brother Jim is trying to reach you. He said he'd meet you at the next truck stop". What a relief! Then he said, "Just follow me, I'll take you to him". He must have thought I was some kind of nut because there was no way I could tell which truck he was in, about 10:00 at night and in the pouring rain, so I just headed for the next truck stop. I didn't know that it was between the two strips of the expressway and missed it as I went by.

About a hundred miles down the road I pulled into a well-lit truck stop. And there was Jim. I don't think he's ever been so glad to see me. He didn't know that I had my gas credit cards and about eighty-five dollars. I had decided that I could stay in a motel and get enough gas to get to Tampa so I wasn't going to worry about it. I didn't know that I only had one usable gas tank, the other one was plugged up, and I couldn't have gone more than a few more miles. Jim had some trouble with the Motor Home he was driving so it took us three days to get home. But, the next time he asked me to go I did.

The last time was in January 1985. We had gone to Indianapolis shortly after New Years and would have a couple days to wait for the particular Motor Homes that he had ordered.

So, I planned on spending some time, a hundred or so miles into Michigan, with my kids. The company that manufactured the wheels went on strike so I spent a month back and forth between Vicki's, Lynn's and Terry's. Finally the twenty-footer that I was waiting for was ready.

~~~~~~

I was waiting at Vicki's in Stockbridge. She came to my room crying that the house was on fire. I said, "let's get out of here". She meant her Dad's house on Ash Street in Lansing.

We rushed to the hospital where Auntie Pat, Max and Ray

171

had all been taken. Pat was not hurt but couldn't be consoled, Ray thought he was having a heart attack. Max was critical from smoke inhalation. He eventually recovered.

The house burned to the ground. A smoldering heating pad that Ray kept turned on between the mattress and springs, to keep his bed, warm caused the fire.

Terry, my youngest son, had convinced his Dad to take out Replacement Cost Insurance for the old house which was over one hundred twenty five years old. He collected over one hundred thousand dollars. A new house, with an apartment for Auntie Pat, was built on the same lot.

~~~~~~

Lynn drove me to Indianapolis, admonishing me all the way about how it was too icy and stormy for me to leave. I wound up in a very bad snowstorm near Lexington, Kentucky. I parked on three inches of ice, from a storm a few days before, while I went in to get a room. I had left the motor running, believing that nobody would steal it in such a terrible storm, afraid it might not start again. When I came back outside the little Motor Home was gone. The motel manager was calling the police when I spotted it across the huge parking lot. There was a very small incline as the lot sloped down to the lower side and there it sat with the motor still running. I got the key, sank in the deepest sleep I'd had for weeks, and vowed that was the 'very last time I'd deliver a Motor Home'.

SQUARE DANCING
WITH BEN

In 1985 I decided that I needed to do something socially so I joined a Square Dance Club in Blairsville. I took lessons from September to April when it was time to graduate from the class. During that time, I had not had a partner of my own so when I got a phone call from Ben, from Summerville, South Carolina, I was delighted. He suggested that he come up for the April graduation. He had gotten my name from a Square Dancer who

172

had visited our club that spring.

I had a guest-room and invited him for the weekend. I had never seen this man but we had been corresponding, sending pictures and calling back and forth since February. I felt like I knew him very well. He got in on Friday night.

We talked most of the night so were a little groggy when my brother and his wife, George and Florine, arrived early Saturday. I didn't know they were going to come by on their way to Michigan. Of course, they were welcome but Ben got there first and had the guest-room, as was the custom at my house. We had a pleasant weekend but George got me aside and passed his opinion on Ben. He thought Ben was not my intellectual level, he was a farmer-type and he talked funny.

Ben definitely had a Southern drawl, Charlestonian, and he did look like a farmer. In my book that wasn't too bad. He had more practical knowledge and skills than most people. When Frank, my cousin Margie's husband, met him he said, " I reckon you'll want to change him to suit yourself". When I said, "He's alright just the way he is" Frank said, "it must be love".

I didn't expect it to be 'love' but I knew that I was lonely and this man did a lot to make me happy. He had come back and forth all summer, I went to Summerville once, so when he asked me to marry him I said, "yes".

We were married in St. George's, South Carolina in August 1986. The plan was for him to move to the mountains with me and sell his trailer park. We spent the next four winters in Hiawassee but decided to go to Summerville for the next two when both he and I had to have surgery. We both recuperated well, he sold his place and we decided to spend the next winter in my last Condo at Place One. I'd sold all the rest by then.

~~~~~~

I had sold that one too but had to repossess it. It was a disaster. The single man who bought it had been run off the property, told that if he came back he'd be arrested, so let his mother, her boyfriend and his twelve year old brother move in.

They proceeded to destroy it. They painted all the

woodwork, doors, cupboards and floor tiles black. They tried to dye the carpet black but it didn't work. They tore out the wall between the living room and bathroom, where a huge walk-in closet had been, and built in a bar which they painted black. It took us six weeks to get it livable, with George helping for three weeks, and over seven thousand dollars to fix it up. We stayed there that winter, 1990, and went back to Hiawassee in the spring.

~~~~~~

Ben loved Hiawassee Haven almost as much as I did and added many features that enhanced the property. He built a framed lattice fence along the driveway that he had paved the summer before. The carport was a work of art but Frank said he was afraid to walk on it because it was extended out over a ten-foot bank. When it was finished he said "I wouldn't be afraid to drive a ten ton truck on it". Ben was a perfectionist so every single thing was level, square and permanent. He also built a picnic table and a swing that I prized.

~~~~~~

The summer of 1992 Lynn and Susan invited us to join them, and Susan's parents, on a weeklong cruise on a sixty-foot pontoon on Cumberland Lake in Kentucky. Susan's Dad took charge of everything. He bought the groceries, planned the meals and gave everyone directions on how to operate the boat.

I didn't know until we were on our way home that Ben had been suffering from prostrate trouble all week. We got back to Hiawassee, packed and left within four days for our condo in Tampa where he had a Doctor who had taken care of him the year before. He was soon all right after another minor surgery. We started looking for a winter place on the ground floor.

Because of the surgeries, he had given a drug that caused a relapse of the Vertigo that he thought he had conquered years before he met me. It was back in full force. He had trouble walking up and down the stairs to the Condo in Tampa and even more trouble when we got back to Hiawassee.

There wasn't anyplace on the lot where he could walk, without the chance of falling, except between the house and the work-shed. He fell many times and I nearly fainted when he fell forward towards a fire on the beach where I had stacked the usual debris that collected every few weeks. I was close enough to grab him. I knew then that we would have to do something about living at Hiawassee Haven any longer. It was too much for me to keep up the yard work and almost impossible to hire anyone.

After months of sleepless nights I decided that I would sell the place. I let my kids know what I had to do. They were all in shock. They had looked forward to coming to the mountains forever.

When I told Vicki she said that she and Ridge would love to buy it but they had just bought a hundred year-old house a few months before so it was impossible for them.

Lynn was really upset and wanted to buy it. I knew that Lynn made very good money but I didn't know how much was available to him. I was pretty sure that he couldn't afford it but promised him I'd give him time to see if he could work it out.

Terry liked to bring his family there. He had even talked about buying a car and leaving it at the Blairsville Airport so we wouldn't have to meet them there and they'd have their own car when they came. Because he had his own plane they could go anywhere and didn't want to feel compelled to go to just one place all the time.

In the meantime, I had two appraisals on my place with a new value of a little more than twice what I had paid for it. I let Lynn know and he said he wanted to be fair and he'd pay me the appraisal price. I took off a ten percent commission and a few more thousand. I knew what I needed, to do what I intended, and didn't want to take advantage of my son and his wife for the full price. He planned on adding on to the house and making it their permanent home. I was glad for all of us.

Ben and I moved to Florida in April 1992. It was a double move because we moved out of the Condo in Tampa at the same time. We loved our modular home in Lakeside Hills Estates. We took part in lots of the events at our Million Dollar Clubhouse. After taking a few courses myself, I started teaching Craft Classes on how to make Petal Porcelain flowers, permantizing silk flowers, and incorporating them in wreaths and flower arrangements. It was interesting and satisfying to me. I made thirteen Porcelain Petal decorated baskets for that Christmas.

Ben built a shed inside the carport, because we weren't allowed to add on, and kept busy with little improvements. He bought a golf cart which he loved to use in driving around the neighborhood and to the stores about two blocks from our house.

In March 1993 he had a major stroke. His left side was completely paralyzed. He spent ten days in the Lakeland hospital before he was transferred to a combination Rehab Center and Nursing Home. He would not, could not, participate in the rehabilitation they offered and after fourteen days I had him transferred to another Rehabilitation Center.

I was with him every day, except for ten days when I had bronchitis and they wouldn't let me see him, from around 7:00 A.M. until 8:00 P.M. Sometimes I'd go home, sleep for an hour or so and go right back. A few people sat with him in my place.

It had been weeks since I'd been anywhere so when Jim and Peggy asked me over to their house in Thonotosassa one night, to play 'Dirty Marbles', I went with my sister Lela and her husband Vern. George, another brother, and a friend came too. It was so good to see my family that I relaxed a bit.

Around 10:00 P.M., June 1993, I got a phone call from the Rehab Center. My family were all with me when I got the message that Ben had died. We held a Memorial Service at the Clubhouse.

He and I had agreed several years earlier that we would donate our bodies to Medical Science for Research and I gave the Undertaker those papers.

We had a Memorial Service for Ben at the Clubhouse in Lakeside Hills.

I've often wondered if Ben didn't just give up after the head nurse told him, "we're going to have to put you in the Nursing Home if you don't cooperate by Friday". He died Thursday night.

176

~~~~~~

I was alone again at seventy-six. I tried to keep busy but had retired in Hiawassee from Real Estate Sales at seventy, and wasn't about to try to find work again. I found lots of time on my hands. I went to the ladies' club meetings, "Chat n' Sew" and Crafts at the clubhouse. I had the kitchen redone, painted, replaced the vinyl and all of the appliances. It kept me busy for months but I knew I had to do something to get myself out of the depressive state I was in.

LIFE WITH HARRY

I started taking dancing lessons to brush up. I was rusty on Ballroom Dancing and the years spent Square Dancing were in the past. I enjoyed those classes and met several nice people. One of the ladies invited me to go to a Singles Club Dance where you had to be fifty to get in.

It was indirectly, through my renewed interest in dancing that I met Harry. He got my phone number and called me to go to an afternoon dance in Winter Haven.

I guess you'd call it a blind date but at my age, seventy-eight, I didn't feel like dating. I did want to get out more, to go dancing and to have a friend to help me fill the lonely hours.

When I met him, in November 1995, he was standing in the parking lot where we had agreed to meet. I had decided to drive my own car so if I didn't like what I saw I could leave. I liked what I saw. The first thing I noticed was that he appeared to be clean cut, had snow white hair, which I seem to have an affinity for, and he was tall.

We went dancing but the music was so loud that we left, so we could talk, and walked in a small park. Before the afternoon was over we found that we had a lot in common and would certainly do something about our loneliness.

He had lost his wife, of fifty-two years, in October 1994. I told Harry that I had Diabetes, Osteoporosis and a few other

177

assorted ailments. He told me about having Myasthenia Gravis and Atrial Fibrillation. We both laughed and decided that we needed each other to look after us in our old age. I was seventy-eight and he was seventy-nine.

We told each other about our families. Harry was a widower with one stepson. He was quite surprised at my large family, which consisted of my remaining three brothers and a sister; my three Children, seven Grandchildren and nine Great Grandchildren.

The next few pages will be a brief summary of Harry's life which I asked him to write for me.

HARRY'S STORY

I was born in March 1916 at the University of Michigan Hospital in Ann Arbor, Michigan. My mother was Inez and I was named Charles Harvey. I was adopted by Frank and Elma and sent to them by train to Mesick, Michigan at the age of six months. Along with adoption papers they filed a name change for me and I was then named Harry Alphonso.

We lived in the village of Sherman where I was raised. I attended school there in a building that used to be the Wexford County Courthouse.

Our next-door neighbors were Joseph (Pony) and his wife Lizzie. They were very fond of me and wanted to trade their best cow for me. My folks wouldn't agree to that. I was very small when Lizzie died. Later, when my folks moved to Ann Arbor, Pony came to live there also. He had his meals with us. Pony would buy me gifts and give me spending money. I was with him when he died at our place in Ann Arbor. He left his property in Sherman to my mother and made her promise that some day it would be mine.

My parents lost their jobs at Ann Arbor in 1927 due to the depression and we moved back to Sherman where Dad began farming. I went to school in Mesick and graduated from High School in 1933.

In 1934 I spent six months in the CCC Camp Kentucky in Michigan. I was assigned to a program conducted by the U.S.

Forest Service to determine what was destroying the pine tree seedlings. This allowed me to use my knowledge of entomology and involved studying the various insects in the pine tree plantations.

I worked at Packard Motors in Detroit for two years and then at General Motors Truck and Coach in Pontiac for two years. During the next year I married and divorced my first wife. I then married Eunyce in October 1942 and entered the Navy two days later. Eunyce had a six-year-old son. I was transferred to a Naval Air Station at Clinton, Oklahoma. Eunyce and her son followed and we lived in Elk City, Oklahoma. I was again transferred and sent to Naval Air Station at Alameda, California. My family went with me by train. I was finally discharged after three years, one month and five days in the Navy. We returned to Michigan.

After working for awhile in Pontiac I decided to re-enter the Navy at Grosse Ile Naval Air Station. We were there for five years. I got out of the Navy in 1950.

I had several jobs and one of the most interesting was with Kaiser Frazer at Willow Run. I started out as a tooling expediter on the C-119 and ended up in charge of all tooling for the C-119 and the C-123 aircraft.

After the Air Force contracts ran out, I had several other jobs and then connected with the Chrysler Corporation Missile Division. They sent me to Huntsville, Alabama to set up the Jupiter Support Management Office. This was a challenging assignment.

During this period Eunyce and I took a trip to Europe with the Porsche Club of America. We took delivery on our new Porsche in Stuttgart, Germany and had a three-week tour of Europe. We were active in sports-car club events while at Huntsville. We won trophies for rallies and economy runs.

After the Chrysler contracts ran out I took a job with the Sundstrand Aviation Division at Rockford, Illinois. This didn't last long. The Bendix Systems of Ann Arbor, Michigan hired me. I was assigned to work on the Eagle Missile. After that closed out I went to the Martin Company in Denver, Colorado on the Titan III program. I was there only three months when Bendix offered me a better deal to return to Ann Arbor. I remained at Bendix until I retired in 1972.

We spent the next winter in Chiefland, Florida running a mobile home sales business for a friend who lived in Gainesville. Later we returned to Mesick and commenced working on the barn that had been left to me by Pony via my mother. Eventually we converted it to a residence.

I got a job with Bureau of State Lottery Bingo Division that lasted for seven years. I finally retired when I became sixty-seven in 1983.

We went to Florida and bought a condo in Winter Haven. We would return to Mesick for the summers and then back to Florida in the fall.

Eunice died in Munson Hospital at Traverse City following heart surgery in 1994. Nineteen ninety-five was sort of a lost year for me. I didn't see a doctor that year and neglected my medicine and failed to follow up on medical tests.

I met Etta in 1995 and she helped me get my life in order. Thank you Etta.

Harry

~~~~~~

I introduced Harry to my brothers, Jim and George, and my sister and brother-in-law, Lela and Vern. They all liked him immediately.

When Lynn and Susan met him, around Thanksgiving time, they approved and Lynn teased me about my 'boyfriend'. Harry told them that we "were going to 'merge' our lives and take care of each other".

Terry and Youlin came the week after Christmas. They also approved but Terry had a question. He wanted to know what Harry meant when he said, "merge". Terry asked, "what does he mean? To get married or just to shack-up?"

I said, "I don't know, he hasn't said anything to me, but next year is Leap Year and if he hasn't told me by then I'll ask him".

About a week after New Years, where Harry and I spent the evening dancing at the Clubhouse with Lela and Vern, I told

Harry what Terry had said. He said, "well, I guess we'll have to take care of that" and took me to pick out rings.

Because Harry was so much into Computers that his equipment took up a whole room at his Condo, and I didn't have room in my small place for it all, we decided to sell both places and buy one together. We found a real nice three-bedroom manufactured home on Linc Lane in Lakeside Hills Estates.

In one week we had become engaged, picked out our rings, set the date for our wedding, put both our homes up for sale and found a home for us to share. When Harry decides to do something he does it NOW! He tells people that "we don't buy green bananas"

I already had a cruise booked for January with Jan, a neighbor across the street. She backed out so Harry said he'd just take her place.

But, before we could get married Harry had to have a bladder cancer removed. He knew that he was having a problem but wanted to wait until after the first of the year to go to the Doctor. I insisted that he go immediately.

He had the surgery and thought he'd be able to come out of the hospital the same day so we planned to go on the Caribbean Cruise leaving three days later. The surgery was performed on Tuesday and we were married on Friday after he told the Doctor and Nurses, " we are going to get married even if we have to have the ceremony in the hospital". The Doctor released him but advised against the cruise so we had to cancel. That ship left without us but we already had another cruise scheduled for April to Bermuda.

Harry took me to the Lake Region Unitarian Universalist Fellowship and after the first visit I knew it was the church for me. We both agreed to join the church and help to support it. We attended services regularly and enjoyed the sermons.

We got settled in our house on Linc Lane and went on a cruise to Bermuda in April. It was as beautiful as ever but Harry was not physically able to enjoy ship life or to share the memories that I had of Bermuda. He was a good sport about it and tried to help me have a good time.

Shortly after the cruise, at the end of April, we left Lakeland headed for Mesick, where Harry had converted his barn to a house, for the summer. He'd spent over thirty years converting it. He had tried to describe it but there was no way he could have made me visualize what it was really like.

On the way we stopped at Vicki and Ridge's for a few days. Vicki had organized a Welcome Party for us at the Country Club near Jackson. All of the family was there. It was wonderful to see all of them.

Harry was having trouble talking. We didn't know then that this was probably the forerunner of the Myasthenia Gravis crisis he had a few weeks later. Because he couldn't talk above a whisper, I got up to thank everyone. I couldn't figure out why everybody was laughing. Harry had sent a note around that said, "she's not talking. I'm a ventriloquist". Everybody liked him from the start.

The barn/house, the 'Farm' as Harry calls it, was quite a shock to me. He really had converted it by putting in two kitchens, three bathrooms, two huge bedrooms, a music-library-computer room, a huge rathskeller in the basement and attached a large greenhouse on the south end of the building. He created solar heat from the greenhouse and had numerous unique ideas built in.

I was overwhelmed by it all because as I stepped into the foyer, barn entrance, through sliding glass doors I was immediately struck by the hundreds of items on display. There was hardly a place where you could see the walls because they were all covered with his collections of pictures, tapestries and posters. The stair railing had ceramic or glass telephone pole insulators every few inches. Off to the right was the great room with living/dining, with a bathroom and kitchen area nearby. Across the foyer was the master bedroom, a bath and kitchen at the other end. All of these rooms were absolutely filled with his collections of vases, dishes, wall hangings, trinkets and unusual items of all kinds on endless shelves. He even had three 'Goya' prints and one 'Rembrandt' of a Lion. The mezzanine was also lined with pictures, unusual lights and two huge pieces, done in relief. One was of a collection of hot-air balloons and the other is a carriage done in gold and beautiful colors. There was a third

182

bathroom beside the stairway from the mezzanine to the guest bedroom that was also filled with memorabilia. His collection of little planters, shaped like cars, was in the greenhouse, along with shelves for all kinds for ceramic flower pots and glass novelties. The hot tub sat next to the windows where the temperature in the greenhouse could be controlled by huge roll-up shades. The basement contained the rathskeller where he had hundreds of glass mugs and ceramic beer steins, a workshop, a craft area for his stained glass and a laundry room. Shelves, filled with everything, lined every wall. Dozens of tables held what-nots, jewelry, and all kinds of ceramic and china dishes. Poles held clothes, ski and boating paraphernalia.

Besides all that there was a pole-barn that was filled with thousands of items Harry had collected over the years. Shelves, three or four in layers, surrounded every wall. They were all full of ceramic items, glassware, whatnots and books and hundreds of books ....besides hundreds more in the house. It was a collectors dream but a nightmare to me because I absolutely could not see how I could ever sort, clean or make a home in such a conglomeration of things.

Harry did his best to make it easier for me. We hired a neighbor lady to come and clean the living area of the house. I decided to live with the accumulation of old dust and clutter in the areas we didn't use and in the pole-barn. None of it was dirty, just layers and layers of dust and one collection piled on top of another. It was not clutter to Harry. Everything in the house and pole-barn had a special meaning for him. I was reluctant to touch anything for fear I'd break it. I just wasn't used to having anything in the house that I couldn't wash, clean or move around.

He took me to visit his friends, to all his favorite scenic places such as the High Rollaway, to Pig Roasts and picnics, to dinner often and to the Unitarian Universalist Church in Traverse City. We took in many events at Interlochen. We had a busy summer before and after he was sick.

~~~~~~

183

I had begun to get used to my surroundings when Harry had a small episode of the Myasthenia Gravis that he had had for about four years.

We should have called the Doctor in Traverse City, who had originally diagnosed Harry's ailment and had prescribed medication, that had taken care of his problem. The rare disease affects the muscles. The cause is unknown and no cure is known. The results are that the muscle and the nerve don't connect after the brain has sent a message for them to coordinate and do whatever the brain tells them to. It could be anywhere in the body but his was in the neck area. He couldn't chew, swallow or talk.

He wouldn't go to the Doctor even though I thought he should. This was during the last two weeks of June 1996. In mid-July he had a major crisis that kept him from breathing. On Sunday I rushed him to Munson Medical Center in Traverse City, twenty-eight miles, where he was put on oxygen and given heavy doses of Prednisone along with other medication. I stayed at a nearby Guest House that night and drove back to Mesick next day.

At 10:30 Monday night the Doctor called to tell me that he had written orders for Harry to be taken to University Hospital in Ann Arbor by helicopter. I was shocked and asked if he was that serious. He said, "I think it may be the only way to save his life. I have him on medication that might bring him out of it but 'if not', I want him down there for this new treatment if it doesn't work. I panicked. When I asked him whether I should come to Munson or go to Ann Arbor, he said, " just go to University Hospital". He had already relayed his instructions to the Doctors there.

When I called Vicki, she insisted that she and Ridge come after me. She lived just thirty eight miles, near Stockbridge, from University Hospital so I would be staying with them and going back and forth every day. She went with me for the first two days because I was so nervous.

She, Lynn and Terry were worried about me. They knew how my world had collapsed when Ben died and it appeared that I was facing another crisis like that. They sure didn't want anything to happen to Harry but they were concerned about their mother.

Harry was in intensive care for ten days, the medication worked, in hospital at U of M for another three days and brought back to Munson for another three days. He was weak but he could chew, swallow, eat, talk and breathe when I brought him home.

He had lost fifty pounds and looked like a ghost but soon was eating good and putting weight back on. I was so happy, and thankful, to have him home that I determined to accept the house like it was and try to bring him back to health.

I tried not to let him know how I felt about the house but I know he sensed it. He said he was going to sell the place but he wasn't up to doing anything about it then.

We planned on leaving for Florida around the first of November but Lynn and Susan got in touch and asked if we could leave earlier, by about two weeks. They would drive us home, in Harry's van, and stay a couple weeks then fly home to DeWitt. We thought that was great and proceeded to make plans.

CHAPTER 6

MY CHILDREN

MY CHILDREN

VICKI

Vicki Ann was born in April 1938 at Edward W. Sparrow Hospital in Lansing, Michigan. Her Dad and I were living on Grand River Avenue in North Lansing. She was born, premature at seven months, on her Uncle Howard's sixteenth birthday.

She was a small-boned baby, at just over six pounds, had dark straight hair and big beautiful eyes. Eventually her eyes became hazel-colored with highlights that pick up whatever color she is wearing. The Doctor said that Vicki was a healthy baby and would have weighed around eight pounds had she gone full term.

I wasn't allowed to see Vicki at first so when the cleaning lady said, "she sure is pretty to be a Breach Baby". I was very upset. I had no idea what a 'Breach Baby' was and panicked. Each time I asked to see her I was put off with the nurse saying "later". I started really demanding that I see her but they still wouldn't bring her to me until my Doctor showed up.

The nurse came in holding a tiny little bundle. It was so short that I thought, 'there can't be any legs' when the Doctor started unwrapping her. She was lying on a metal frame, like a small wire shelf in a refrigerator, with two metal arms that met at her navel. I never knew why the metal rods met and held her umbilical cord tight to her body. They left a flower impression in her navel. The Doctor did say something about her not being able to stop bleeding but I was so concerned about her legs that I didn't inquire further.

I was scared to look but the Doctor kept talking as he removed the wraps around her hips. There were two legs all right. They looked perfect but were folded so flat to her sides that it looked like they weren't joined to her hips. The tight wraps were to hold them in place. The Doctor explained that because her bones were so delicate they hadn't been able to tell, on x-rays, whether the hip bone was in the socket or not. I was hysterical. He tried to console me by saying that it could be

189

taken care of but to just give her time. She might be fully developed after all. He didn't recommend doing anything until she had a chance to grow a bit.

That wasn't much comfort after my mother-in-law stood at the foot of my bed crying. She said, "she'll never walk, I know it". I thought of my crippled brother-in-law, Max, who had been born with the umbilical cord wrapped around his waist and had never fully developed below that.

I didn't know, until after my third baby was born 'Breach', butt first. that in my case, it was caused by the lower vertebra in my back being fused together since I had Spinal Meningitis when I was about five years old. The Doctor said, "if you have a hundred babies, they will all be Breach because during the pregnancy your back is supposed to give so the baby can turn". There was nothing anybody could do about that. I was very lucky because, at that time, three of five Breach babies didn't live.

When Vicki was three weeks old, I pulled her bassinet into the kitchen where I was working. I had left the covers a little loose because I didn't think she'd ever be able to use her legs if they were bound up so tight. I kept them tight at night. I was looking at her as she cooed and thinking how beautiful she was when the covers moved. I threw them back in time to see a tiny movement in both legs. I screamed for everybody to come and look. We all cried and thought that it was a miracle. I called my mother-in-law to tell her the news. She warned me about being too optimistic.

Vicki had colic her first three months. I had to give up on breast feeding her in about three weeks because the Doctor said she wasn't getting enough nourishment. I cried. Because she was my first, I determined that I was going to give her the best care possible so I fed her a formula every four hours, strictly by the book. I know that she might have been hungry at times. I've been sorry for that ever since. She's been healthy most of her life so I guess it didn't do any real damage.

She continued to develop and within three months her legs were as firmly in place as any other baby. Her hair grew so fast that when the top baby hair began to come out she looked like a little old man, from the back, with a long fringe of hair around her head.

When she was three months old, her Dad lost his job as a Taxi Driver. We had to move in with his parents on Ash Street. I went back to work within days so Mother watched her during the day. Within a few days Vicki had her first tooth

Vicki soon learned that if she cried at night, between 3:00 and 4:00 o'clock, Pop would come into our room, pick her up and take her for a ride in his car. This happened every night for weeks. He'd take her for a ride while I lay wondering where he had taken her and missing the badly needed sleep I had to have to go to work every day. Finally, I said, "This is enough. Nobody goes into that room after I've put her to bed". He was very upset.

The first night she screamed for an hour. The second night was maybe a half-hour. The third night she whimpered and that was that. No more 'middle of the night rides'. I didn't know it but I had started my 'Tough Love' program before it was ever heard of.

She would stand on her feet, in anyone's lap, by the time she was four months and was scooting around at six months. She scooted right past the crawling stage. At eight and a half months she walked everywhere. She was so tiny she could walk under the dining room table, climb in and out of chair rungs and loved doing things for herself. She was very independent and the joy of our life. We were so grateful that she could walk.

Mother said we should not let her because she surely would be bow-legged. There was no stopping Vicki. She isn't bow-legged. She would scream if anyone picked her up while she was walking and she walked all the time. The house was full of people, all bent on spoiling her it seemed to me, when I told them I'd been able to save enough money for us to move out on our own. They were all upset with me, especially Pop.

As long as we stayed there, and Ray wasn't working, our marriage was in jeopardy. He would hang out with his buddies, working on old cars or motorcycles, until I actually threw a fit. I got Pop to take me to where I knew he was and blasted him in front of his friends. I knew it wasn't the way to handle it but wasn't experienced enough to know what to do. Pop praised me for doing it and Ray got a job. We moved about a block away in a big house on Larch Street.

I delighted in decorating for our first Christmas in our own home. Vicki wanted to touch everything but when it came to the tree I told her not to. The bulbs were too hot and it might tip over on her. She looked like a living doll standing in front of the tree, with her hands behind her back and saying "Ooo, Ahh". She had been saying 'Daddy', 'Duck' and 'Doll' at eight months, a few weeks earlier.

I made her some 'little girl' dresses rather than the baby clothes she'd been wearing. I was so pleased with my work that I wanted to show it, and her, off to everybody. One of my sisters-in-law, inspected the inside seams of everything I made and commented that I was "making an old lady of her" by dressing her in colors. That hurt but everybody else encouraged me to dress her in colors, rather than pastels, and to pay no attention to her.

I thought she would burst one of her own seams when I made Vicki a little white net dress, from my graduation dress, for her first birthday. It had a square neck with puff sleeves, a waistline with three rows of ruffles below. Lace eyelet, with tiny pink ribbons run through the eyes, edged the neckline and sleeves. The hem of the skirt was fifteen feet around. Because it was made of see-through net, I had to make her a tiny A-line petticoat. She wouldn't sit down in it and loved to watch the ruffles as she walked and twirled around.

Somebody gave me a beautiful piece of black velvet materiel so I made Vicki a tiny little A-line coat, lined in pink satin, with removable pink organdy collar and cuffs. It was outstanding. Everywhere she wore it she knew she was being admired so would do a little turn for them. People just wouldn't believe that I made her clothes but I've thought many times since that probably my sister-in-law contributed to my being an expert seamstress because of her criticism.

Vicki was sixteen months old when she got her first little brother, Lynn. She loved helping take care of him and would scold him when he cried. Luckily he was a good baby and didn't have the colic like she did.

I've always been sorry that she had to be neglected when Lynn was sick so much, three episodes of pneumonia before he was one year old, but she seemed to be very content. She would do things herself that others wanted to do for her.

When her Auntie Pat knitted her a little mauve-colored coat, with cable stitches that formed a princess A-line, I was very pleased. Pat went on to make her a red knit sweater top with flared attached skirt, dresses and jumpers, skirts, tops and even a little tam to match the coat. Vicki had the most darling wardrobe of any little girl we knew. She was three when she got the coat but I had it blocked and stretched each time I had it cleaned so she wore it through first grade. As she outgrew the little knitted clothes we gave them to her cousins who were younger.

The year that Vicki was three in April, her second little brother, Terry, was born in July. She always enjoyed her brothers and I can't remember her fighting with them like many children do.

That spring, while we were living on Turner Road, South of Lansing, she was standing on the axle of her baby doll buggy when it rolled out from under her and her head hit the cupboard doorknob. It cut a gash about an inch long in the back of her head. Blood was pouring when I called the Doctor to see what to do. He instructed me, over the phone, how to make a 'Butterfly Bandage' after I had cut the hair away from the gash. I did what he said and was glad that the scar was on her scalp and would not show. I was grateful that it wasn't on her pretty little face.

SONS-A-BITCHES

Our three-year-old daughter, Vicki, sometimes amazed us by her ability to absorb information and come up with some startling deductions.

She only had neighborhood boys to play with, all of them older than she was. She had to be lectured quite often about a current new word they had added to her vocabulary.

Her latest one was quite a shocker. I told her that it was such a bad word that even grown-up men didn't use it because if they called each other this word they were mad enough to fight.

The first time I knew about the new word she was singing it to her doll as she pushed her doll-buggy around the house. I stood, listening, a few minutes before I was positive that she was singing, "sons-a-bitches, sons-a-bitches, sons-a-bitches, sons-a-bitches".

Trying to sum it up so a three-year-old could understand it I said, "Honey, it's the worst word anyone could say".

A few weeks later she was visiting my mother who was determined that she get some of the same religious training that she taught her Sunday School Class.

Since it was Easter time, she told her the story of how Jesus was crucified on the cross. She vividly described, with emphasis, the very bad men who had done this terrible thing to Jesus.

After some minutes of absolute silence, with big tears in her expressive eyes, she looked up and said, "Grandma, they were sons-a-bitches weren't they?"

Shortly after that we moved to Viking Road to a Redi-Bilt house that had been put up on our lot. We finished it over the next few years.

Her Grandpa, Pop, gave her a dollhouse for Christmas when she was five. I thought it was too much for her age but he insisted that we let her play with it.

He had made it several years earlier for a client who had him construct several small buildings for a display in the window of her Real Estate Office. He told me that the woman had given him a Ford car, worth seven hundred dollars, for the schoolhouse he had done for her but she wouldn't take the house because she already had enough to fill her office window.

The little house had real glass windows with curtains, congoleum floors, individual little hand-made shingles and plant boxes at the windows with tiny little artificial flowers. It was furnished with little furniture that Pop had made. The roof lifted up from the front and was hinged at the back. There was an electric light bulb hanging inside but Pop agreed that the cord should be taken out because of the danger. She took such good care of it that it was in better shape than when she got it. We'd painted the outside, wallpapered the inside and made new curtains. Vicki absolutely loved that little dollhouse and was devastated when we had to give it away, when she was twelve, because we were moving into a smaller house with no room for it.

We gave it to her three girl cousins. I was sick when I saw it later, out-of-doors in their sandbox. I was relieved that Pop never saw it like that. He died when Vicki was six.

We were still living on Viking Road when Vicki fell out of a swing at The Ledges Park in Grand Ledge. It was the Fourth of July and we were visiting my parents with a family picnic. Vicki was standing up in the swing, I had just told her to sit down, when she fell face first on the ground. When she started to get up the swing board hit her in the back of her head. It didn't bleed but she was sick to her stomach immediately. We took her home and tried to call the Doctor. Because of the holiday he wasn't available so I called emergency at Sparrow Hospital. That Doctor said, "just keep her quiet, put cool compresses on her head and she'll be alright in a couple days".

On the next Sunday she was sitting in a child-size hammock when two little neighbor girls jumped in with her. The hammock broke and Vicki got up vomiting with such force that I took her to emergency. The young Doctor said, "I know how these young mothers are, they panic at everything. Just take her home and keep her quiet for a few days and she'll be all right". He told her to sit up on the examining table. When she did she vomited all over him, the Nurse standing behind him and the wall. He decided to keep her in the hospital for observation. This was during the years that Polio was rampant and every parent panicked when their children got the least bit sick.

By Tuesday they still hadn't decided what was wrong with Vicki, but were conducting Polio tests on her, when Terry got sick. I rushed him to the hospital and they put both of them in isolation. I was absolutely a wreck. My oldest and youngest were both terribly sick and the Doctors couldn't seem to find out what was wrong.

On Friday Ray and I were in Sears store, buying things to take to the children, when I got sick. He rushed me to the hospital where I got immediate attention.

It was determined within a few days that we all had Streptococcus Infection in our throats. It was not a well-known disease at the time and Doctors didn't know what to do about it. Penicillin was a new drug and it was given to Vicki and Terry. They were discharged from the hospital within a few days but I had to stay a week.

I was determined to find out how all three of us got infected with the 'Strep Bug', as the Doctors called it. We had everything, including our house, the well water and our outdoor toilet, checked. The tests didn't reveal anything that indicated that the Bug had come from our house. The Doctor said that Vicki must have picked it up somewhere and that Terry and I probably got it because our toothbrushes were standing next to each other in a glass by the sink. I threw those toothbrushes away and made sure that none of them were left out in the open or touched each other again.

Just before we got into our new house, Auntie Pat gave the kids a puppy for Christmas. It was a blond, honey, taffy colored Cocker Spaniel. She put him under the tree at Mother and Pop's house with a cute red ribbon around his neck. The kids named him 'Taffy'. He was adorable with his curly fur and cute ways. Even I, who never liked dogs, fell in love with him but we had to wait to bring him home until we moved into our new house.

After we moved to Norwood Drive, in 1950, Vicki did a lot of baby-sitting. She was proud of the money she earned at thirty five cents an hour. Sometimes, I thought, she spent it foolishly, like the time she paid nine dollars for a small leather purse because all the other girls had one. I gave her a hard time about it because I'd never spent that much for a purse in my whole life.

She had a girlfriend, Peggy, across the street who copied everything that Vicki did. If Vicki had a new dress, skirt or anything at all Peggy had to have one like it. Broomstick skirts and saddle shoes were popular. Vicki bought her own shoes but I made her several skirts of small pleated materiel that was sold by the inch. The next thing I knew here was Peggy with material for me to make her a skirt. I obliged that time but when her mother bought her a regular pleated skirt and sent it to me to be hemmed, I rebelled.

When Vicki was about fourteen, I made her a full-length winter coat. I'd made snowsuits and jackets for her and her brothers since they were babies. Her coat was green wool from materiel that I bought at the Eaton Rapids Woolen Mills. They sold blanket scraps of all sizes that I bought for winter clothes for years. She wasn't too happy with the coat but it was in style with what other girls were wearing and green had been the only scrap large enough to make a coat. From that time on I never made outer clothing for any of my kids.

We moved to St. Johns, in 1954, where we lived in a car dealership building that I converted into a nice livable apartment. Vicki's bedroom was in what had been a nice pine-paneled office. The safe for the business was in a hole in the floor in her room.

While we were moving it started to pour rain. I could hardly see the road. Vicki was with me in our Mercury and the boys and the dog, Taffy, were in a borrowed pickup truck with Ray. He was hauling a huge wooden wardrobe, that Pop had made years earlier, filled with my clothes and Vicki's. He also had our new 1952 console combination Television, Record Player and Radio, our first TV, in the back of the truck.

About halfway to St. Johns Vicki and I came upon a big pile of clothing in the middle of the lane on U.S. 27. I could see one of Vicki's dresses on the top of the pile. We stopped and walked, through the blinding rain, to it. I went into shock. Neither the boys nor the dog were anywhere to be seen. The TV was still on the truck bed but the wardrobe was in splinters all over the pavement and in the ditch. The truck was gone.

A police car pulled up behind me and was concerned immediately as to where the boys were. The last time we'd seen the truck the boys and the dog were in the back of the pick-up. We didn't realize that Ray had stopped before the rain became so intensified and put the boys and dog up front with him. What a relief. He had to drive several miles before he could make a turn around, on U.S. 27, to come back to where he had lost his load due to strong winds. We had almost forty dollars worth of dry cleaning done to get back to normal.

Vicki had her first, official, boyfriend while we lived in St.

197

Johns. She was sixteen when she went to Don's senior prom. I bought her a beautiful formal at a resale shop. It was the best I could do for her and nobody knew except her and me. She looked like a doll as they walked out the door. Don was a nice boy but ugly as sin as far as I was concerned. He worked at a Kroger store, where he'd been offered a training course which would eventually make him a manager, and he had an old car. They were in love.

So, when we moved to Albany, Georgia, in 1955, she didn't want to go. He wanted to marry her and keep her in Michigan. At sixteen there was no way I'd allow that but did make a deal with Don who was eighteen. I told him to "save your money, at least two hundred dollars, do something about a car and come to visit us in Georgia. Then, we'll see what happens".

Within two months he was in Georgia. I had told him he could stay two weeks 'for free' but after that he had to pay board and room. Milk was a dollar a gallon and he drank a whole one per day.

I had the boys chaperone them every minute. Vicki and Don got pretty sick of the boys' chaperoning them. Vicki got sick of Don but he wanted to stay longer than the two weeks I had promised him. He was running out of money so asked if he could stay if he found a job. I told him to try it so he got a job at Lykes Meat Packing Plant in Albany . He spent his first days' pay, in advance, for the shirt, pants, apron, gloves and boots, all white, that he had to wear on the job.

When he got home from his first day, his hands were still bleeding. The solution that he had to use to wash the baking pans had taken his warts off, and he hadn't had lunch. I sat on the bed beside him while he was looking at his poor hurting hands. I tried to console him as he cried and finally told him that if I were his mother I'd want him home. I also told him that I thought he should take advantage of the offer that the Kroger Store had made him. He left the next day. The romance had lost its bloom. That summer, when Vicki went to visit her Dad, she didn't resume the relationship.

Vicki, reluctantly, got used to the South and picked up the dialect right away. Within a few months she was answering with "yes Mam" and "yes Sir" which she had sworn she'd never do. She made a cute little Southern girl.

She got a job through the job training program in school and went to work for a lawyer part time. She learned quickly and was a big help to him, especially after he became a victim of Muscular Dystrophy. That experience came in handy later when she worked in New York City for attorneys.

I used Vicki's boss to get my divorce from Ray in 1956. She typed the paperwork and knew exactly what the terms were. I was supposed to get seven dollars per week per child but never collected a penny. My divorcing her Dad nearly broke Vicki's heart. He went back to Michigan. She, the boys and I stayed in Albany where all of them were in school.

She didn't date anybody particularly until I introduced her to a handsome Marine that I had met at a friend's wedding.

He, Dean, and another Marine invited themselves to my house by offering to buy the turkey and all the trimmings for Thanksgiving. My finances were very limited so I was delighted to cook for them and my family. We had a great time and they both continued to come to our house and bring food. They picked up pecans at the Marine Base and brought us over two hundred pounds that year. We had pecans in everything and gave lots of them away. They were lonely fellows and we liked both of them.

It was quite a surprise to me when Dean asked me if I would mind if he gave Vicki a watch for Christmas. She needed one badly to get from school to her job on time. I agreed, but with no strings attached. He gave her a beautiful watch that she treasured.

Ray came back at Christmas time and wanted to get remarried for his 'family's sake'. We remarried in February 1957 and two days later he said, "you should have known better". Our impaired family life resumed, temporarily.

Soon after they met Dean was asking to take Vicki to the movies, I still sent the boys along sometimes, and their love for each other developed. I could see it before my eyes but wasn't too worried because she was still in school and he was eight years older than she was. By the end of January he knew he was getting his 'orders' to be transferred out of the Marine Corps Supply Center in Albany to the Brooklyn Navy Yard. He got serious and started talking about getting married.

Again, she was too young and hadn't graduated from High School. I finally agreed that when he came back on leave, both had April birthdays, we'd talk about it and maybe, if they still felt the same way about each other, they could make plans. There was no doubt about it. They wanted to get married in June, a week after she graduated from Albany High School.

I had gotten in touch with a friend of mine, who raised flowers for local florists, in January because I suspected I might have a June wedding coming up. She started planning and planting flowers that would be ready in time. She already had pink and red roses, baby Gardenia plants, pink carnations and several kinds of white perennial flowers but had to plant gladiola and dahlias. She was determined to have what I needed for a church wedding.

I bought off-white satin, chiffon net and lace along with a size three pattern for her wedding dress. I worked on it weekends and after work for weeks. It had a sweetheart neckline bordered with tiny satin rosettes covered with a single lace rose, a bodice of lace and long sleeves with tiny buttons, a full skirt of satin with net overlay and filmy chiffon net over that. The hem was lined with horsehair braid. There was no train. I was pretty proud of the finished product but my heart sank when the front panel of the satin underskirt, which was cut on a bias as the pattern recommended, sagged in the middle. I lost some sleep before I figured out what to do with it. I pulled tiny little creases together, about an inch long, all over the front and sewed miniature satin ribbon bows on top. It turned out so well Vicki wanted to wear that part on the outside.

Before the wedding could come about Vicki had lost weight, she was down to eighty-nine pounds, so I had to alter the seams.

The veil was made of the filmy silk net to fit around a cluster of curls on the top of her head. She had worn her hair like that for months. I made a circlet of mother-of-pearl orange blossoms, bordered with individually cut lace roses hand-sewn completely around it.

The day of the wedding she came home from the beauty shop wearing her hair in a pageboy style that the girls in the beauty shop had talked her into. The cluster of curls was gone. I cried and remade the veil to fit the new hairdo. I had to remove my thimble to put on my gloves to go to the Candlelight Wedding Ceremony.

In between all the other things I had to do for the wedding, I made one bridesmaid's dress, all of the flower arrangements, corsages for the mothers and grandmothers, nosegays for the bridesmaids and Vicki's arm bouquet. I fastened a beautiful corsage to the end of her arm bouquet, for her to wear on their wedding trip. She forgot and threw the whole thing out to the waiting girls.

Dean had given me twenty-five dollars to pay for the flowers. I couldn't believe the amount of flowers that my friend gave me for that amount. It would have cost hundreds of dollars at the flower shop.

I arranged two huge baskets of white dahlias and gladiolas, flanked with candelabra trimmed in Ivy and white candles, for the altar of the church. The Bride's Table had a sectional flower holder filled with baby gardenias and pink carnations. Another table was decorated with unusual dahlias, half of a single petal was red and the other half was white, where the Wedding Cake and punch were later served. White candles and Ivy decorated the marble windowsills and a table in the vestibule had a huge blue basket of red roses at the end of a long white tablecloth where the Marines lay their hats, gloves and swords.

Dean's friends did a Color Guard for them after the ceremony. It was a beautiful show of affection and very impressive.

A friend, from the Marine Base made the all-white wedding cake, except for the tiny little Marine in dress blues and a bride doll wearing a dress that I made to match Vicki's gown. It was gorgeous.

I'm sure that I never did anything for Vicki that I enjoyed more than her wedding. It was my dream come true, along with hers.

They went for their honeymoon in Jacksonville, Florida,

back to Albany and then to Brooklyn, New York where Dean was stationed.

Ray and I were divorced the second time in March 1958. He went back to Michigan where he lived with his mother and brother, Max. The boys and I were alone. We all missed Vicki. We kept in touch with letters and an occasional telephone call.

Vicki and Dean lived in a basement apartment that she decorated with colorful slipcovers and curtains for the small windows. She had a flair for making cute things for her home, which she still has to this day.

Their entrance was in the back of an attached house. The lot was so small that the fellow who mowed the lawn had to stand on the outside of a hedge and lift the lawn mower over it in order to mow the small patch of lawn.

Vicki lost her first baby almost a year after they were married and was given a real hard time by her landlady. She thought she was too young to be married and blamed her being 'Southern', for that. She thought all Southern girls got married by the time they were twelve or thirteen and didn't believe that Vicki was nineteen.

For a long time after she lost the baby, Vicki was so depressed that Dean convinced me to come to visit them in Brooklyn.

I worked at a second job so was able to go that summer, 1958, by plane.

It was the first time I'd flown anywhere so was quite flustered when I got to Atlanta, from Albany and thought I'd missed my plane. I couldn't understand the southern drawl when they made the announcements.

Vicki had told me that she hadn't seen any flowers growing in Brooklyn. So, I was carrying a huge florist box, my friend had wrapped each flower in wet cotton and foil, a carry-on bag, my purse and wearing a big-brimmed hat. In the confusion I dropped the flower box, flowers went everywhere, I lost an earring and my hat got knocked off. When I arrived at their apartment, Vicki had about half a dozen vases filled with red roses all over the place. She forgot to tell me that they had come in bloom and the backyard was full of them.

202

When I got off the plane at LaGuardia, I thought the plane must have been hi-jacked because every face I could see was either Cuban or some dark-skinned person. They were fleeing to the United States by the planeload during those years.

Vicki's landlady was quite impressed with me but I was insulted when she said, "I hadn't expected to see such a well dressed and educated lady from the South". She thought she was paying me a compliment. I didn't tell her that I was educated in Michigan.

She had never been out of New York, seldom out of Brooklyn. When she said "I thought about getting tickets to an Art Show but decided not to because you might not appreciate Art". I told her " I won a scholarship in Art to the Chicago Art Institute in 1936". I didn't tell her that I won the scholarship while I was a senior at Eastern High School in Lansing, Michigan. She had some second thoughts about what she believed about 'Southerners'.

I was so proud of Vicki. She had become a real little homemaker. She had made Toreador pants for herself out of a pair of Dean's dress blues and fixed up their apartment real cute. Dean took time off and we rode the Staten Island Ferry, had a picnic lunch and spent a beautiful day. Vicki seemed to be cheerful when I left.

Vicki and Dean came home for Christmas that year. I had made matching jackets for them for Christmas of quilted red plaid, in a Mandarin style, with black trim. They were very pleased with her lounging jacket, to go with her Toreador pants, and his smoking jacket. They were so well finished inside, thanks to my sister-in-law, that they could be worn reversible.

Vicki told me that she wanted me to come to Brooklyn when her baby was to be born in May 1959. I made plans to arrive, by train, a few days after the baby was born so I could be of more help to her. I couldn't do anything for her while she was in hospital.

Jeffrey was born at St. Albans Hospital, the Naval Hospital, in Queens on Long Island, New York. Vicki didn't want him to have to say, "I was born in Brooklyn".

I met friends at the train station, leaving Albany, who were escorting a group of Boy Scouts to Washington, D.C. They were short one escort so I filled in. I had no trouble with twelve boys. I gave them the freedom of walking around and talking to each other, which some of the other escorts didn't, so we got along fine. I knew they couldn't get off the train until it stopped. By the time we got to Washington we were all buddies, especially after I spent the afternoon with them at a ball game that was in their schedule.

Vicki was home with her beautiful baby, my first Grandchild, when I arrived. He had loads of black hair, even some on his back. His eyes were big and brown. I loved every minute of helping Vicki take care of him and was sorry to go home. It is hard to describe the feeling of joy as I held my first Grandchild.

On the return trip, shortly after the plane took off from Atlanta, I could see that it appeared to be making a big circle. Soon the Captain's voice came on. He said, "we're having a little trouble on the dash".

'I thought My God-the dash, who does he think he's kidding... the dash is where he controls this darn thing!'. We we're heading back to Atlanta when he said, " This won't take long so please remain in your seats".

Two hours later we were still on the ground. I was supposed to be back to work the next day and was worried about a layover. When I asked, and was told that the next plane wasn't until 8:00 that night I went inside and bought a hundred thousand dollars in Life Insurance. I got back on the plane thinking that would take care of Lynn and Terry until they got on their own. They were going to be eighteen and sixteen their next birthdays.

Jeffrey was about ten months old when Vicki and Dean brought him to visit me in Albany. During this visit I got a chance to get acquainted with my first little grandson. He made us all laugh when he called 'birds' "boids". We teased Vicki about her little 'Brooklynite' baby even though he was born on Long Island.

When Dean had to go to Korea in 1958, on his second tour of duty there, Vicki went to Michigan for the eighteen months he was to be gone. She was about a month pregnant for Randy who was ten months old when his Dad got home.

I promised Dean that I would be with Vicki when Randy was born. He was a darling blue-eyed, blond-haired boy.

When Dean got back from his tour he was to be stationed at Cherry Point, North Carolina so on their way to that base, they stopped to visit me in Albany.

Jeffrey was two in May that year. We thought he was so cute in his little Rebel's hat and holding up his little hand, waving a confederate flag and saying, "Save your Confederate money. The South will rise again". Randy didn't talk but I taught him to whistle. He'd pucker up his lips and whistle until his own laughter cut his whistle short. Those were precious days for me.

I visited Vicki, Dean and the boys once while they were stationed at Cherry Point. Vicki had a good job at the Commissary and I thought all was well except that Dean was obsessed with becoming a Captain in the Marine Corps. He put several restrictions on Vicki. He thought that her association with certain ones of her friends might hinder him in reaching his goal. When he demanded that she not associate with them, she deeply resented it.

Shortly after they had gone to Cherry Point, I made my move to Bermuda.

I kept in touch with her by letter as often as possible and she always wrote right back. When I started missing her letters I got very concerned. I later learned that Dean had been having a neighbor woman take Vicki's letters, to me, out of her mailbox because he didn't want her to tell me what was going on.

Vicki finally realized, from my letters to her, that I wasn't getting hers. She mailed one from the Post Office, which put me into shock. I called and talked to Dean. I told him that because of the way he was treating her I would report him to his Commanding Officer. He knew that would end any aspirations he had for making Captain. And… he knew me well enough to know that I would do it! I got a long letter from Dean, apologizing and saying he'd never do it again. Of course, something had happened to their love but Vicki would not file for divorce.

After I had lived in Bermuda for four years, married John

and was living on Long Island, Vicki and her family came to visit us. We begged Vicki to live with us for the duration of another tour that Dean had to make. They went to the to the 1966 World's Fair and on to Michigan where Vicki and the boys stayed for another twelve months. On his return they were divorced. I felt badly because Dean was such a nice fellow. I looked on him as my third son. And he was the father of my first two Grandsons.

Soon after her divorce from Dean, Vicki married Rex. I felt like I had lost my daughter for the next four years. He brainwashed her in such a way that it was hard for me to accept what was happening to my smart little girl. She was a Legal Secretary among other things. I spent many sleepless nights worrying about her and the boys.

I was very relieved when she moved out and went to Florida, where she worked a few months and went back to Michigan where she married Ridge in 1972

Ridge was the owner of Owen's Barber Shop in Stockbridge, Michigan, inherited from his Grandfather. He provided well for Vicki, Jeff and Randy.

Both Vicki and Ridge's Dads built them a nice house near Stockbridge. In no time, Vicki had it looking like a charming Country home. Her homemaking instincts took over as she used her many talents to decorate every room.

Vicki had her third son, Ridgie, in 1974. I stayed with her about a month, helping her where I could. She had a beautiful, healthy baby boy and did a good job taking care of him.

She soon realized that commuting about forty miles each way to Lansing for her Legal Secretary job was too demanding. She took a job driving school bus intending that it be temporary until she found something nearer home. The 'temporary job' lasted over twenty years with her distaste for it growing by the day.

Ridge helped her convert their two car garage into a woodworking shop. She had every conceivable tool a person could need for her hobby of designing and making wooden toys. She made a Noah's Ark cradle complete with all the little hand-painted animals and a small Ark which made the cradle into a toy box, small tables and chairs, rocking horses and a double deck Fire Engine bed for Ridgie.

Her talent in thinking up these ideas, making patterns and actually finishing the huge variety she had was amazing to me. I knew she had artistic ability but I didn't realize that she was talented in so many ways. She made items of wood and painted them, articles of cloth sewn and painted or embroidered. Anything she saw once she could do, or make, with her own ideas to improve it. She sold many items but was not ready to quit her bus-driving job.

And then, one day she sawed into the main joint in her right thumb. The thumb was saved but the joint had to be removed. That put a damper on her woodworking days and eventually she quit entirely. She still has most of her heavy equipment with the thought that she might go back to it some day. All that time, she was still driving the bus.

In 1984 she opened a Fabric Shop which she named 'Odds n' Owens'. She carried all kinds and colors of quilt fabrics, crafts of every description and many sewing articles. She taught classes in her shop as well as at home. She really tried to make a go of it so she could get away from driving the School Bus.

She would leave the house, taking Ridgie, she took him with her from the time he was a tiny baby in a carrier, at 6:30 A.M., do her first run to the school. When she opened her business she would go to the shop a few hours in the morning until her noon run to take kindergartners home; then back to the shop for another couple hours; then back to the school to pick up the rest of the students and take them home and end up her day back at the shop. Luckily, she had a lady who worked in the shop while she kept her unusual hours. I thought her shop was a dream come true but worried about the fact that almost all of her customers were local and Stockbridge wasn't a very big town. Her customers loved her shop and many participated in her quilt-making classes at her house.

She kept this schedule for about five years when she finally realized that Stockbridge wasn't large enough to support a business like hers. She tried to negotiate for a bigger, already established shop, in Chelsea, but couldn't work it out so had to sell her stock of supplies and go out of business. Some of her customers cried as she closed her shop with a heavy heart. She couldn't sell everything so had shelves and shelves of materials, sewing items and crafts at home for years.

School bus driving had become a necessity during all those years because of the needed benefits but she still had dreams of doing something to get her away from it.

Ridge's days of barbering were behind him except for the pets. He could get more for cutting and trimming them than he could make on people. He set up a pet-trimming business in the basement complete with shower facilities for the animals. It turned out to be a lucrative sideline between the years of 1974 to 1984.

Family members kept him in practice for years, usually at no charge. He did about twenty haircuts a month at a Care Home for men where they were under Adult Foster Care Programs of one kind or another. Some were Veterans, some on Medicaid, others were State Wards but they all had to have haircuts.

During 1984-1986 Ridge got into and out of timber cutting and merchandising. He and his two brothers had a rough time making a living for three families so Ridge started on construction jobs.

Vicki and Ridge bought a one hundred-year-old, plus, home on Oakley Road just North of Stockbridge in 1992. It wasn't long before she had the place looking like something in a decorator's magazine.

She utilized my antique steamer trunk as a coffee table by wallpapering the surfaces between the brass trim. The antique lady's drum top oak desk, which I had stained green, and the seven foot tall Etagere with its black wood frame, shelves and legs with hand carved flowers, an inch in relief in some places, and its rose-pink counter with a scalloped edge in the decorating of her old-new home. I had given her these three pieces, over the years, so was pleased to give her my converted kerosene hanging-lamp for her dining room. It goes perfectly with her theme.

She took up stained glass as a hobby and made many beautiful pieces. She could have sold her first piece, consisting

208

of several kinds of fruit in a frame, for five hundred dollars but it hangs in her kitchen window.

She discovered that her Grandson, Jeffrey, was dyslexic and proceeded to learn how to teach dyslexic children. She took several courses and was able to help turn his life around. Because he had trouble reading, he thought he was dumb. He has pretty well mastered the problem and has done excellent work in school. During the time she was so concerned about Jeffrey she also learned that Ridgie, her son, was suffering from the same problem. He was helped a great deal too and finished his last years in High School with a much better attitude.

Vicki was not able to pursue getting a license to teach dyslexic children, partly because a lot of time was demanded and the work didn't pay enough to make a living. Both boys are grateful to her for helping them to overcome their problem.

Vicki decided to take College courses that would qualify her to be a Medical Transcriber.

While she was still driving the school bus and going to College at night, Ridge and the rest of the family took over the cooking and housekeeping. They worked it out on weekends while Vicki studied.

When she completed her classes, she found a job working for three Doctors. She was able to bring some of her work home. She quit her bus-driving job in 1993.

Vicki and Ridge became Grandparents when her grand daughter, McKenna, was born in 1995 to Ridgie and Donna.

McKenna is a pretty, tall and ambitious little girl with big brown eyes and a winning disposition. She has the face of an Angel with a determination of her own. Smart too. Her little brother, Coltyn, is two years younger and already weighs more than she does.

Ridge had been doing construction work for several years when he hurt his back and shoulder so badly that he couldn't work on heavy construction. He later had to have surgery on his back. I thought it unusual that the incision was on the front of his neck.

Somewhere along the line, while Ridge was doing the cooking, he got the idea of establishing an Adult Foster Care

Home similar to the one where he gave haircuts. He and Vicki talked for hours, days, weeks before they decided to try it. They made plans to build a new facility on the six acres where they lived on Oakley Road.

They were several weeks into their plans when the owner, of the one where Ridge cut hair, offered to sell them that place. It took a lot of decision-making before it was finalized but they went ahead and bought it. They became the owners of 'Elder Ridge Manor' in December 1995.

Vicki had to take courses, get permits and train staff for this undertaking. Ridge said he'd do the cooking and clean up the s--- if she would manage the place. They hired some family members and staff to run the place. All had to undergo required courses of training in how to handle the 'residents'.

The responsibility and care for twenty men is tremendous. All medications and home treatments are part of the job. They must be taken for Doctors appointments to Ann Arbor, Battle Creek or wherever they have to go for treatment. Some wind up in hospitals, then back to the Manor for home care, while others have to be sent to other facilities.

Vicki and Ridge bought a sixteen-passenger van in order to take groups of residents to the Doctors or wherever they need to go. They also used the van to take groups of their men on shopping tours to the Malls, ballgames and to the circus.

In 1998 they bought a summer home on Thousand Islands lake in the upper peninsula. They take several of their men, at a time, there so they can enjoy the lake, the fishing and scenery.

I couldn't be more proud than I am to be Vicki's mother. She has fulfilled my dreams of what a daughter should be and given me the pleasure of having a 'real live doll' for my very own … all these sixty years.

LYNN

Lynn was born in Lansing, Michigan. He became the fourth member of our family, which consisted of his dad, me and his sister, Vicki, who was sixteen months old.

He was a Breach baby and premature. Had he gone to full

term, the Doctor said he would probably have weighed over ten pounds. He had big boy-feet, blue eyes, practically no hair and a pointed head. I was scared that it would stay that way but the Doctor rubbed his hand over his head and said he'd have a beautifully shaped head. He did, within a few days. His head shaped up so nicely that it was one of the contributing factors to his becoming a handsome man.

When we brought him home, to our little house on Knollwood Avenue in Lansing, his Grandma Wilson was there to welcome him and stay for a few days to help out until I got on my feet.

Lynn seemed to have some trouble breathing at times but the Doctor said that was because he was premature and that he would be alright. He gained weight well and weighed fifteen pounds by the time he was three months old even though he had Pneumonia when he was two months old. The Doctor said that his bronchial tubes were weak and that was the cause of the Pneumonia. Within a few days he was fine.

We had fixed up our little rented house on Knollwood. We cleaned, painted inside, wallpapered the nursery, where Vicki shared her room with Lynn, and were pleased with the results.

When our landlord came to collect the December rent, he saw how nice the place looked and decided that his newly-married daughter would love it. He gave us notice on the spot. We had to get out by January 1st.

We were lucky to find a house on Turner Road, south of Lansing, and with help from some of our friends we moved.

During this time Lynn was whining but I thought it was because of all the confusion until he started having breathing problems. He couldn't breathe when I laid him down so I carried him over my shoulder for several days. I was completely exhausted from trying to take care of him and getting settled.

I called the Doctor who told me how to make a steam tent with a coffee pot. He seemed better after I put him in his room and set the electric coffee pot on a vanity bench. Suddenly I smelled smoke. It came from the nursery. The coffee pot had scorched a hole in the top of the bench and was smoldering. It was between Lynn and me. I knew that I had to get it out of my way to reach him so I pulled the plug, grabbed the bench and threw it out the window. When it hit the air it burst into flames, which were immediately put out on landing in the snow. Lynn would have suffocated in a few more minutes. I grabbed him, ran downstairs and dissolved in tears.

The following Sunday my parents came to visit the new baby and see our new house. My Dad took one look at me and told Mama that she should stay a few days and help me out. She complained that she hadn't brought any clothes with her and that she would miss church on Tuesday night. Dad said, "I don't think that will keep you out of Heaven". I loaned her some of my maternity clothes, which fit pretty well.

Lynn looked surprisingly good in spite of his breathing problems. His cheeks were pink and he smiled at everyone. Mama didn't think he was sick but his problem with breathing soon convinced her. She took a turn sitting up in bed, leaning against the headboard, while I tried to catch up on some sleep.

Suddenly she woke me and said, "He's stopped breathing". I shook him. He gasped, breathed a few breaths and stopped again. I ran to the phone and called the Doctor. He said to get him to the hospital as quickly as possible.

I woke Ray and we made a dash for the car. Just as we ran under the overhead garage door it unrolled and knocked both of us down. I managed to hold onto Lynn and we sped toward Sparrow Hospital. On the way, we had to take the ditch, for several feet, to avoid hitting a milk truck that had pulled out of a side road.

When we got to the hospital they had an incubator, with a tiny oxygen tent over it, ready for him. The nurses stripped him and turned everything on. Within seconds he turned from blue to pink and started breathing regularly. We cried.

We thought he was alright but he didn't improve even though I was bringing him breast milk every day. After six days I was really upset that he didn't seem to be getting better.

I spoke to the Doctor and he said that he didn't know what else to do unless he could give him blood transfusions. He knew that Ray was an RH Negative and that I had so many allergies that neither of us would be a good donor. We started asking

212

everyone in the family if they would donate. Several were tested before a match was found. Ray's sister matched. They made a small slit in the top of Lynn's foot and put the blood into his tiny vein. From the moment of the transfusion he began to show signs of improvement and we were able to take him home within a few days. Again, the Doctor said that his Bronchial Tubes were the problem.

Lynn bounced back quickly and by the time he was six months old he weighed 18 pounds 10 ounces. He was a good baby who seldom cried.

When he was eight months old he had Pneumonia again. I was so afraid that he would die that I had never left him and Vicki with a baby-sitter. It seemed like he was determined to beat his problems and survived his third bout with Pneumonia. I had had to wean him at five months when he was so sick but he thrived on his formula and weighed twenty three pounds at one year. As he grew, he became cuter every day and so roly-poly that we called him 'Punkin'.

At ten months he turned everything that anyone gave him in the opposite way it was handed to him and looked it over before he put it into his mouth. At nine months he would pucker up and blow a little whistle, then stop and laugh. At eleven months he crept by lying flat on his stomach and pulling with his arms and hands. He had seen his crippled Uncle Max get around like that. At fourteen months he climbed on top of the kitchen table and looked out the window. He didn't walk until he was fourteen months old.

I was concerned that he would never learn to talk out-loud because he whispered everything. I think that was because everyone whispered around him thinking that he would wake up when he was so sick. He would whisper, "Hi Daddy, What's dat? See da' snow, Where's Ray? and " It's cold" at fourteen months. This was so different from Vicki who had talked a blue streak at eight months and was making sentences of two or three words at one year. Again, I blamed it on his being sick so much.

When he was five there were no more traces of Bronchial trouble and he never had breathing problems from then on.

Vicki was three in April and Lynn was twenty-three months

old when Terry was born.

I had not been able to stand crying babies so when Mama came for a few days while I was in the hospital, I told her that she didn't have to listen to their crying unless they were hurt or sick. I could tell the difference and was sure she could.

We had a 'crying corner' so whichever one wanted to cry had to stand there until they stopped crying. She didn't know which corner it was so had shoved the big toy chest against the wall in that corner.

When Lynn started crying she sent him to the 'crying corner' and watched to see what he would do. He walked over to the toy chest, looked at it for a minute, and began throwing toys out of it until it was empty. Then he pulled the chest out of the corner, stood there a few minutes, shed some tears, turned around, pulled it back in place and piled all the toys in it. She thought he was such a smart kid for figuring that out.

Our family enjoyed our little stone house on Turner Road. We planted a garden and I did lots of canning... green beans, tomatoes and even tried to make chili sauce with jalapeno peppers. The juice burned my fingers so bad I had to be taken to the hospital and came out with both hands in ice bags. I'd found out another of my allergies.

I took a temporary job at Sears for the Christmas holidays when Lynn was sixteen months old. It was the first time I'd ever left him for more than a couple hours. I was pleasantly surprised at how well the children got along with our neighbor lady as a sitter.

After Christmas, our family went with my Uncle Leon and his family on a trip to Georgia to visit relatives. While on that trip, their son was sick most of the time while we were at Grandma Rachel's place.

Grandma asked me when I was expecting my third child but I was sure that I wasn't pregnant. Shortly after we got home we discovered that the boy's sickness was because of measles. Lynn had a few spots on his chest but Vicki had a bad case. They were in her hair, up her nose and on her whole body. It was confirmed that I was pregnant for Terry who was another premature Breach baby.

The Doctor said that "if you have a hundred they would all be Breach because of the fusion of the vertebrae in your lower spine".

Lynn was two when our landlord gave us notice to move. We couldn't believe that this had happened to us again. We had fixed up the rental place, bought used furniture which I had recovered and made drapes to match. Our friends called it a "doll house".

We felt lucky to find a company that built Redi-Bilt houses that they would erect, on your lot, within one day! We found a lot on Viking Road and went to the Loan Department at the Bank.

The first winter after we were in our house on Viking Road I had to hang the laundry in the attic. I begged Ray to nail down the boards I walked on because they tipped if I got too close to the ends.

Once I forgot and the board flipped up, hit me in the rear and dropped my legs through the ceiling. I was stuck. As I sat there, Lynn looked up at me and said, "Momma, you broke our new-new house". I had to laugh at the predicament I was in until I realized that I had to get myself out because all three of my babies were below me. I finally wiggled around enough that I could drop down. Luckily the couch was directly beneath me. The boards got nailed down and new wallboard put up.

When Lynn was two and a half, Terry was eight months old, I went back to work. First, at the Capitol building issuing Drinking Permits. World War II was on and this was not my idea of helping so I soon got a transfer to the State Office Building where I delivered mail throughout the entire building. Even though I was replacing a man who had gone into service, I was not satisfied that I was doing much to help the war effort.

During the years I was working we had a series of housekeepers, baby-sitters and even a live-in lady with her seven-year-old daughter. One woman, who represented herself as being middle aged, was in her seventies. When I found out that she was mistreating Vicki, she loved little boys, I tried to fire her but she wouldn't leave. I finally had to call the Sheriff who threatened to come and get her. I felt sorry for her but later learned that the references she gave had lied to get rid of her.

One young woman stole jewelry that she was wearing when I went to her house to ask her if she knew where it was.

Another one, who had a little girl, was trying to earn enough money to get her husband out of jail for getting two fourteen year old girls pregnant.

I was really upset by all this when my next door neighbor, the kids called her 'Aunt Blondie", offered to keep all three until I got the boys into the Day Care Center. It was sponsored by the War Department after I was hired at the War Plant. Vicki went to Pleasant Grove School and the boys went there, as they became old enough. 'Aunt Blondie' kept them until I got home from work.

THE BUTTERFLY

During World War II I worked at Fisher Body in the Parts Department, in Lansing Michigan, where the B-29 Nacelle, the part that holds the engine, was assembled My job was in the office where we kept records and issued parts, some 5,000 different ones, for the huge plane that played a very important part in the bombings over Germany.

My children were small so I worked out a system where my next door neighbor, Blondie, kept Vicki after school and I took Lynn and Terry to Nursery School in Lansing at Walter French Junior High School. The boys were four and two when we had the experience about the Butterfly.

I'm sure that I have described the differences between my two boys in some of the other stories I've shared but it was quite evident that the boys' characteristics were constructively developed during those two years at the Nursery School.

Terry had always been the most outgoing and, for want of another word, rambunctious while Lynn was more compliant. Both boys loved going to *school and* I felt secure in knowing that they were in good care.

It was quite a surprise to me when I was called at work to come and get my son who was causing a problem. All the way there, I was thinking, 'what in the world could Terry have done to make them call me'.

When the teacher met me at the door with Lynn at her side, I blurted, "you've got the wrong one". She looked at him, then at me, and said, "he is yours isn't he?" Of course, he was but I couldn't imagine him doing anything so drastic as to cause them to call me.

She said that he was causing a disturbance and wouldn't cooperate and asked me to step aside to tell me that she thought that he might be retarded.

I was flabbergasted and sick to me stomach. I tried not to cry as I took him to the car wondering how she had determined this. I thought of the comment I'd heard many times "the Mother is the last to know" about her children.

I went over in my mind the agonies of his first year when he had pneumonia three times. He was born with Bronchial problems but had recovered from all that and I was proud of his development as a profound thinker. He seemed to think over things, like the crying corner, before he did them even when he was two.

Lynn and I sat in the car a few minutes while I tried to get my wits together after the shock that my little boy might have a real problem.

It came to me that our pediatrician would know what to do. The Doctor took Lynn by the hand, after I had tearfully explained what the teacher had said, and took him in the examining room.

While I was waiting my mind was going crazy trying to figure out what happened. I couldn't think of anything that might have caused this problem to this sweet little boy with such a gentle disposition and personality of his own.

Even our family Doctor had assured me that the boys were just different. Lynn was quiet and reflective while Terry was outgoing and always busy doing whatever came to his mind. Our Doctor had warned me about trying to make the boys alike. "Just don't try to mold their personalities, their characters yes, but not their personalities". Had both of us missed some detail that would have been a clue?

When the Pediatrician brought Lynn to me, about an hour

217

later, he said, "What makes you think there is something wrong with this boy?". His tone of voice made me feel rebuked but I told him again what the teacher had said.

He got her on the phone and asked her what she was basing her opinion on. He practically roared as he said, "YOU MEAN TO TELL ME THAT YOU THINK THERE IS SOMETHING WRONG WITH HIM BECAUSE HE DOESN'T THINK HE'S A BUTTERFLY - WELL, YOUNG LADY, YOU'D BETTER GO BACK TO SCHOOL ... FURTHERMORE, I DON'T WANT TO EVER HEAR THAT YOU ARE DIAGNOSING CHILDREN WITHOUT A DEGREE IN PSYCHOLOGY. I am sending Lynn back to you and YOU WILL NOT MAKE AN ISSUE OF THE BUTTERFLY AGAIN".

When I took Lynn back, it was an embarrassed young lady who led him back into the Nursery. She tried to explain to me that when all the other children marched around the room waving their arms and singing, "I'm a little Butterfly" Lynn wouldn't do it. He went and sat on the floor and wouldn't cooperate. He knew that HE WASN'T A BUTTERFLY.

In March 1943, I was waiting for an interview at Fisher Body, where the B-29 Nacelle was being assembled, when I met Millie. We both were hired and became friends and have remained so for fifty-six years. My job was in the parts control office out in the plant.

The B-29 Nacelle, the part that held the engine, was assembled at Fisher Body.

When two of my three brothers, Howard and Leo, both Marines, came to the plant, I was very proud of them and myself for doing something that I thought would help them win the War.

The War Department sent military men, in full dress uniform, to the War Plants as a morale booster for the workers. It really did help.

After the War was over, our family went camping in several state parks during the kids 'growing-up' days. We would keep a trailer packed with a tent, that we bought used after a cow had mistakenly gotten trapped inside and tore one side of it out, which we repaired. We had a gas camp stove, lanterns, cots and everything we could leave outside from week to week.

On Friday nights after Ray got home from work we would finish packing and drive to Wilson State Park where we'd set-up after dark. Several times we went to the Upper Peninsula, where we visited Tahquamenon Falls twice, and various places depending on how many days off we had. The kids always loved to take bread or peanuts to feed the chipmunks.

They all enjoyed collecting 'rocks'. I called them 'stones' if they were rounded instead of jagged edges. We eventually had about a ton, which we gave away much later, when we moved from Michigan to Georgia in 1955.

During the summer of 1949 we camped near a field of wild blackberries. We picked and ate until we nearly burst. I got the idea that I could make blackberry jam so we went to town, bought some jars and sugar. I made dozens of pints of blackberry jam. It was delicious.

The day before Christmas Eve, Ray got sick. He heaved so hard that the small veins in his eyeballs burst.

I thought it was caused by the paint fumes from our doing so much painting on the beds that we had built for all three kids. We had made them of scraps of pine, painted them gray and covered the headboards with gray leather.

I had made cowboy/cowgirl outfits to help because our finances were so low that we couldn't buy them anything for Christmas. Ray had been laid-off a month earlier.

The kids hurried to bundle up and I drove Ray to Sparrow Hospital. I had to leave the kids in the car until someone from the family could pick them up. They weren't allowed in the Emergency Room.

The Doctors operated immediately but wouldn't take his appendix out because they had already ruptured and Peritonitis had set in. They filled him with blood plasma, inserted drainage tubes and sewed him up. The Doctor said, "if he lives, we will operate on him later".

In February 1950 Lynn was operated on for a ruptured appendix. The next day we kept Vicki packed in ice to keep her appendix from swelling any more than it already had. She didn't have hers out until much later.

I panicked. I questioned the Doctor about this siege of

appendicitis that our family was undergoing. I had had mine out when I was sixteen and Terry didn't show any symptoms at the time. He said that they had found lots of what appeared to be berry seeds inside the appendix and that was probably what caused the problem. My blackberry jam!!!! After that I usually made jelly.

Lynn recovered beautifully and only had a small scar to show for all his trouble.

Ray didn't do so well and had another recurrence in March. His appendix ruptured again. After he was fed lots of vitamins and foods to make him stronger, his appendix was removed.

He was off work a whole year and I was having a real struggle to make ends meet.

After the war I had done very well in Stanley Products and was a Unit Manager over seventeen dealers. There was no salary but commissions were very good until I, with all the worries at home, and all my dealers, lost the ability to maintain record sales within a few months. We had won several state championships, two trips to the home office in Springfield, Massachusetts and National recognition.

I knew that I had to do something to get us out of our financial difficulties so I went back to my salaried job at Wolverine Insurance Company. I had worked there before I was married. It was a good feeling to have a regular paycheck. I couldn't handle a year of no regular income for myself and none from Ray.

We finally decided to sell the house on Viking Road, in July 1950, to pay the hospital bills and get ourselves out of debt. After the sale we had nine-hundred dollars left to buy another house.

Ray and his nephew found a subdivision where new houses were being built and we could buy one for only five hundred dollars down. The drawback was that we couldn't get in for six weeks.

In the meantime, we made arrangements for Lynn and Terry to stay with my brother, George and his wife, and Vicki to stay with my sister, all in Grand Ledge. Ray and I stayed at his parents so we could get to work easier and because no one had room for all of us.

The six weeks turned out to be six months plus. It was difficult for all of us but we survived another setback and picked up our lives in our new home on Norwood Drive in February 1951.

We were thankful for family that understood and accepted what we could afford to pay for the children's support.

'Auntie Pat', Ray's oldest sister, gave the kids a Cocker Spaniel puppy for Christmas but we had no place to bring him 'home' until we got in our new house. When we did, in February, there was no lawn yet. When the snow didn't cover the ground, there was mud.

I was determined that the puppy, 'Taffy', would be trained 'to go' outdoors so the poor little guy was put out where he sank to his belly in snow or dragged it in mud. Because I insisted that he not bring all that mess into our new house, the kids would pick him up at the back door and put him in the shower, rinse and dry him before he set foot on the floor. He was so well trained that, for the nine years that we had him, he would not move from the rug at the back door, if his feet were wet, until somebody wiped them.

After the War, Ray drove truck for several years so was gone more than usual. He loved truck driving.

It finally got to the place where we had to do something. Our marriage and the children were suffering from his neglect.

He agreed to stay home more if we sold the house and invested in a gas station in St. Johns, Michigan. He had learned that the Drake's Gas Station on U.S. 27 was for lease so we sold our dream house on Norwood and moved.

The boys often teased me about making their bedroom in the oil-drum room. There was no smell from the empty oil drums but the boys knew they were there even though I had put up bamboo blinds as dividers.

It was in what had been an auto dealer's building, which included a four-bay car repair set-up with a gas station in front and offices that became our home. I had converted the whole place into quite nice living quarters for our family.

I was still working in Lansing and driving the twenty miles

to work every day, coming home and getting dinner, pumping gas until eleven and doing the books.

We had only lived at Drake's from June until October 1954 when the owners told Ray that we were not producing enough sales, of gasoline, to make it worthwhile to them. We were paying them a percentage. Ray had invested several hundred dollars in tools and equipment for the garage but it hadn't paid off either.

We had to move again. We found an old cement block house on Clinton Street in St. Johns.

Ray was really down in the dumps. I was still working in Lansing but he wanted out of St. Johns. There was no way that I could handle a move, higher rent and other expenses that it would take to move. Besides, I wanted the kids to finish that year in the St. Johns schools.

I was having a lot of back trouble and knew that the cold weather wasn't helping. So, when I got a letter from my sister-in-law, Peggy in Albany, Georgia, telling me that the warm sun would feel good on my back, I wished there was a way we could go there.

In a matter of days, after I wrote that Ray wasn't working and there was no way we could make such a drastic change, my brother, Jim, called and offered Ray a job. He would be supervisor of a crew of men who worked for him installing window awnings that he manufactured. I was thrilled but Ray balked. He finally decided to go ahead, in February 1955, while I stayed and worked until school was out in June.

Ray took our Mercury to Georgia and I got a ride to work with a neighbor. The kids and I made a go of it even when the furnace broke down, it got to forty degrees inside the house, my back continued to get worse and the house itself was a nightmare.

One evening, after the furnace was fixed, I asked Lynn to go put some more coal on the fire. A few days earlier I had injured my back further by lifting a shovel full of coal and throwing it in the furnace.

Lynn was watching Television. He ignored me until I told him the third time. He knew by the tone of my voice he'd better move. As he ambled across the floor in front of me I knew he was mad. When he got about ten feet away, he turned to me and said, "Why don't you ever do anything yourself?"

Before he got to the cellar stairs I grabbed him by the neck of his sweat shirt and yanked. I must have caught him off balance because he fell flat on his back. The wind was knocked out of him and he lay still. I stood there so shocked that I didn't know what to do. I thought, 'Oh, my God, I've killed him' but he stirred and blinked his eyes. I knew he'd be OK so I said, "Next time I ask you to do something you'd better do it!" He said, "Yes, Ma'm", got up, fixed the furnace and later told Vicki and Terry that they'd better listen because "Mom knows Jujitsu". I never told him that I didn't until he was grown up.

When school was out in June, Ray brought Jim's truck up to St. Johns to move us to Albany.

Vicki and I were going to fly but my sister decided to drive down. We visited my parents, near Toccoa, Georgia, for a few days. I hadn't seen them for over two years after they had moved from Grand Ledge to Atlanta and then to Albany, Georgia. The folks had moved to the mountains because Dad's eyesight had failed, a result of his diabetes, and it was too hot in Albany.

Both Mama and Dad had Diabetes by then but would not stay on any kind of diet. Instead, they would go to church and have their Brothers and Sisters pray for them to be healed. They were told, "if you had enough Faith you would throw away the Insulin and eat what you want".

They did just that and had already suffered through several crisis besides his blindness. Once was from burns that Dad got on his feet when Mama put the heating pad, that I had sent them, on high. His feet were always cold so she thought the higher the heat the better. She had called me, back while we still lived in Lansing on Norwood, and told me that Dad was having both feet amputated the next morning because of gangrene from the burns. I was crushed. I never dreamed that something I was trying to do to help them would cause such a horrible thing. Luckily, the Doctors decided to try one more medication and it worked!

Mama had gotten help and cleared much of the seven acres that she had bought from her brother. We enjoyed fresh vegetables and some wild plum jelly that she had made.

Arriving in Albany was quite a shock. Ray had found a house about two blocks from the High School where Vicki and Lynn would go and a few more blocks to Terry's school.

Our backyard fence separated us from one of the many black sections of town. The house had pine paneling throughout and an oil space heater in the hall for winter. We had sold some of our furniture before leaving St. Johns so had to buy a living room set and a few other pieces. We cleaned the place entirely and set up housekeeping.

Within days I had found a Doctor who recommended that I go to Atlanta, one hundred and seventy three miles away, to have back surgery after he had seen the x-rays of my spine.

Ray and the kids took me there, after he insisted on a side trip to see the Cyclorama, and I checked into Emory University Hospital. A spinal tap reaffirmed that I had had Spinal Meningitis and convinced the Doctors that surgery was not the answer. I wound up in a body brace from my collar bone to the bottom of my hips.

I objected when they tried to give me Morphine for the pain because I had had a severe re-action from it in Lansing years before. They tested me for Morphine and brought my chart in to show me that it was marked, in red letters an inch high, "NO MORPHINE'. I was in the hospital a week when I called Ray to come and get me. He hadn't notified anyone, not even my brother in Albany, that I was in the hospital so I had seen nor heard from anyone all week.

A few days later, I took the written exam for a job at the Marine Base. I passed it but couldn't pass the physical exam because of the back brace. About two months later I went to work at the base in the Transportation Department.

The kids started school in September. Lynn didn't like it from the start but he knew he had to go so made the best of it.

The assistant principal called me and said, "Lynn is getting involved with the wrong people". He named the boy who was supposed to be 'the bad influence'. I told him that I would talk to Lynn but that I usually let my children pick their friends unless they were really bad.

224

Lynn said, "Mom, don't you think that I can be a better influence on him that he can be a bad influence on me?". I agreed to let him try. The boy needed a friend and Lynn seemed to take Jerry under his wing.

Lynn started bringing him home with him. They went everywhere together. Jerry took Lynn home with him where Lynn saw the living conditions. Jerry's dad was an alcoholic, his mother was sick, they had a house full of kids and were on welfare. Lynn felt sorry for him and showed him that could have fun together in spite of his homelife.

I'm not sure how they got involved with the Civil Air Patrol (CAP). It wasn't long before they had uniforms and were attending meetings every week. They really enjoyed the group and the leadership of the Senior Officers of the Air Force Auxiliary.

Boys had to be fourteen to get in at that time so Terry felt very left out. In the meantime, Lynn and Jerry went on bivouacs, did marching exercises and had some good times.

As soon as Terry was fourteen, the boys got him into the CAP. From then on it was the prime source of activity in their teenage lives. They made friends with other boys in the Squadron and brought them to our house many times. Among them, besides Jerry, were John, Gary and Jim. They all called me 'Mom'.

Lynn made Major. He had worked his way up from Cadet, which inspired Terry to do the same. They turned out to be the only two brothers who made Major, during the same time, in the history of CAP.

When Lynn was promoted and an article in the paper read as follows:

"It isn't every day that a woman gets to kiss the Commander, but when he's only eighteen and your son, a lady can get away with it. Etta did just that recently. She has just reason to be proud of her sons. Lynn who came up through the ranks of the Civil Air Patrol, Albany Squadron, and was promoted to Cadet Commander of the patrol. Terry was promoted to lst Lieutenant. Lynn has been a Cadet for three years and has earned certificates of accomplishment in Survival, Search and Rescue and Summer

Encampments. He holds the Certificate of Proficiency, the highest award given to a Cadet. Terry holds the same certificates, except the Certificate of Proficiency and he's working on that. Terry is Supply Officer of the Squadron and is earning his Observer's Wings. With two years as a Cadet behind him, he says, "You can have your picture taken with me when I make Major, Mom". Lynn got a job at Mr. B's gas station when he was fifteen. Mr. B liked Lynn and let him work some very irregular hours, partly because of his CAP duties, after school and on Saturdays. Lynn learned to tear down a motor, rebuild and replace it among other jobs while working for Mr. B. Lynn and Mr.B shared a mutual admiration for each other that lasted a life time.

By the time Lynn was sixteen, his Dad and I were divorced, remarried and divorced again. After all the upheaval at home it was a wonder that Lynn, Vicki and Terry, kept their heads and carried on with their lives.

Because of all this, our little family, the four of us, had moved twice and were living in a duplex next door to my mother and Frank, her second husband.

Lynn used the 1940 Ford, that Mama gave me, to get to work at the gas station and I got a ride to the Marine Base.

He was leaving the house to go to work one day when I called home to make sure that Terry didn't miss his dental appointment. While talking to Terry, I heard a loud crash over the phone. I assumed that it was an airplane from Turner Air Force Base nearby. I told Terry to go see if he could see anything.

He came back to the phone and said, "Yep, Lynn's been in an accident". I felt faint but I hung on while Terry ran to the corner to see what happened. He reported that "Lynn's alright but there's a Negro lady bleeding all over the curb".

The Marine Sergeant sitting behind me said that even my ears turned white. He offered to take me home and we arrived before the police did. When one finally did arrive he started blaming Lynn until he saw the skid marks, the damage to the front of the other car and the back wheel of my Ford. My car had been hit so hard that it was turned around and was heading back where it came from. It was totaled because the axle was bent so badly and the car was too old for a replacement.

I reported the accident to my insurance company, as State Law required. The colored lady's head had hit the rear view mirror and required several stitches. A colored man drove that car. A white man owned it and there wasn't supposed to be anyone else in the car. I was out a car and there was nothing I could do.

Then I got a notice that I was being sued, two-hundred-fifty dollars, for damages to the other car. I called my insurance company again. They appointed a lawyer for me who counter-sued for four-hundred dollars as a total loss on my car. We went to court.

I could not say a word in court because I was not a witness. Mama was. She had seen the whole thing from her kitchen window as she was doing lunch dishes.

The attorney for the defendant told of the colored man's exemplary driving record and his good character.

The policeman testified that his car had slid over two hundred feet after impact and that he would have had to be speeding.

My attorney disproved the driving record by reciting twenty-eight charges of speeding, minor accidents and leaving the scene. When he questioned the colored man he said, "I didn't even see the boy, Lynn, because I was looking at a white woman at her mailbox".

The defendant's attorney then called on Mama as a witness. He started cross-examining her in a rude and callous way. He made the statement that "Lynn was scratching off" to which Mama very emphatically replied, "He was not!". The attorney said that he doubted that she knew what 'scratching off' meant. She said, "I do so know. It's standing still and starting off in a hurry". The audience twittered. She had responded as civilly as she could until he said, "I know how Grandmothers are. Even my own mother would lie a little bit if it was to help her Grandson". Mama took a deep breath and said, "well, your mother may be a liar but I'm not". The courtroom erupted in laughter and he threw up his hands. I won the case but never got any money. The other driver didn't own the car, had no driver's license or insurance and no money. Lynn's record stayed clean.

Lynn enlisted in the Air Force in 1958. Because of his years in CAP he had been selected to go to the Air Force Officer's Candidate Academy but there were no immediate openings. The enlistment officer told him that he would be notified when the time came. That time came but he was stationed in Germany. He was never notified. It embittered him towards the Air Force and he counted the days until he got out.

He left Albany in March 1959 and arrived in San Antonio, Texas for basic training. From there he was sent to the Tech School in Amarillo. By September he was stationed at Spangdalem Air Force Base in Germany. According to his recollections he was there for three years, four days and two hours, except for three months when he was on leave. He actually spent a total of four years and three months in the Air Force.

While stationed in Germany, he hitchhiked to Albany, on military planes and vehicles, when I was again scheduled for back surgery.

In February of 1960, I injured my spine again when I stepped in a ten-inch hole, with one foot, on the grounds near where I worked at Turner Air Force Base. I had transferred after having worked at the Marine Base for four years.

As it turned out, I did not have surgery but spent twenty-one days in traction in Phoebe Putney Hospital.

I was released just a few days before Lynn arrived in Albany. He had taken a bus from New York where he had missed Vicki by a few hours. She and her family had just left Brooklyn to drive down to Albany because of my problems. They didn't know he was coming.

Lynn's first job, after the military, was at a gas station on South Logan Street in Lansing, Michigan. From there he went to Mill Supplies Corporation in where he was hired in 1963. He began as a truck driver.

Lynn met Susan before he went in service but waited, until Susan was almost eighteen and he was almost twenty-six, to get married.

I teased him about his child-bride and told him that he would have to allow her time to grow up. They were married in June 1966. She surprised me, I thought she was too young, and made a good wife. She was the love of his life.

My one, and only grand daughter, Jennifer was born in September 1967. She was a beautiful baby with a ready smile but no hair.

When she was just fifteen months old, Lynn and Susan brought her to Long Island, New York to visit John and me. She was adorable in her little white fur coat and hat to match. Lynn made quite a production of taking off her hat to show me her red hair.

We had a Christmas tree that turned and played Christmas carols. Because the adults got tired of the ten selections, we pushed a little button on the floor that turned it off. Jennifer found the button but her little fingers weren't strong enough to make it work. She held on the arm of a chair, turned around and stepped on it with her heal. We thought she was a genius to figure that out.

I was not around my grandchildren very much because by the time they were born, all in the Lansing area. John, my second husband, and I were living in Albany. We had thought we would retire to Florida but my mother had a slight stroke so we settled there until she no longer needed us and moved back to Michigan. We made our move to Florida in 1972 so only were able to visit my family occasionally.

After John died in August 1983, I met Ben in 1986 through a Square Dance Club in north Georgia.

Lynn and Susan collected figurines of 'old couples'. They had several pairs but I saw an 'old couple' of dolls at the Fair in Hiawassee in August 1990. I suggested to Lynn that he buy them for their twenty-fifth anniversary gift the next year.

The dolls were about three feet tall made of bisque. A couple of local people made them. The husband poured the heads, hands and feet that included high brogans and rolled stockings on the old woman and high-top work shoes on the old man. His wife painted the faces and even showed veins in realistic looking hands. She also made the bodies that were stuffed cotton forms and made their clothes to the specifications of the buyers.

They both had snow-white hair and wore silver wedding bands, at Susan's request, and tiny eyeglasses. Susan selected a pretty pink for the sun bonnet and apron with a gray striped dress, which had tiny pink stripes of flowers running lengthwise for the Grandmother. The Grandfather's shirt matched the dress and his full length red underwear showed below his bibbed-overalls. A small farmer's straw hat sat on his white hair which was complimented by a white mustache. The workmanship was absolutely perfect so the price of four hundred fifty dollars was not too much for the pair. Susan will treasure them forever.

The next year, 1991, Lynn and Susan celebrated their Twenty Fifth Wedding Anniversary. Susan wore her original wedding gown. Lynn needed a little larger tux for the outdoor ceremony in the park in DeWitt. It was a beautiful ceremony with all their children participating.

Lynn had given Susan a ring out of a Cracker-Jack-Box, when they were dating, with a promise to give her a better one some day. He had a jeweler make an exact replica of that ring and surprised her with it on their Twenty Fifth Anniversary. It was a sensation for everyone as we shared their happiness.

The next day the four of us, Lynn, Susan, Ben and I, left for Hiawassee in preparation for a trip to Bermuda that we had planned for months.

I thought they should do something very special to celebrate this occasion and suggested they go to Bermuda. Because I had lived there for four years, and it was the Mecca for Honeymooners, it seemed perfect. They made it a condition that we go with them. At first we declined and our enthusiasm was dampened when Ben had to have surgery six weeks prior to the wedding. But when the time came, he was determined to go. We spent six days at the Princess Hotel and all had a wonderful time.

~~~~~~

Here's a quote from a note that Susan sent to us after the trip. To say 'Thank you' isn't much after all you did but hope you know how much it all meant to both of us. The 'dolls', which Lynn had given her, 'the money', our anniversary gift, 'seeing Bermuda with you' and especially for coming and sharing our day with us".

"I don't think we've come out of the clouds and gotten over the good times we had with both of you in Bermuda. It was because of you we all got to go and we're real glad. The memories will last a long long time. Take care and remember we love you both. Lynn and Susan".

~~~~~~

Their oldest son, Danny, married his high school sweetheart in 1989. We flew to Lansing for the wedding. It was a storybook wedding as Roxanne stood beside her handsome husband. Susan looked as pretty as the bride, in her long lavender chiffon dress with a ruffled train down the back. She looked like she just stepped out of an oil painting.

After Hurricane 'Hugo', the day before the wedding, we tried to make contact, from DeWitt, with the Disaster Team in Charleston so we could take food, or whatever they needed, to Ben's two daughters who lived there. We were told not to come because of downed trees, traffic jams and mass confusion. We were very concerned until we got word, after three days, that both daughters and their families had not been hit by the hurricane.

Danny and Roxanne became the parents of their first child, Casey, in December 1990. He is a darling little brown-eyed sandy-haired boy. He is quite shy most of the time.

Their second child, Megan, was born in July 1992. She is a beautiful child. She has curly strawberry-red hair and makes up for the talking that Casey doesn't do.

When she was about three, she was sitting on my lap and looking intensely at my face. She said, "Grandma, you're pretty". I was on cloud nine, I hadn't heard anything like that for a long long time, basking in her admiration when she said, "But Grandma, you're OLD". My cloud burst and we all had a good laugh.

Danny and Roxanne's third baby, Zachery, was born in

March 1995. He's a cutie with blue eyes and reddish/blond curls. He reminds me a lot of George, my brother when he was two.

Their last baby, Andrea, was born in January 1997. She is a living doll with rosy cheeks, bright blue eyes and red hair.

Every one of Danny and Roxanne's children are absolutely beautiful. If they grow up to be as handsome as their Dad and as pretty as their Mom they will be knockouts.

Danny always, from the time he was about three, wanted to be a policeman. He made that dream come true and is now a Michigan State Policeman stationed in Three Rivers.

Of course, all my grandchildren are gorgeous. Some will have to work on their personalities, as I did, but they have the makings of good people. I hope they don't try to 'get by' on their 'good looks'. I will be disappointed if all of them don't live up to their full potential.

~~~~~~

When my third husband, Ben, died in June 1994, all of my family came from Michigan and Ben's daughters came from South Carolina to the Memorial Service that I had for him in the Clubhouse at Lakeside Hills Estates in Lakeland, Florida. We lived there since moving from Hiawassee, Georgia in 1993.

At the Memorial Service, people were invited to make some remarks about Ben. One of my brothers told Ben's favorite story of his First Date. Ben could tell it with his southern drawl that kept your attention with every word he said.

His story went, "When I was sixteen I was sent to CCC camp in the northern part of South Carolina. I saw this real purty girl in town and asked her if I could come and see her. She told me where she lived and I walked out in the country to her house that very night. It was my first date.

We was a sittin' in the livin' room with her maw, her paw and her little sister jus' talkin'. Atter awhile her mother said she reckoned they'd all go to bed so all three went up stairs. I skooched over on the couch, next to that purty little gal and was about to put my arm around her neck when her little sister came to the top of the stairs and hollered, "Is Ben gone yet?". I said, "tell her yes". She told her and her sister hollered down, "Well, Momma said for you to pee in the yard 'cause the pot up here is full".

The people had a good laugh and that was the way Ben would have wanted. He always wanted to leave you laughing. I was ready to choke my brother.

~~~~~~

Lynn and Susan's third child was Mark, born in November 1971 on Thanksgiving Day. He was a cute curly dark-haired baby. He was a typical boy but not as large boned as Danny.

He had lots of problems with allergies that caused him to have to have shots when he was real young. I remember going with him, and Susan, one time when he was about three. He just walked up to the nurse, held up his little arm and smiled. She gave him his shot and a sucker and he walked away ready to go. Not even a whimper. I felt real bad that the little fellow had all those allergies, many of them handed down from me.

He, like Danny, was very active in Boy Scouts and only lacked his written report on his project to become an Eagle Scout when he quit. His special project was the procuring and supervising of the planting of dozens of trees along a section of new street within the city limits.

Mark has a daughter, Britney by his first marriage. Britney is a cute little blue-eyed blond. She has just entered Nursery School so will be spending less time at her Grandma Susan's where Mark lived until he married Brandi in June 1997.

~~~~~~

As the children were growing up, Lynn was progressing with Mill Supplies Corporation and eventually became Secretary/Treasurer. Only one step higher and the owner held that. Lynn eventually became tired of the hassle and talked about quitting.

When he told me of his frustrations, I told him that he

needed a hobby because all he had done for years was that job.

He got interested in community affairs after they had lived in DeWitt, Michigan for two years and was on the City Council for one term. Running for Mayor was next, where he won easily and was re-elected for four more terms. During his tenure, the city built a combination city hall-police station and a fire barn and established sewer, water and fire protection agreements with DeWitt Township.

During the winter of 1987-1988 he built a roll top desk for Susan. It has four drawers on each side, two pull-out shelves, the slatted roll top with compartments inside. It is made of oak. It was his first major project in woodworking but it turned out beautifully. He was not satisfied with it and wanted to do another desk some day.

Before he resigned as Mayor he was able to see the 1989 budget through, completion of the city fire barn, appoint a new fire chief and performed a wedding. I hadn't known that he could do that but as Mayor he had the power to perform weddings, like a justice of peace or a ship's Captain.

In an article in the Lansing State Journal, Greater Lansing news section, on June 21, 1989, he said, "after a period of time, you're just not as effective as you once were and it's time to change, and that time is here. The fact that it didn't come at election time is irrelevant to me".

When Lynn first became Mayor, he showed me his office and the city hall. One item that I never forgot was the 'holding facility' for prisoners. It was so simple that the prisoner just sat on the floor with wrist manacles fastened to the wall and leg irons fastened to the floor. They were usually there only long enough for someone to take them to the county jail. Of course, the new police station included a holding pen for prisoners.

During his years at Mill Supplies Lynn designed an insurance policy that gave employees many extra benefits, like dental and eye care, which the company accepted. He also set up the computer system, itemized, categorized and recorded stock flow for the thousands of machinery parts that Mill Supplies handled. He was in charge of all financial aspects for the firm. He looked forward to retirement and was eligible, with thirty years, at fifty-three.

In anticipation of that he and Susan bought my house on Dogwood Trail in Hiawassee. He and his family had been coming there for years on vacations, to visit me, and they loved it. It was located on Lake Chatuge with a view of the Blue Ridge Mountains.

The owner-president of Mills Supply died suddenly in 1994 so Lynn had to drastically change his plans. He, and two other men in the company, eventually bought the company and became owners in December 1995.

In the meantime, Lynn's family recognized a need for a place to go in the summer that was closer than the seven hundred miles to Hiawassee. They bought a house trailer and two lots on Hog Back Lake near LeRoy, Michigan.

Eventually, they bought two lots next door and built a beautiful house on one of them. Lynn made the remark to me, "I think I missed my calling. I should have been a carpenter because I love it so much".

During the years he was building the house, he took several courses and got his Contractor's license. He did his own plumbing and electricity as well as the construction. It was a complete surprise to me when he said he had the licenses needed and could do all those things. He said "I didn't want to tell you in case I didn't make it". I knew that he could do whatever he set his mind to do.

Susan, and the rest of the family, mostly Danny and Roxanne, helped him during the three summers of spare time that it took to build the house. Ben and I spent three weeks helping in the summer of 1993 when they were just starting and needed a stairway from the basement to the hall. Ben built it.

After Ben died, I had time on my hands and Lynn again started insisting that I write the many stories that I had told him, Vicki and Terry when they were small. Vicki had encouraged me too. Terry wasn't too enthused but did furnish me with the dates and statistics that I didn't have on him.

Vicki bought a used computer at the Stockbridge High School when they were replacing theirs. I acquired it but was concerned about having to buy a printer, a desk and supplies.

Lynn and Susan shipped the computer and a printer to me and replaced it with an updated one the next Christmas. Ben bought me a very nice computer desk.

After I married Harry, we began to spend our summers at his barn-house in Sherman, Michigan, near Mesick.

Harry and I were invited to Lynn and Susan's house on Hog Back Lake, before it was finished, many times the summer of 1996. Sometimes we would call them, or they would call us, and we'd meet in Cadillac for dinner.

Even though Harry had a crisis and nearly died, from Myasthenia Gravis, we met twenty two times during the summer of 1996 either in Sherman, Cadillac, at Hog Back Lake or DeWitt. And they came to Florida once.

Because of Harry's severe illness, and my brief collapse afterwards, Lynn and Susan called and offered to drive us to our home in Florida. They wanted to leave two weeks earlier than we had planned because of Lynn's work. We planned on leaving in the middle of October. We were very grateful that they offered to drive.

On October 11th they offered to come on up to Sherman to help us pack that night. We told them we had it all done and would drive to their house in DeWitt on Saturday, October 12th.

The next day, October 13th, the family all met at Terry's house on Columbia Road, Eaton Rapids for one last get-together before we went south for the winter.

Everybody brought something and a big dinner was in the making when Terry decided to take those that wanted to go for a ride in his Star Duster II. It was a small bi-plane with an open cockpit. A fun toy.

I had just taken pictures of Harry as he deplaned and was talking with Lynn and Terry when they both turned to me and said, in almost identical wording, "Mom, have we got time for one more?" I said, "I don't think so. The girls are getting ready to put dinner on the table now".

They looked at each other and I knew from the twinkle in their eyes that they were going. I turned to go back to the house when Terry turned around and said, "Mom, we'll just make it a short one".

With that, they boarded the plane and taxied to the end of the mile long airstrip. They had gotten as far as the opposite end of the strip and about two hundred feet in the air when the plane made a nose dive and burst into flames.

I had my back to it when Terry's next door neighbor, screamed, "somebody call 911". I turned around. I could see the flames reaching about thirty feet in the air just beyond some bushes approximately nine hundred feet away.

My heart froze. I knew that Lynn and Terry had been securely strapped in, because of the open cockpit, and could not have gotten out even if they survived the two hundred foot crash. I heard a woman screaming and screaming. I didn't know that it was me.

Corey, Terry's son, and Josh, his cousin ... my Great Grandson, saw the plane go down from where they were sitting on top of the playhouse-gym combination. They both came screaming to the house. I hugged them as Harry eased me into a chair. We were all crying. Corey thought that his dad was doing tricks. As soon as he realized that it was an accident, he went to his mother.

I was paralyzed with grief and couldn't stop crying. Both of my beautiful sons were dead in seconds.

For years I had tried to steel myself to the fact that something like this could happen to Terry, even though he'd been flying over thirty years and had trusted my life with him many times. I knew that he was an excellent pilot.

I couldn't believe my eyes. To have lost both boys at the same time was more than I thought I could bear

When Vicki realized what had happened, she ran to her Jeep and drove out to the field. She had been in the house helping get dinner. Susan was running and got about three-quarters of the way to the scene when Vicki came along and picked her up.

At first, Susan didn't know that Lynn was on the plane. Vicki and Susan ran as close to the plane as they could but had to stop because of the flames.

Vicki said "I could see Terry ... he was slumped over in the back seat ... but I couldn't see Lynn at all".

A neighbor, whose house was closer to the scene, had called

911 before Youlin, Terry's wife, did. Their son, a fireman, was visiting them and was already at the scene. He could not get near the plane even though he had put on his fireman's clothes. Vicki couldn't understand how a fireman could get there so soon and without a fire truck.

Susan collapsed at the scene and was carried away from it by Mark. When Vicki realized that I wasn't there, she drove back to the house and got Harry and me.

When I was finally able to get to the scene, I found Youlin and Corey on the grass clinging to each other. I joined them. All of us were in a state of shock. It was like a very bad nightmare that none of us could believe.

The fire trucks and ambulances came but could not get close enough to get, what they called, 'the remains' until the fire was entirely out and the area cooled down. There was absolutely nothing left of the plane but the metal frame.

Someone, probably at the hospital, retrieved Lynn's watch and money clip and Terry's billfold. The bodies were taken to Edward W. Sparrow Hospital, where they were both born, for autopsies and testing for alcohol and drugs. Neither of my boys drank or used drugs.

Lynn's son, Danny, viewed the body. He said there was nothing recognizable and he wished he hadn't seen him.

Both wives, Susan and Youlin, decided to have a double funeral at Tiffany's Funeral Home on Saginaw Street in Lansing. They each selected the casket they wanted for a 'Closed Casket' funeral. The accident was on Sunday, October 13, 1996, and the funeral was on Thursday, October17th.

There were about fifteen State Police from Danny's post in White Pidgeon, Michigan in attendance. They were on motorcycles, along with local police, at every intersection.

The funeral procession went to DeWitt Cemetery first, by the way of Airport Road and the west side of town passing the new Fire Station that Lynn had instigated. All of the men were in full uniform and saluted as the two hearses passed by the new fire station. I thought my heart would break as I watched them honoring Lynn.

There was a short ceremony at the gravesite in the DeWitt

Cemetery where we had to leave Lynn.

Most of the people followed the procession to the Dimondale Cemetery on the way to Eaton Rapids where a burial ceremony was held for Terry.

Harry and I left for Florida on Saturday, October 19th. I felt absolutely drained. I had lost both of my wonderful sons in such a tragic way. There was just no understanding it. Without Harry, I would have been completely lost.

A few weeks later, while we were in church at the Unitarian Universalist Fellowship in Lakeland, I came across this writing:

WE REMEMBER THEM

In the rising of the sun and in its going down,
    we remember them,
In the blowing of the wind and the chill of winter,
    we remember them,
In the opening of buds in the rebirth of spring,
    we remember them,
In the blueness of the sky and in warmth of summer,
    we remember them,
In the rustling of leaves and in the beauty of autumn,
    we remember them,
In the beginning of the year and when it ends,
    we remember them,
When we are weary and in need of strength,
    we remember them,
When we are lost and sick at heart,
    we remember them,
When we have joys we yearn to share,
    we remember them,
So long as we live, they too shall live,
    for they are now a part of us,
        as we remember them.

From Roland B. Gittlesohn

Susan let us know that there was going to be a ceremony at

the City Hall in DeWitt on May 21st, 1997. We were in Sherman, having left Florida in April, so it was easy for us to get there.

I wouldn't have wanted to miss it. Several dignitaries spoke and the new City Hall was dedicated to Lynn E. Thayer, former Mayor of DeWitt from 1980-1989. About eighty people attended. I said, "I always knew that Lynn was all the things you said. I just didn't know that so many other people knew it too".

Lynn's wife, Susan and his children, Jennifer, Danny and Mark and their grandchildren Jordan, Casey, Megan, Britney, Zachery, Justin and Andrea, who was born in January after the accident, and I, his mother, will always remember him as the wonderful son, husband, father and grandfather that he was. His many friends will not forget.

TERRY

Our Family, Ray, Etta, Vicki and Lynn lived on Turner Road, off Jolly Road, just south of Lansing, Michigan when Terry was born in July 1942. He was a Breach baby, as his sister and brother were. He had a bruise at the bridge of his nose and one ear was folded and lay flattened to his head. The Doctor said that his nose was broken but that it would be alright. It never caused any problems and shaped up nicely. I pressed my fingers on his ear until it no longer was folded. Terry was cute, with a well-shaped round head, dark slightly curly hair and a smile, almost from the day he was born. He was a good baby and seldom cried. He adapted to all kinds of circumstances and was a joy.

Within a month we were given notice to move because the owner had sold our rented house to a man who was going into the military and needed a place to leave his family.

We made arrangements to have a Redi-Bilt house put up on Viking Road just north of Jolly Road. We had many problems trying to make the house livable but Terry was a survivor and adapted very well.

The house was so cold that he was not allowed on the floor to learn to crawl or walk so he just learned right in his baby bed.

He would not go to sleep when Vicki and Lynn did because he seemed to be too wound up to lay down. We would hear him singing sometimes after everyone else had gone to bed. I was worried about his not sleeping and talking to himself in his little bed. The Doctor explained that some babies didn't require as much sleep as others do and thought I was lucky that he didn't cry all night just because he was awake. The Doctor told me that I should not try to make him like the other two. He was different.

When he was about three, his Grandpa, "Pop", had a stroke and was never able to move any part of his body, except his eyes, for the six months that he lived. Mother put a twin size bed in the living room so Pop wouldn't miss anything.

We went quite often to see him. Terry would climb up on the bed, in spite of his Aunts trying to stop him, and talk to Pop. None of us could understand what they were saying. Pop tried to make words that were indecipherable to the rest of us but Terry would 'talk' to him in words that none of us had ever heard. Pop's eyes would light up so we knew that they had something going on between them that was beautiful to see. Terry brought joy to his stricken Grandpa.

Many times, when he was about five, a little five-year-old neighbor girl who had a brain tumor that caused her to digress to an infant, ran down the hill to our house. I'd find her and Terry talking up a blue streak. I couldn't understand a word either of them said but after awhile she would wave, smile and run home. Whatever Terry had in the way of understanding and giving happiness to others, I was never able to find out. I thought it was remarkable and a gift.

While I worked at Wolverine Insurance Company, I had to have a baby-sitter for the children and tried several who had turned out to be unsatisfactory. Eventually my next door neighbor offered to keep Terry and Lynn during the day and let Vicki come to her house after school while I worked.

The children called her "Aunt Blondie". She told me that one-day, when Terry was about four, he knocked on her door. She cried when she saw what he had done. Not because he had his arms full of her first Parrot Tulips but because he looked so cute as he said, " Aunt Blondie I brung you some flowers". She took him in her arms and hugged him. I asked her how I would ever be able to teach him not to pick her flowers. She said that she showed him how pretty they looked in her yard and told him "I don't have any toys, just flowers". He started dragging his toys over to her house to share them with her.

During the War I worked at Fisher Body under a World War II contract for fifty dollars per week. The government paid one third, the state paid one third and I paid ten dollars a week for both of my boys so they could go to Day Care Nursery School at Walter French High School. Terry was two and Lynn was four. When the War ended that was the end of the Day Care Center.

When Terry was seven, his Dad and I built bunk beds for all three of the kids. We painted them gray and used gray leather on the headboards.

His Dad got so sick, we thought it was from the paint fumes' that I took him to the hospital. He had a ruptured appendix two days before Christmas in1949. He had to have emergency surgery but the Doctors wouldn't take it out because it was so full of peritonitis. They said, "it would be certain death if we did". They filled him with blood plasma and drains and operated the next March. He didn't work for a whole year.

It was that Christmas that I made tan cowboy shirts trimmed with maroon for all three. We made three sets of wrist gauntlets, and chaps for the boys, of maroon leather and I made a tan skirt for Vicki. Relatives bought cowboy hats, guns and holsters to make their outfits complete. They were so cute but looked so sad because their Dad was in the hospital for Christmas.

By the middle of 1950 I knew that I couldn't keep up with the payments on the house and pay the exorbitant hospital bills that Ray had incurred. We had to sell our house on Viking Road.

We felt lucky that we had nine hundred dollars left after paying off everything and even luckier when we found that we could have a house built with less than that as down payment. We had to wait a long six months for our house to be built.

~~~~~~

During the time that Terry was going to Windemere School,

I took a temporary job doing payroll for the teachers. I was on medical leave from my regular job since I had a back injury and was wearing a back brace.

I came out of the principal's office to collect payroll slips and stopped short when I saw Terry's third grade class marching down the hall to the music room. Terry was marching right along with the other kids but he was zigzagging from one side of the hall to the other and touching the wall each time. He didn't see me. I thought his teacher would straighten him out but she acted like she didn't see him.

While I was standing there, a young teacher came up and stood beside me. She started a conversation by asking me if I knew that boy. I just nodded my head. She proceeded to tell me that he was one of the worst kids in the school.

She seemed surprised that I had heard about his breaking a ceiling fixture the week before. I knew because I had paid for the fixture. The principal had told me that she had punished both boys who were tossing their helmet-type snow hats in the hall but Terry's hat was the one that broke the light.

The young teacher added, "my husband is a policeman. I have told him about this boy and he says that Terry is 'typical delinquent materiel'. "Well, I get him next year and I'm going to take that out of him".

I tried to control my temper as I said to her, "when you find out how to do that please let me know. His father and I have been trying to do that since he was born".

She turned several shades of red and said, "Oh I didn't know". I responded "we think that if all that energy is turned in the right direction he just might turn out to be a good and useful citizen" and turned on my heel and went back into the principal's office.

When I told the principal what had transpired she said, "I will personally see to it that she doesn't get him". Luckily the school was large enough that there was more than one fourth grade.

Fourth grade was a breeze for Terry but there probably was never a student who cleaned as many blackboards, beat as many erasers or ran as many teacher's errands as he did. I had told his new teacher that all she had to do was keep him busy to use up all that extra energy because he'd find something to do with it.

TO VISIT ROY ROGERS

It was spring vacation for school kids so Terry and Lynn planned a camping trip. Not together as they each had their own group of friends. They had permission to take a lunch. They were both experts in making peanut butter sandwiches. The rules were that they were not to go near the river and they had to be home by 4:30 when I got home from work.

My boys didn't have watches but some of the boys did. I trusted them to keep their word. They were ten and twelve. Terry was the youngest and was usually the leader of his group.

On this particular day Terry and Johnny, who lived up the hill on the street behind us, weren't taking anyone with them. That seemed a bit odd to me but Johnny was the new kid in the neighborhood, just having moved in the Willow Woods subdivision from Arizona, and Terry had taken a liking to him. They were still fixing their lunch when I left for work.

Lynn and his friends had already gone and Vicki had plans with her girl friend, Peggy, who lived across the street. I felt secure knowing they all had plans for the day.

It was when I got home at 4:30 that my world seemed to fall apart.

Terry and Johnny were not back yet. Vicki said they took lots of stuff with them but she hadn't paid too much attention to what it was. Both boys knew their limits as to where they were allowed to go and neither had ever broken the rules before.

Thoughts of kidnapping immediately filled my mind... or maybe they had gone to the river and fallen in. My mind went crazy with thoughts of terrible things that could have happened to them.

Just a week or so before two little children, four and five years old, had fallen in the river. It had taken days to find their bodies. Because of the spring thaw the river was high and the current strong. I could still see, in my mind, the newspaper pictures of the little boy and girl shoes that were found on the edge of the river.

Vicki was devastated but I assured her that it was not her fault; that Terry had mad his own decision about what he was going to do for the day.

We checked the neighborhood. Nobody had seen Terry and Johnny all day. I called Johnny's mother and she blamed me, saying that Terry was always the ringleader and had gotten Johnny in trouble before. That was the first I'd heard of that but I was too upset to question her about it right then.

Later I thought she was referring to the time that Terry and Johnny were tossing their snow helmets to each other in the hall at school. Terry threw his a little too high and broke a ceiling light. Both boys were punished at school but I had to pay for the light.

I called the Sheriff's office and told him the two boys were missing. He told me to call any friends or relatives that lived within twenty miles to see if possibly the boys had hiked to visit them.

I called my brothers and sister who lived in Grand Ledge, my Uncle Leon who lived just a few miles from us across the river and everyone I could think of. They all arrived shortly. Each had his or her own idea as to where the boys might be. Before long there were about seventy people gathered at our house. They searched the neighborhood but didn't find a trace.

While everybody was milling around, not knowing what to do, a neighbor came in with his little girl in tow. Faith was called 'Terry's girlfriend' because she usually went everywhere with him and the boys. She was a real cute little Tomboy.

Her Dad made her tell me, tearfully, that the boys had tried to get her to go with them to see Roy Rogers. They were going to hop the train and go to Arizona because Johnny knew that he lived on the ranch next to the one they had just moved from. She didn't want to go. Her Dad brought her to tell me what she knew.

I called the Sheriff with this information and he gave me the number to call the Railroad Police.

I thought my heart had stopped when the Railroad Police told me, "if they left at 8:30 this morning, they could be in

Chicago by now." We lived over two hundred miles away. He said "they probably climbed on the freight train when it stopped to take on water about a mile or so from your house". He tried to reassure me by saying "all little boys try running away from home at least once in their life".

It seemed like forever before the Railroad Police called back to say that they had checked every stop between our house and Chicago. Nobody had seen the little boys.

I guess the Sheriff thought he had done his duty when he turned it over to the Railroad Police and got in touch with Terry's Dad and told him to get home. Ray was on his truck route. I had no idea where.

The hours dragged by and some of the people began to leave. No one offered to help search further for the boys that night. I was too scared to leave the house in case somebody found them and called.

At 11:20, I'll never forget the time, the doorbell rang and there stood Terry. I grabbed and hugged him, dirt and all, until he was squirming to get away. He was covered from head to foot with soot. His face was so black and his eyes so white that he looked like little colored boy.

They really had tried to hop the freight train but it started moving too fast. They had walked about fifteen miles thinking the train would stop again. The Railroad Police confirmed the distance when we learned of some of the places the boys saw before they turned back. When the train didn't stop they turned around and headed home. They had eaten some of the canned goods they had taken with them and carried the rest back with them. All their water was gone and Terry was exhausted.

He had worn two jackets and two pairs of jeans plus his other clothes. He had stuffed canned goods and everything he could think of inside his jacket. His pockets were loaded so he must have been relieved from carrying all the things. We found them under his window the next morning.

He saw all the cars in front of the house and went around to his back bedroom window. It was locked so he had to come to the front door.

I took him to the bathroom and helped him get out of his

filthy clothes and into the shower. I fixed him some soup and hovered over him until he nearly went to sleep at the table. He slept very late the next day.

That was the only time I remember that his Dad ever did anything to discipline him. He did give him a good talking to. He sat on the front steps with him the next day and said, "See the thirty foot sidewalk from here to the street? Well, it would take all the cans you could put on it for you to have enough to eat to get to Arizona." Terry was impressed.

Needless to say, Johnny's mother was mad at me. She didn't call or come around to help look for the boys as we scoured the neighborhood. She had nothing more to say about Terry when I told her that he didn't know where Roy Rogers lived until Johnny told him.

There were several people, who had various ideas as to how Terry should be punished, including my Uncle Leon who said, "I'd beat hell out of him".

I felt that Terry had been punished enough. He would never do that again but I knew he would think of something else.

With him there were no dull moments. He was the one who kept things going. No matter how hard I tried he was the one that kept my on my toes. I never knew what he would do next. He was not a mean child…just a very busy one.

And now, over fifty years later, I can still say that we were never a dull family.

~~~~~~

After four years, we had to sell our little house on Norwood, mostly because Ray was gone most of the time. He was back driving truck after the War and seemed to love it more than ever.

There was nothing else that he wanted to do except possibly own a gas station. He heard about a Drake's gas station that was part of a car dealership building where they were looking for new management. That was his heart's desire so we sold our house and moved to St. Johns, Michigan.

The children adapted to living in the building, that had once been a car dealer's place with the gas station attached, that I had converted into a nice apartment. It was clean and livable but some different than the new house they had moved from. We were only there from June until October when the owners told us they wanted us to move because the gas station was not productive enough.

It could have been but Ray was not a businessman. He would let his friends use the four-car garage and all of his equipment, including the pits and hydraulic equipment, to fix their own cars... free. He made a lot of friends who liked to hang-out and talk.

I was working at an insurance company in Lansing so we managed but had to move into an old house on Clinton Street in St. Johns so the kids could continue in school. None of us liked St. Johns so when my brother offered Ray a job in Albany, Georgia he took it and drove to Georgia in February 1955. The rest of us stayed in St. Johns until school was out in June.

During that time I was still working in Lansing and felt that Vicki, Lynn and Terry were old enough to stay by themselves after school.

~~~~~~

When I got home from work one day, Vicki was crying her heart out. I tried to find out what was wrong but a police car drove up about that time and my attention was diverted when they came to our door. They wanted to see Terry. He was upstairs and refused to come down.

One of the policemen called up to him and said, "Do you want to tell your mother what you did or should we?".

Terry came slowly down stairs. His eyes were almost swollen shut from crying. He sat on the sofa and I put my arm around him. The policeman kept urging him to tell me. By then I was crying too. Vicki didn't know what was wrong but she was feeling sorry for Terry.

He finally blurted out "I stole a car". I was dumfounded. How could my little eleven year-old boy steal a car? He couldn't drive. My mind was going crazy when the policeman said to Terry, "tell your Mom what kind of car it was and where you got

248

it".

I didn't know whether to laugh or cry again when he sobbed, "it was just a little one from the Dime Store".

I knew that this was serious and Terry had to learn a lesson from it. I told the police that I would see to it that Terry paid for the car and apologized to the storeowner who had called the police. When I did, the man said that he had had so much petty thievery that he was trying to put a stop to it before it put him out of business. He also commended me for making Terry face him. He said most mothers refused to believe him and that those boys were still stealing. I was glad that he caught Terry in his first, and last, attempt to take something that didn't belong to him.

~~~~~~

When school was out for the summer of 1955, we moved to Albany. Ray drove my brother Jim's truck up to haul our furniture back. He took the boys and our dog, Taffy, with him. Vicki and I planned on flying down until my sister, Lela, showed up at our house in St. Johns on the Saturday before we were to leave for Georgia. As it turned out, Lela drove her car and took Vicki and me.

When we arrived in Albany, we were quite surprised to see that Ray had rented a house, with only a fence between us and the black section of town.

Within ten days after Lela left I wound up in Emory University Hospital in Atlanta, because of a back injury that I had suffered since November while shoveling coal into the furnace in St. Johns.

On the way home from the hospital Ray told me that he wished he had never come to Georgia. He hated it, his job and being away from his family. There was no way, financially, we could turn around and go back so we decided to stay and work it out. When I was able to get out of the back brace and pass the physical, I went to work at the Marine Base.

The kids enrolled in school but had some problems because the other kids didn't speak the same language, it seemed to them. Some called them 'Nigger Lovers' because they didn't refuse to participate in sports and activities where blacks were involved. The white students would act like the blacks were dirty and the girls would not touch hands for games. It was rough on Terry, Lynn and Vicki because they were not used to that kind of attitude. Terry adjusted to the Junior High School situation quite well and made several boy friends.

Lynn became involved in the Civil Air Patrol (CAP). He had been a member quite awhile when Terry became interested. The boys had to be at least fourteen years old and go through some strict training to become a member of CAP. They had to have uniforms, similar to the Air Force khakis, and learn to salute their officers. They went on bivouacs, search and rescue parties and marched in parades. They learned First Aid, survival in swamp areas and to discipline themselves. They both made Major in the Civil Air Patrol. Terry made Major when he was seventeen.. When they became officers they were issued 'dress uniforms' like the military in the Air Force.

Going back to 1955 - Terry's Dad went back to Michigan only six months after we moved to Georgia-----I'm sure the changes in his home life were hard on Terry but he never complained. He just didn't understand it. As far as he knew, his parents had a good marriage. At least, it had not affected him until his Dad left two days before Christmas in 1955. Ray gave both boys an identification bracelet with his name in it so "they wouldn't forget their Dad".

~~~~~~

I divorced Ray, the first time, in March 1956. The three kids and I moved into a duplex on Cleveland Street in Albany and I took a second job working nights at Phoebe Putney Hospital to supplement my income from the Marine Base.

The children and I lived in a duplex until the building was condemned. There was scalding water in the toilet tank and on the wrong side in the sinks; the roof leaked and the wiring was so mixed up that when we pushed the light switch in the living room the light in the bathroom would go on.

The fire department condemned the duplex after the

neighbors saw steam coming above the housetop and called the fire department thinking that there was a fire. The Fire Chief said he'd never seen so many gross violations.

While we were in the process of moving, to another duplex on Gordon Avenue, my Dad became so ill that Mama called Jim, Peg and me to come to Toccoa.

The kids finished packing and, with the help of some of my friends from the Marine Base, moved everything to Gordon Avenue. They had all the furniture placed the pictures on the walls and the dishes in the cupboards when I got home from Dad's funeral in September 1956. Our neighbors thought that three teenagers had moved in without parents. I was so proud that they showed such responsibility and seemed glad to do it.

At Christmas time that year, Ray came back. He said, "all I want is my family, this family". I decided to give him another chance and we remarried in February after he made one more trip back to Michigan. Two days after our wedding he said, "you should have known better". I was crushed.

I'm sure that all of our turmoil affected the kids and Terry in particular. He became very self contained and would never return my message when I told him that 'I loved him'. It was as if he knew that the word 'love' didn't mean anything. I was never able to get him to say that 'word' but he did things for me, bought me gifts and treated like he really cared. He just wouldn't commit himself verbally.

SOCIETY AVENUE

Terry and some of his friends, John, Gary, Jim and a couple others cleaned five truckloads of trash out of the basement on Society Avenue. Former tenants had tossed all their trash down the stairs instead of taking it outside.

The boys made themselves a Club Room in the stone house where I had moved while Terry was in Michigan that summer with his Dad.

They pooled their money and bought an old commercial size pool table. They had to have a couple of black men, with a truck using a winch, to get the table into the basement. When I saw it

251

I couldn't see why they wasted their money.

They had transformed the basement into a 'neat' clubroom. They had scrounged furniture, lamps, carpet and an old refrigerator. They had some good times down there, playing cards, talking and sharing dreams of conquering the world.

They had also pitched in and bought a Ham Radio. They put the antenna on the roof and the operating apparatus in the attic. It was great to know that my boys, all of them, would rather be at my house than anywhere.

Terry was helping me paint some inside walls a pretty soft shade of green when something happened to the reception on the Ham Radio. Some of the boys were operating it while Terry painted. Terry climbed up on the slate roof to fix it. When he started down he couldn't grasp the slate shingles and slid all the way to the ground. He landed on his elbow and back in a pile of stones.

His right elbow came out of joint. He stood up, ashen faced, in agony. His arm was grotesquely out of place. We took him to the hospital where the Emergency Room Doctor told me to wait outside.

When I walked into the waiting room, there sat all of my 'boys'. They had used their Ham Radio to contact those not at our house and told them to get to the hospital because they thought Terry might need blood. I burst into tears.

While they were comforting me, a young fellow who worked in ER came up to me and said, " I've never seen Gangrene before". He thought the green paint was Gangrene. We couldn't help laughing. The poor boy didn't know what he had said that was funny.

Terry told me later that the Doctor put his foot in his armpit and pulled on his hand. The elbow slurped into place and he came out of ER with a cast from his shoulder to his hand. He wore it for the first six weeks of his Senior year. One small bone protruded from his elbow but he never complained about. It caused him no pain.

All the boys had plans as to what they were going to do after graduation. None of their parents could afford college. Terry decided that he would go back to Michigan and enlist in the Air

Force. Instead he enlisted in the Michigan National Air Guard.

All of his friends had been in Civil Air Patrol in Albany with him but none of them wanted to pursue a career in flying. He knew he'd have to work his way into flying and the Air Guard was a start.

When he told me his decision, I decided to take Peggy and Will up on their invitation to go to Bermuda and started making plans to leave at the end of my lease. Terry left for Michigan on Friday and I left on Sunday for Bermuda in August 1961.

~~~~~~

It was sometime around then that Terry started going to the Albany airport every weekend and working, for next to nothing, just to be around the planes. Some of the owners would let him wash their planes, gas them up and clean the interiors. I checked with the airport manager who said, "Terry is no trouble, the owners like him and I think it is good for him to have such an interest in planes". He got to know men who would take him up and eventually learned to fly.

He joined the Civil Air Patrol in 1956 and very often went on Search and Rescue Missions and later escorted Cadets on Bivouacs to Alabama, Mississippi and other places. He knew that he wanted to be a pilot but also knew that I couldn't afford the lessons he would need to accomplish that. He worked and earned his way during his second try at being a senior.

Lynn enlisted in the Air Force so Terry and I moved into a new house trailer near the Air Force base. Terry loved having his own bedroom and bath.

We got along well and were happy there until I stepped into an eighteen-inch hole at the Base and injured my back. I was in traction for twenty days and never worried once about Terry. I knew that he was capable of taking care of himself and I trusted him.

Terry apparently had missed a lot of school, no one ever notified me, and failed his senior year. He was a good student, only having to read something once and he knew it, but he had too few hours in to graduate.

I was sick at heart when he went to Michigan that summer. He got a job doing some menial work, which he hated. Maybe that's why he came back when I wrote and told him that I wanted him back with me but he was going to have to work, buy his own clothes and earn his spending money. I would furnish him a home and meals. He came and I was over-joyed. I knew that I was being tough but I knew that he had to grow up and take responsibility for himself. I could not and would not do it forever.

His CAP uniform shirts had to have three pleats in the back and it was part of the High School dress code at the time, by choice, to have creases in their blue jeans. I refused to do it for him so he figured out a way to get it done. It was good training for him and he always dressed fastidiously from then on.

When he came back from Michigan, he started his second round as a senior and got a job at a dry cleaners so he would have some spending money and get his shirts and his jeans cleaned pressed and pleated.

He continued going to the airport near Albany, Georgia on Sundays and any spare time that he could while going to school full time.

They were always pulling jokes on me. It was all in fun and I got a kick out of it too except for the time they put a red light bulb by the entrance to the basement which faced a well traveled alley. Nobody ever stopped and I didn't know what they had done until I noticed cars slowing down as they went by. I asked the boys what was going on. They thought it was very funny until I told them what that red light bulb could do to my reputation. It was hastily replaced.

During this time I had my heart broken by my fiancee who had embezzled money from the insurance company he worked for. That made me want to break the lease but the owner wouldn't allow it.

Terry kept his job, went to school, worked at the airport and stayed busy for the remainder of the ten months I had on my lease. I knew that he was sacrificing his summer in Michigan for me and I really appreciated it.

I bought a little English Ford but Terry was embarrassed to

ride in it. It was transportation for me. His friends liked the little car and his friend, John, would trade cars with me, for the day, every once in awhile. He had a convertible but didn't have a driver's license so Terry always drove when they were together. Terry wound up driving the Air Force Blue, painted with a spray can, English Ford with the steering wheel on the right side. He finally got to like it and the attention it drew. He bought it from me and sold it when he went to Michigan for fifty dollars more than he paid me for it.

On Baccalaureate Day, the boys took the little car for a long drive in the country. They got stuck and had to actually lift the car out of the mud. They were almost late to the ceremony. John, always my favorite, called me recently from Albany and related some of the fun times the boys had. They were stopped by the police once for having thirteen boys in the little car. How, I'll never know. Terry's friends called me "Mom". They were always welcome at our house.

My lease on Society Avenue was up August 1961. Terry stayed with me until then. We both had plans to leave Albany at the same time. He went to Michigan. I went to Bermuda to live with Air Force friends, who were stationed there, and find a job.

I had been divorced from Ray for eight years, and survived a traumatic experience, when I met John on a Christmas Cruise from Bermuda. We were married eighteen years, from March 1965 until he died in August1983.

He saw many of Terry's qualities as he worked his way up the ladder. John was very proud of my boys and told several people that he wished he had sons as capable and responsible as they were. He even thought that I had something to do with that.

Terry transferred to Lansing, Michigan as a CAP Major, He was the only one in Michigan at that time. He joined the Senior CAP Program in 1962 where he became Captain, the highest rank in CAP, and was Squadron Commander in Lansing and Grand Rapids, Michigan.

During that summer in Grand Rapids he learned to fly a Glider. He got his Pilot's License in 1963 and later got a Commercial Pilot's License, as well as Glider and Instrument Pilot's licenses. He became an Advanced and Instrument Ground

Instructor and taught Aviation Technology at Lansing Community College from March 1976 until June 1978. His dream was crushed when he failed the eye exam.

He went on many Search and Rescue Missions out of Lansing. One of those was to hunt for his cousin, Dick, who was the pilot of a small plane that crossed Lake Michigan to Milwaukee, Wisconsin in the summer of 1968. Dick did not file a return flight plan and went down somewhere over the lake on the way back. After weeks of searching, no traces were found of Dick or his three passengers.

Between them fourteen children were left without parents. Dick had seven children, the couple had four and the other man had three. Dick's wife had a nervous break down and had to go on welfare. Insurance companies would not settle for seven years because they claimed that there was no evidence that the plane had gone down. Nothing has ever been found. In 1969 this accident was recorded in the book of 'Plane Crashes and Ships Sunk in the Great Lakes'.

Terry got his Instructor Rating and taught Aviation at Lansing Community College and was an instructor for three years. Lynn, his brother, took those classes and got his Pilot's license but never used it like Terry did.

~~~~~~

To get back into sequence to when Terry first went to Michigan... His first, what he called 'real', job was with Domestic Finance during 1961 and 1962. He quit when he had to repossess a baby crib and furniture financed by them.

He went to Pioneer Finance of Kalamazoo as Assistant Manager where he worked from 1963 until 1967.

He worked for the Credit Counseling Center from 1967 to 1975 as Counselor, Branch Manager and as Training Manager with offices in Lansing, Flint, Grand Rapids, Detroit and Royal Oak.

It was while working in Detroit that he met Paulette who had two sons. After they had been married a year, Terry adopted her two boys.

In 1975 he moved his family to Lansing and opened up Financial Counseling Service Inc., as owner, with an office on West Saginaw Street. He reverted to Proprietorship in 1982.

Terry bought his first, and only, house on Columbia Highway, Eaton Rapids, Michigan on an airstrip in 1978. He built a hanger and bought his first plane, a Luscombe 8F in 1980. He upgraded to a 1960 four passenger Bonanza in 1986. In 1989 he bought a 1967 five passenger Bonanza. He used that for trips to Albany, Georgia, to Largo, Florida and to Hiawassee, Georgia when I was living in those places and for business trips

He was very successful in helping families to control their spending, setting up budgets and paying off their bills. He had seen too much mishandling of funds by families while he was a bill collector.

Many of his clients were employees of the State; General Motors and others with good incomes who just didn't know how to handle their money.

He was President of Image Makers, a Restaurant Consulting Service, for several years. He showed those businesses how to handle their finances and make money.

Terry and Paulette were divorced in June 1982 but he continued to pay child support for his two adopted boys until they were eighteen.

He closed his Financial Counseling Service because lay-offs, strikes and other business failures made his business one that no one would use. Because so many were having financial problems then, most everyone was in the same boat, it didn't seem to matter whether anyone paid their bills.

In 1984 Terry went with the Ohio Company, a member of the New York Stock Exchange, and worked as an Account Representative for seven years. He met Youlin while he was still in training with the Ohio Company.

Not long after he met her she was in a terrible auto accident when a drunken driver hit her head-on. She is so short that her face was severely damaged by the steering wheel. Terry took care of her sons during her long hospitalization and helped through her recuperation. She had plastic surgery on her face. Her mouth was wired shut so her teeth could reset themselves

257

and bones could heal They were married a few months after the accident.

Their son, Corey. was born in August 1987. Then Terry had two adopted-sons, two stepsons and a son of his own. He took Youlin on many trips so we always said that Corey was flying before he was born.

Terry left the Ohio Company and went with PaineWebber as Executive Investment Counselor in 1991. He left that position in 1995 to form his own business, which he called 'Investment Management and Research'..

During their thirteen years together, Terry, Youlin and Corey traveled extensively. Their travels included Orlando, Florida, New York City, Switzerland, Hawaii and Bermuda. They took cruises to Mexico, Grand Cayman Islands and the Caribbean Islands.

Most of the time they took Corey with them but I remember once when Terry flew to Hiawassee, Georgia and took me to stay with Corey while they went to Hawaii.

Corey was two and wasn't talking too well yet. He would take me by the finger and lead me to what he wanted. He tried to tell me that he wanted his "foo boo hemit" but I couldn't understand him until he led me upstairs where he got his "football helmet" which turned out to be a sand pail turned upside down with the handle under his chin.

Terry learned how to make furniture including a baby cradle shaped like Noah's Ark, like Vicki had made earlier, and a full length oval mirror on a stand and tables for the living room. He was a perfectionist and each piece was a work of art.

He learned to install doors and put in new oak doors in the house. He had a bedroom, kitchen and dining area combined into a huge kitchen-dining area with all oak cabinets, an island in the center and a special baking counter made for Youlin. She is so short that other surfaces were too high for her. She loves to bake and Terry would often help her. Once she and Terry made over twenty pies for Thanksgiving just to give everyone the special kind they wanted. It is Youlin's dream for a kitchen. They spent many happy hours working together in their kitchen. Terry loved to make salads particularly and was a good helper with pies.

In 1993 he bought a Starduster II, a small open cockpit, double wing aircraft, as he called it, "my toy". He loved to take people up in it, fly around the Capitol dome in Lansing and around the countryside. I went up with him during the summer of 1995 while visiting from Florida. I thoroughly enjoyed it. He repeatedly asked me, through the earphones, if I was OK. He got a kick out of buzzing Vicki and Ridge's house near Stockbridge but never did any stunts with anyone unless they wanted to.

The next year Lynn and Susan got in touch with us and offered to drive us home, back to Florida for the winter. Lynn could take time off better then than later and they were concerned about us driving so far since Harry had had an almost fatal crisis with Myasthenia Gravis during the summer. We were glad to have them spend some time in Florida.

That was no problem for us so we drove from Sherman to DeWitt to their house to be ready to leave on Monday morning.

In the meantime, Terry and Youlin planned on everyone in the family coming to their house, near Eaton Rapids on Skyway Airport, for Sunday dinner before we were to leave for Florida the next day. All the girls fixed food and planned a beautiful get-together for all of us.

During the afternoon Terry had been taking everyone who wanted to go on a short flight in his 'toy' Starduster II. Mark, one of Lynn's sons, wanted a little fun so Terry did a few stunts that thrilled him but when Harry went up he told Terry "no tricks" and he didn't. Harry enjoyed the flight .

I was out by the hanger taking pictures where Terry and Lynn were standing talking to me when both of them turned to me and, in almost identical words and at the same time, said "Mom, have we got time for one more"? I said, "I don't think so. The girls are putting dinner on the table".

They looked at each other, grinned and I knew they were going.

The plane had gotten up about two hundred feet and nose-dived to the ground. My legs wouldn't hold me up even though Harry had his arms around me. Both the boys put their heads in my lap as soon as I sat down. Josh stayed with me and cried too as he tried to comfort me.

Youlin didn't know that it was Terry's plane that had crashed when she called 911 until they asked her if it was about the plane that had crashed there.

The family was in shock. Somebody had to notify Ridge, Vicki's husband, who was golfing near Jackson. He thought she was on the plane with Terry. I don't know who went to Jennifer's, Lynn's daughter's house, and someone called Danny, Lynn's son, in White Pigeon where he is stationed as a State Policeman. He brought his wife and their children. They were all there in two hours. The rest of the family was already there.

It was the worst day of my life.

This is a letter that I shared with family and friends after the accident:

December 13, 1996

Dear Ones,

I have had an experience that I want to share with you.

Last night, December 12th at about 11:00 P.M. I was half awake, half dozing but not asleep when a circle of, what I would call diffused, light appeared before me.

Terry appeared wearing a dark business suit. He was standing in front of me but a little to the left, in profile, with the light appearing to be at his left shoulder. I could see his face but it seemed in semi-shadow.

He was leaning forward slightly and reached his hand downward to the biggest, most colorful long stemmed roses I've ever seen. They seemed to be in florist flower containers, by the dozens, of every color. They covered a circle about three feet across.

He said, "Now, do I have to prove anything more"?

I was speechless and tried to figure out what he meant when it occurred to me that maybe he was trying to tell me that 'He Loved Me'.

For years he and I had this little game going between us. I wanted him, desperately, to say that he loved me but he would not. I would tell him that I loved him and would sign off on phone calls with "I Love You" and he would say "OK", "So

260

long" or "Talk to you later". It got to be a ritual. One day I forgot to say it and was waiting for him to sign off when he said "You forgot something". I said, "Oh yes, I love you". He laughed and hung up.

I didn't see Lynn in this circle of light until he spoke up. He was wearing an Argyle sweater of light blue, pink and yellow with casual slacks.

He was facing me but looking at the flowers. He was sitting on a slab of rock, like something in a rock garden, and leaning against another rock. He had his knee pulled up with his hands clasped around it.

He said, "She always knew that we loved her".

The circle of light disappeared and they were both gone. I don't know why or how this happened but I felt a wonderful peace come over me as I realized that my boys were together and appeared to be alright.

I got out of bed and wrote this experience down, afraid that I might not remember it in the morning but it seems embedded in my memory and I will never forget.

I have told this story to many people and have shared tears with them as they told me how lucky I was to 'have heard' from my boys.

The following poem was given to Youlin after Terry's funeral. I'm sure that she appreciated it.

"Wings in the Wind"

On wings he soared across the sky,
Sometimes quite low, other times high,
A life among the clouds was fun,
At morning light, or setting sun,

In building his own, he took great pride
To assure success in his long, long ride
O'er hill and vale and forest green
And many sights no other has seen,

Five thousand miles with nary a map

Except the reverse side of his lap;
He flew as did old pilots of chance,
Who called it "by the seat of your pants",

Two wings, and time to search and find
Where rivers flow and highways wind
Across this great land of the free;
I wish his passenger had been me,

I'll ne'er forget the summer roar,
O'erhead in rolls and loops he did soar
In celebrating his return to the air
As if he wanted to stay up there,

Little did we know how soon the call
Would come to fly up over the wall
Where clouds are silver, soft with love
From the Mighty Sky Pilot up above,

Some day he'll fly by once again
For passengers to the golden plain
Where all may share without a tear
Life in the skies of "Another Sphere".

Sunflower Son
E. Dale Knepper

Terry's sister, Vicki adds a Postscript ---------------

August 4, 1997 - Terry's name was placed on a Memorial Wall at Osh Kosh, Wisconsin.

Terry's wife Youlin, son Corey, Sister Vicki, brother-in-law Ridge and Great Nephew Josh traveled to Osh Kosh, Wisconsin to attend the Memorial Service which was very moving and beautiful. There is a Chapel, with a dozen or more stained windows with airplanes, that is peaceful and dignified.

I am not certain if Terry knew of this Memorial Wall but we feel that he would be very pleased to have his name there among so many pilots whose love of flying was like his own.

Next to his family, flying was the ultimate joy of his life. Terry was one of the fortunate ones who could work hard and accomplish much and then change gears and concentrate fully on family and flying.

He and Lynn both were such vibrant, active accomplished men that it seems even more tragic that they would die in what seemed to be the best times of their lives.

I Love You Both
and
Will miss you very much......

Vicki

CHAPTER 7

AFTER

AFTER

THE ESTATE SALE

After many months of grieving we headed back to Mesick for our second summer.

Shortly after we arrived Harry followed through on his plans to sell the farm. He contacted the owner of Mesick Resale Shop, who immediately came up with plans to hold a Living Estate Sale. She hired several people to help her get organized. They priced Harry's collections for fourteen days. It was a humongous job. They had signs made and fliers advertising over ten thousand items. Harry's intentions were to clear the buildings to the bare walls and sell the farm.

Our idea was to be moved out of the house/barn so the crew could take over and get ready for the sale planned for June.

In the meantime Harry pursued the e-mail contacts, made before we left Florida, in locating a Condominium in Traverse City. We looked at several but settled on one that we really wanted in Traverse Hills. It had belonged to a couple who had only lived in it for seven months when they both passed away. It was difficult getting in contact with the owner's son, a lawyer, who handled the contract and closing, but Harry persisted and made all the contacts.

We signed a contract and started moving some of the items we planned on keeping into the garage of our new place and closed the sale in June, 1997. We became the owners of an almost new condominium, which included three bedrooms, one for our computer room, three bathrooms, and a kitchen/breakfast area, living/dining room combination, a large foyer and a two-car garage on the first level. The huge family room, one of the bedrooms and one bath and a room for Harry's trains on the lower level. With a total of twenty four hundred square feet plus a double garage and two decks, we now have all the living space we could use.

Before we moved from the farm Harry invited his friend, Yuri, to come and take all the books he wanted. Yuri came

267

several times taking with him hundreds of books. There were still several hundred books to be sold but they brought practically nothing. Yuri and his wife, are avid book collectors and are building many shelves in their re-built house to accommodate those that Harry gave him. Harry promised Yuri the Rembrandt of the Lion but isn't ready to part with it yet. It hangs in our foyer.

I selected dishes, pots and pans, decorator items and everything we could use in our new place. The special one, to me, is the Cinderella Coach, about four feet long and two and a half feet high, made of a laminated materiel, in relief, and painted in beautiful colors with a gold overlay. When Harry hung it on the highest wall in the living room, I told him that "it's to remind me that I married a Prince".

Eventually the Living Estate Sale, which ran for nine days, was over and Harry could relax somewhat. I knew that parting with all his personal treasures was hard but what seemed to upset him most was that someone stole a Ski Bee. It belonged to Toby, his step-son. It was one of a kind... a motorized fan that he strapped to his back for cross-country skiing, or when riding a bicycle or on a small boat to convert it to an air-boat. One-of-a-kind.

ROOM MATES

We went to our place in Florida for our second summer together. It was pleasant enough but I had two serious falls that left me with some anxiety about walking and later the pain, that had started in my left knee about a year earlier, began to cause me extreme problems. I didn't want to have the knee surgery, that was recommended, in Florida, so waited until we got to Traverse City. By this time Harry's knee was giving him a lot of trouble, from an old injury, so we talked to our Doctor about having surgery on both of us ... on the same day.

The Doctor was dubious at first but he and his assistant agreed to do it in May. We shared a room at the hospital for four days then went to a Rehab Center where we shared a room again. Some patients who walked down the hall and saw the two of us in the same room did a double-take. One lady even stepped into our room and asked us if we were married. We assured her that we were and she spread the word.

The nurses were so impressed that they suggested that we had a newsworthy story but I had some complications so that idea was abandoned. Harry was driving his van, within three weeks, to come and see me. He brought Chinese food one evening. We ate in the little park-like area. I was the envy of many of the women who watched from the inside recreation areas. I couldn't wait to get out of there. I had ten weeks of physical therapy, ten weeks of pool therapy and seven weeks of acupuncture.

I had a lot of problems with my knee all summer but Harry kept encouraging me and started talking about both of us selling our cars and our house in Florida. We didn't need two cars and it was getting to be a problem to drive the fourteen hundred miles back and forth from Michigan. We sat down and figured what it cost us to maintain two places. We were quite surprised.

EUROPE

We sold my car in Florida and put that house on the market, telling ourselves that 'when we sold it we would go to Europe and take delivery on a new car'. In the meantime, we looked at Volvo's and BMWs. Harry sold his van and bought a little Escort Ford to use while we were waiting for our BMW to be built in Munich, Germany.

In the meantime, Harry made all of the arrangements for our trip which would be in May. It was fun to get all the literature and information from all those places. We knew that we'd be flying into Amsterdam, then to Munich to pick up our car.

We had to wait several hours at the delivery center so were very tired from no sleep for twenty six-hours. Both of us were too excited to sleep the night before we left.

After what seemed like an eternity, the car was brought out. It was a beautiful metallic, what was supposed to be Glacier Green, color. It looked Grey to me. Between the distributing agent and Harry, they convinced me that it really was our car. It just looked different under the showroom light.

During our second day, we discovered that we had the wrong car! It was not the one we ordered.

We stayed in Munich for two days and saw several Museums, Cathedrals, took bus tours and found obscure places to eat. The most interesting was Wirtschaus-Zurmefs-bluen Rose where huge blue and white fresco roses adorned the walls to the ceiling.

From there we went to Salzburg. I insisted on seeing the origin of "The Sound of Music" and the show at the Marionetten Theatre. We took the tour and saw the show. A thrill for me.

The Bed-and-Breakfast Hotels that Harry had booked turned out well so we had no hassle about a place to stay. Most of them were Hotels converted to Bed-and-Breakfast.

We went to the dealer in Salzburg but it was Saturday and they couldn't do anything about it until Monday

We were not about to drive back to Munich so suggested that they meet us, with our car, somewhere along the way and trade cars. Apparently that didn't appeal to them so they asked if it would inconvenience us too much to just drive their car for the rest of our trip. We agreed. The company put us up in a beautiful Bread-and-Breakfast, Rubezahl, near Neuschwanstein, where we had planned to see the Castle.

We went on to England, saw the Stonehenge, English countryside in the Cotswald area, Madame Tussaud's Wax Museum in London and headed for Amsterdam where we were to leave our car for shipment home.

It rained almost every day during the whole three weeks but the flowers and greenery everywhere was beautiful. My pictures turned out well in spite of the rain.

Our car was delivered to us, in Traverse City, six weeks after we left Europe. It had three miles on the speedometer. Their car had one thousand eight hundred and eight when we left it in Amsterdam.

Final Note: It took me three years to put together my first book, "Scraps of Family History", which was never published.

We had seventyy-five copies printed and gave seventy two of to family and friends who thought that some of the 'Stories' from that book might be interesting to someone other than family. I hope that my readers will enjoy it and attempt to write some of their own "Family Stories".

Etta Wilson Lawrence

ABOUT THE AUTHOR

Etta W. Lawrence, the eighty-two year old author of "Memories" was born in rural Georgia in 1917. She bore and raised three children. She divorced their father, remarried him and divorced him again. She married twice more and outlived both of these two husbands. She later met and married her fourth and present husband in 1996. She lives with him in Traverse City, Michigan.

Etta started collecting stories about her family as a very young girl and writing them down as she heard them told. She was gifted with a tremendous capacity for recalling details and dates. She had been urged by her children to write a book and include these stories which she had told and retold to them in their childhood.

One of her sons provided her with a computer and printer and the book was started. Her new husband, a computer buff, agreed to help her with his more advanced equipment. Together they completed a book entitled "Scraps of Family History". Seventy copies were printed and distributed to relatives and close friends. This book contained a lot of genealogical data, pictures and family trees as well as many stories. Etta decided to put together another book of just the stories and call it"Memories"